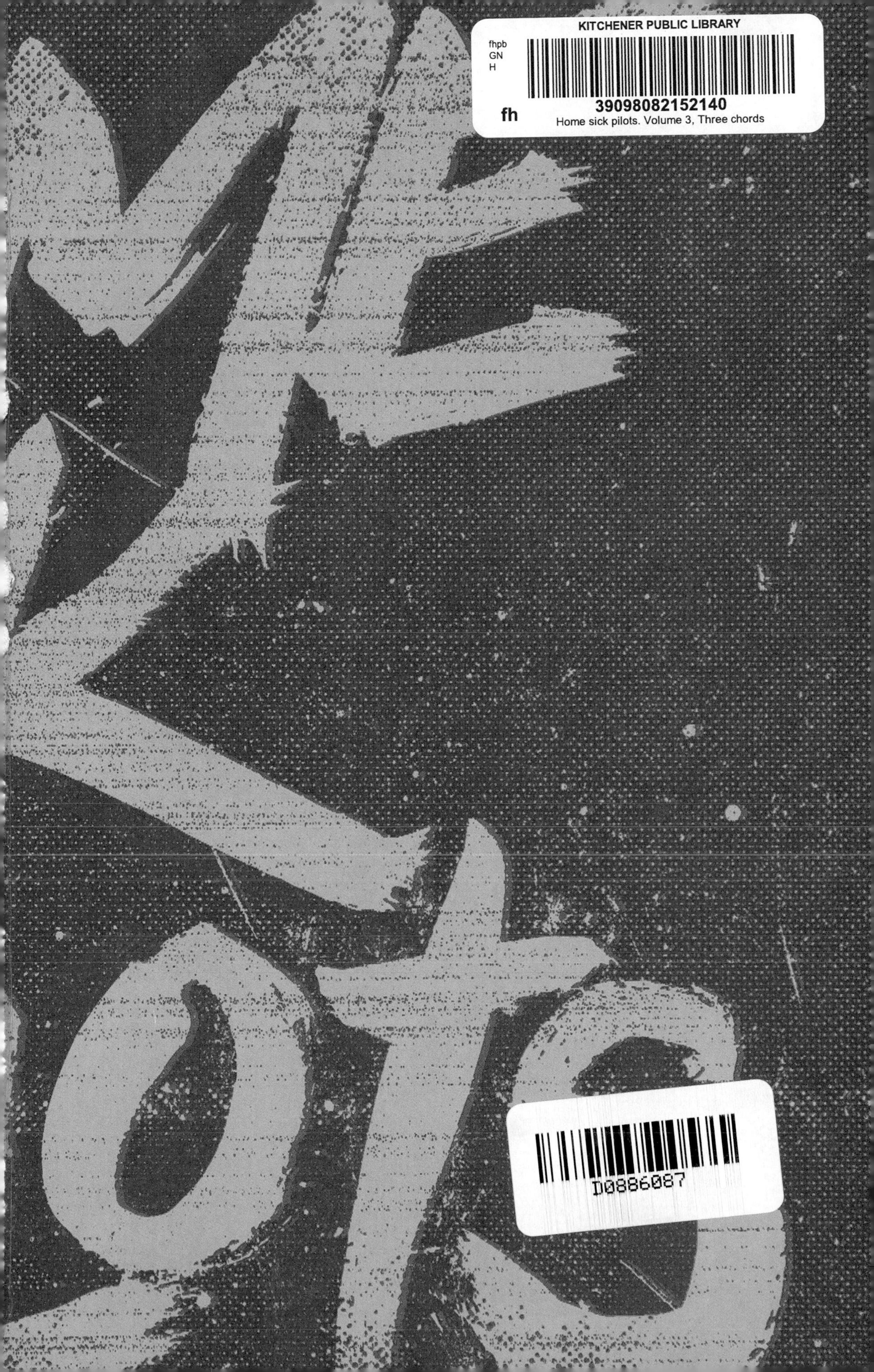

TONIGHT!

Dan Watters, Writer
and Caspar Wijngaard, Artist

With:

Aditya Bidikar: Letterer
Tom Muller: Designer
Erika Schnatz: Production Artist

PRESENT:

IMAGE COMICS, INC.
Robert Kirkman: Chief Operating Officer
Erik Larsen: Chief Financial Officer
Todd McFarlane: President
Marc Silvestri: Chief Executive Officer
Jim Valentino: Vice President

Eric Stephenson: Publisher / Chief Creative Officer
Nicole Lapalme: Vice President of Finance
Leanna Caunter: Accounting Analyst
Sue Korpela: Accounting & HR Manager
Matt Parkinson: Vice President of Sales & Publishing Planning
Lorelei Bunjes: Vice President of Digital Strategy
Dirk Wood: Vice President of International Sales & Licensing
Alex Cox: Director of Direct Market Sales
Chloe Ramos: Book Market & Library Sales Manager
Emilio Bautista: Digital Sales Coordinator
Jon Schlaffman: Specialty Sales Coordinator
Kat Salazar: Vice President of PR & Marketing
Deanna Phelps: Marketing Design Manager
Drew Fitzgerald: Marketing Content Associate
Heather Doornink: Vice President of Production
Drew Gill: Art Director
Hilary DiLoreto: Print Manager
Tricia Ramos: Traffic Manager
Melissa Gifford: Content Manager
Erika Schnatz: Senior Production Artist
Ryan Brewer: Production Artist

Tara Ferguson: White Noise marketing

Private property
Keep out

ice

STRICTLY
NO

HOME SICK PILOTS

*Home Sick Pilots
created by
Dan Watters and Caspar Wijngaard*

Originally published as HOME SICK PILOTS #11–15

HOME SICK PILOTS, VOL. 3: THREE CHORDS AND THE END OF THE WORLD. July 2022. Published by Image Comics, Inc. Office of publication: PO BOX 14457, Portland, OR 97293. Copyright © 2022 Dan Watters & Caspar Wijngaard. All rights reserved. Contains material originally published in single magazine form as HOME SICK PILOTS #11-15. HOME SICK PILOTS, and the likenesses of all characters herein or hereon are trademarks of Dan Watters & Caspar Wijngaard, unless expressly indicated. "Image" and the Image Comics logos are registered trademarks of Image Comics, Inc. No part of this publication may be reproduced or transmitted in any form or by any means (except for short excerpts for journalistic or review purposes), without the express written permission of Dan Watters & Caspar Wijngaard or Image Comics, Inc. All names, characters, events, and places herein are entirely fictional. Any resemblance to actual persons (living or dead), events, or places, without satiric intent, is coincidental. Printed in the USA. All inquiries: licensing@imagecomics.com.

IMAGECOMICS.COM

ISBN: 978-1-5343-2313-1

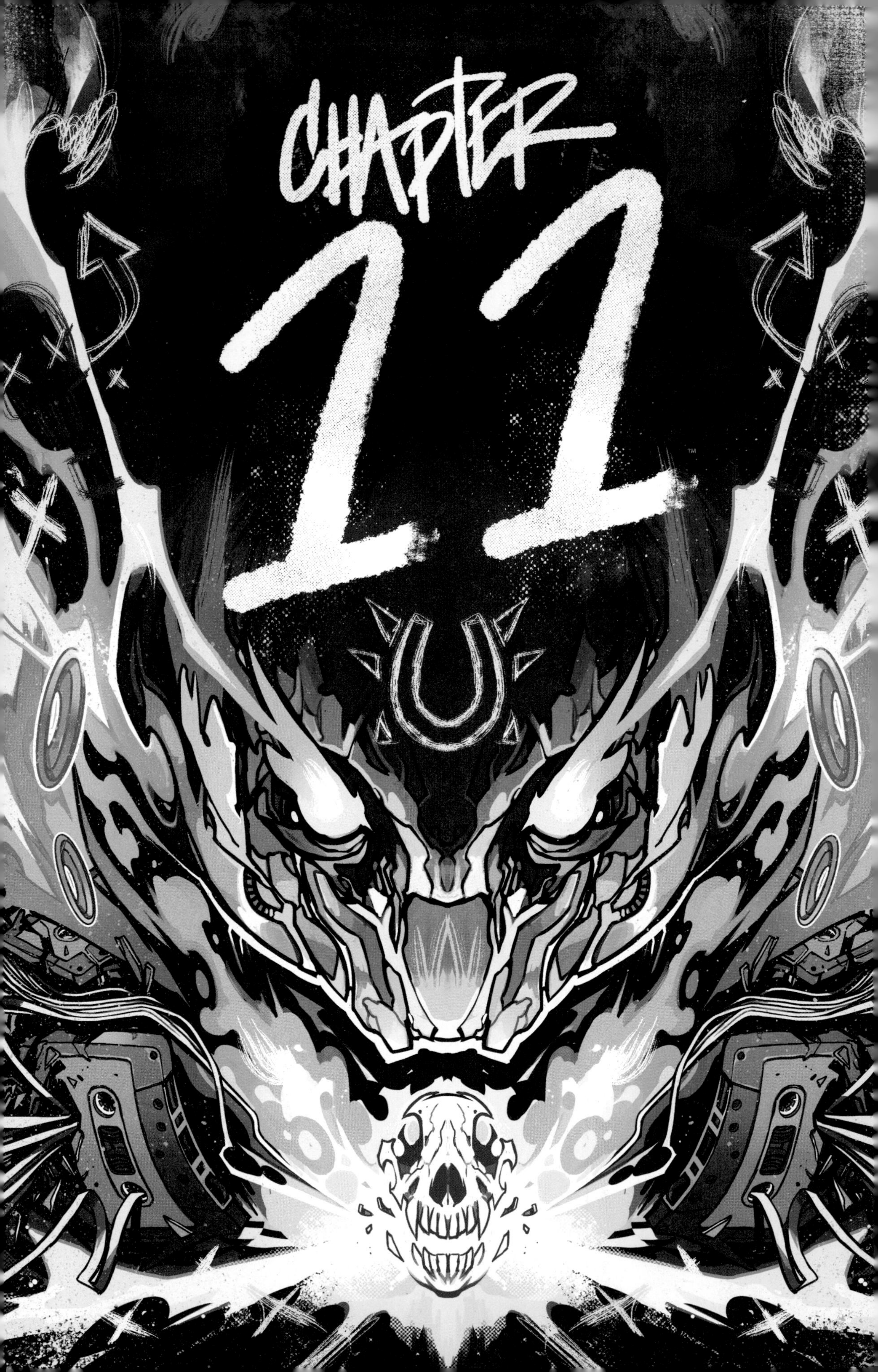
CHAPTER
11

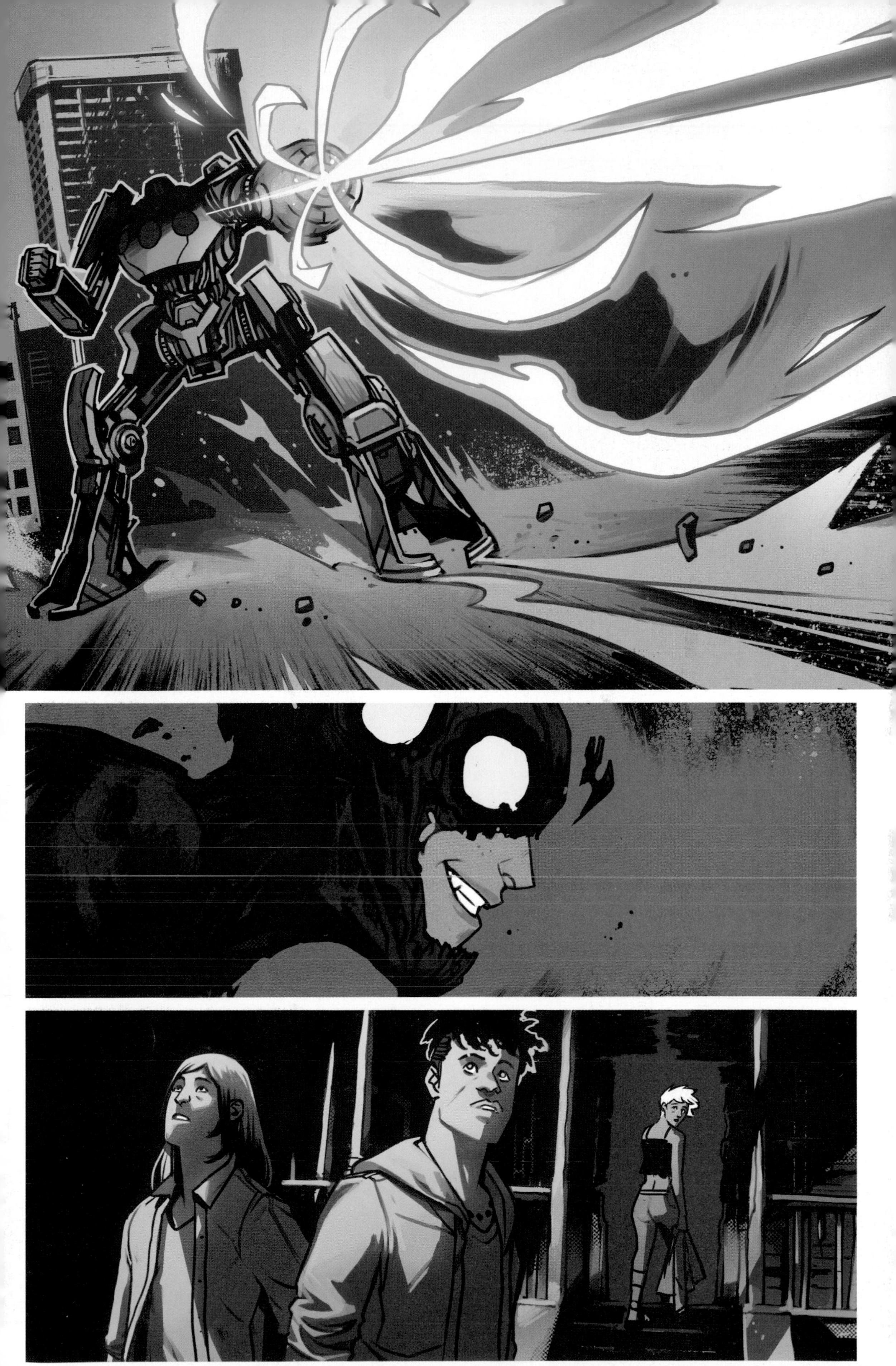

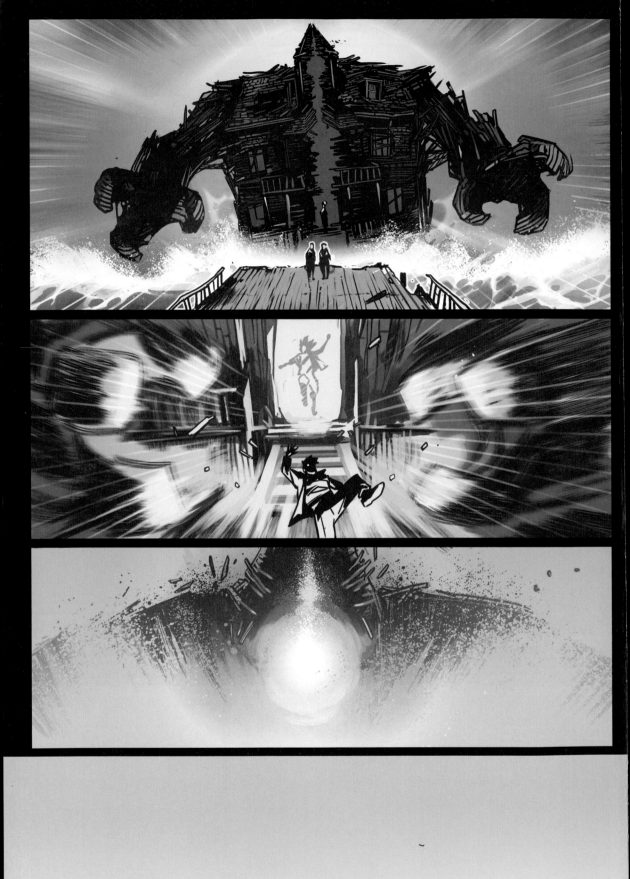

BUZZ. ARE WE DEAD?
NO...

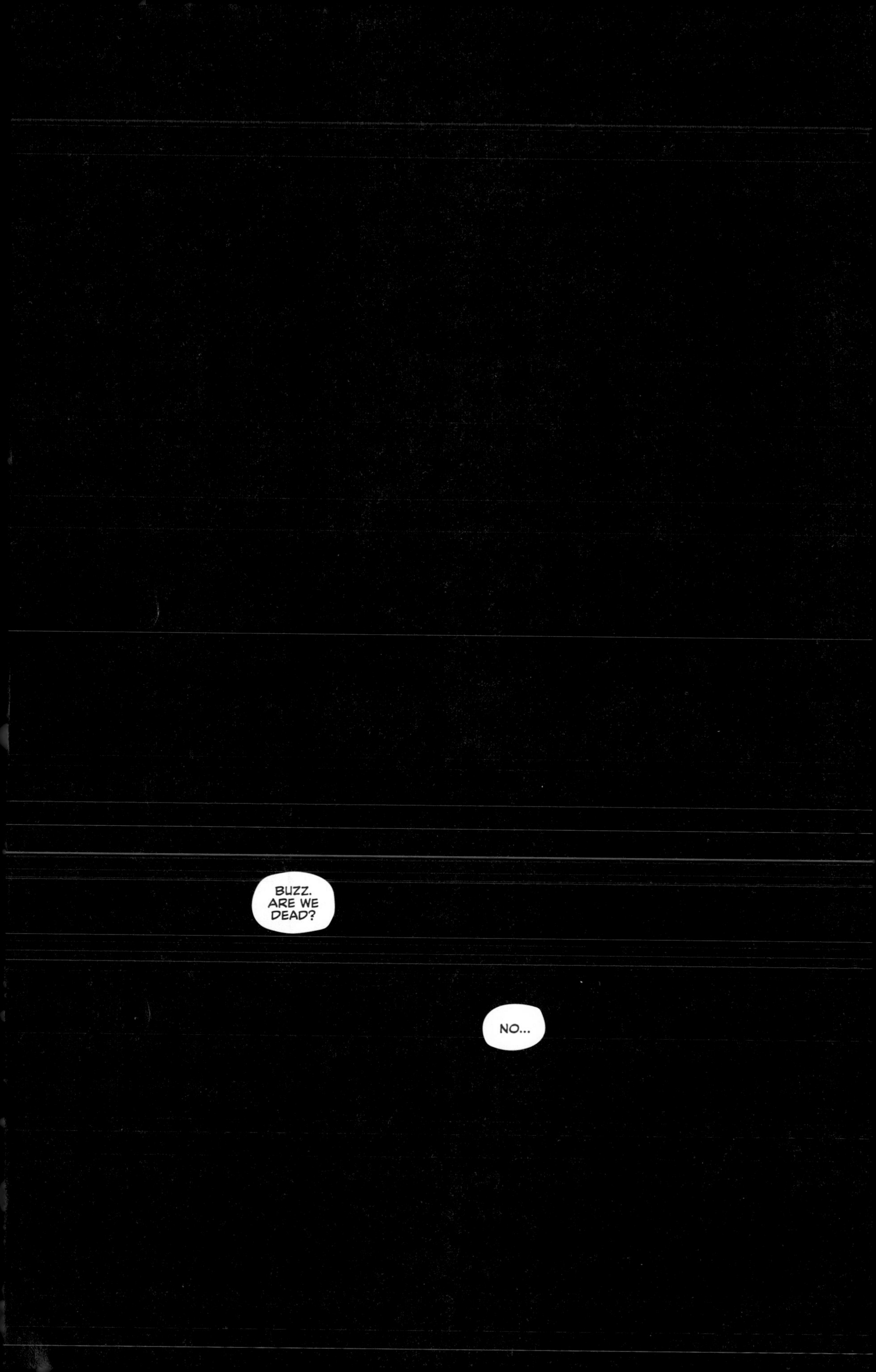

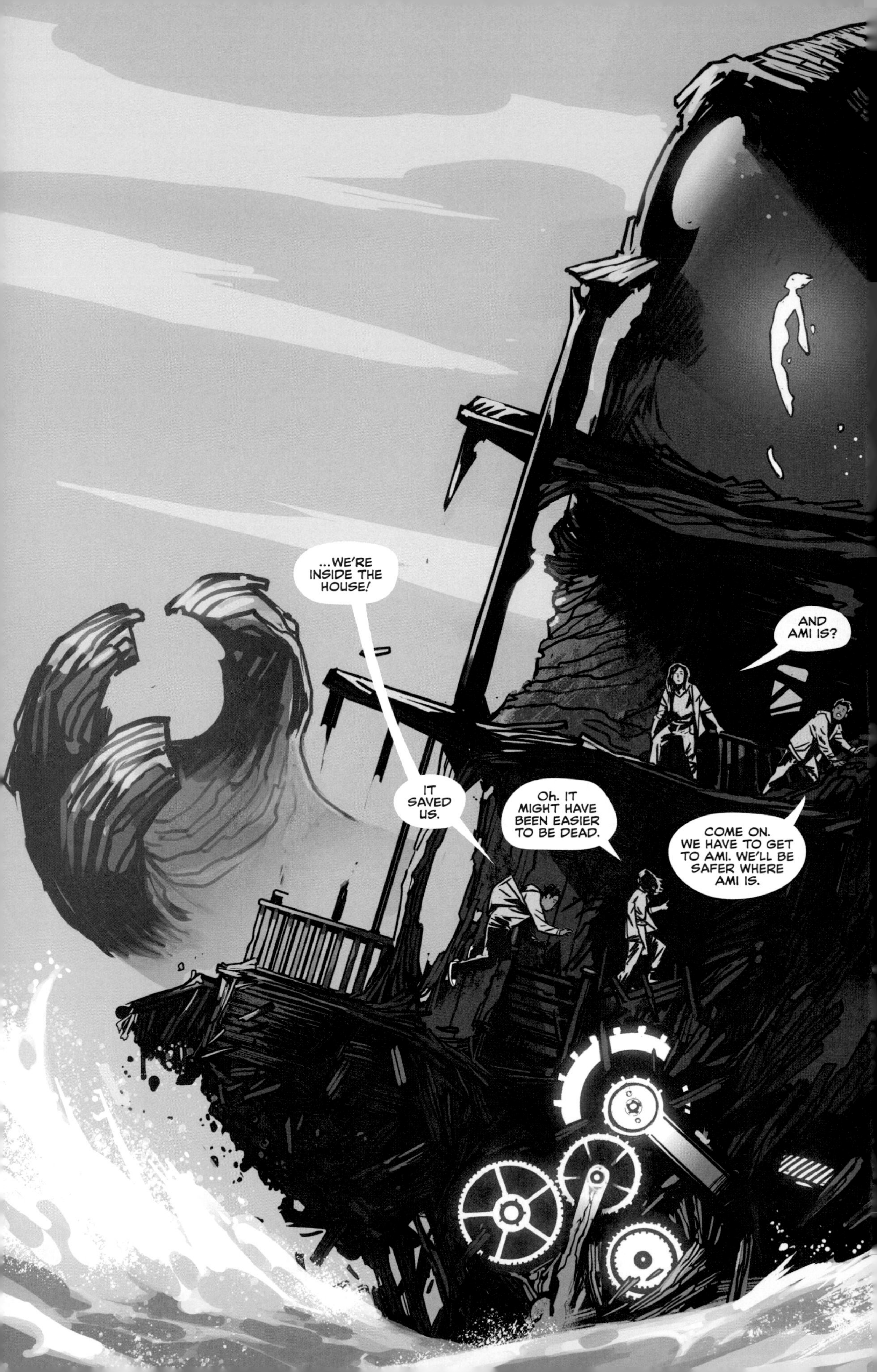
...WE'RE INSIDE THE HOUSE!
IT SAVED US.
Oh. IT MIGHT HAVE BEEN EASIER TO BE DEAD.
AND AMI IS?
COME ON. WE HAVE TO GET TO AMI. WE'LL BE SAFER WHERE AMI IS.

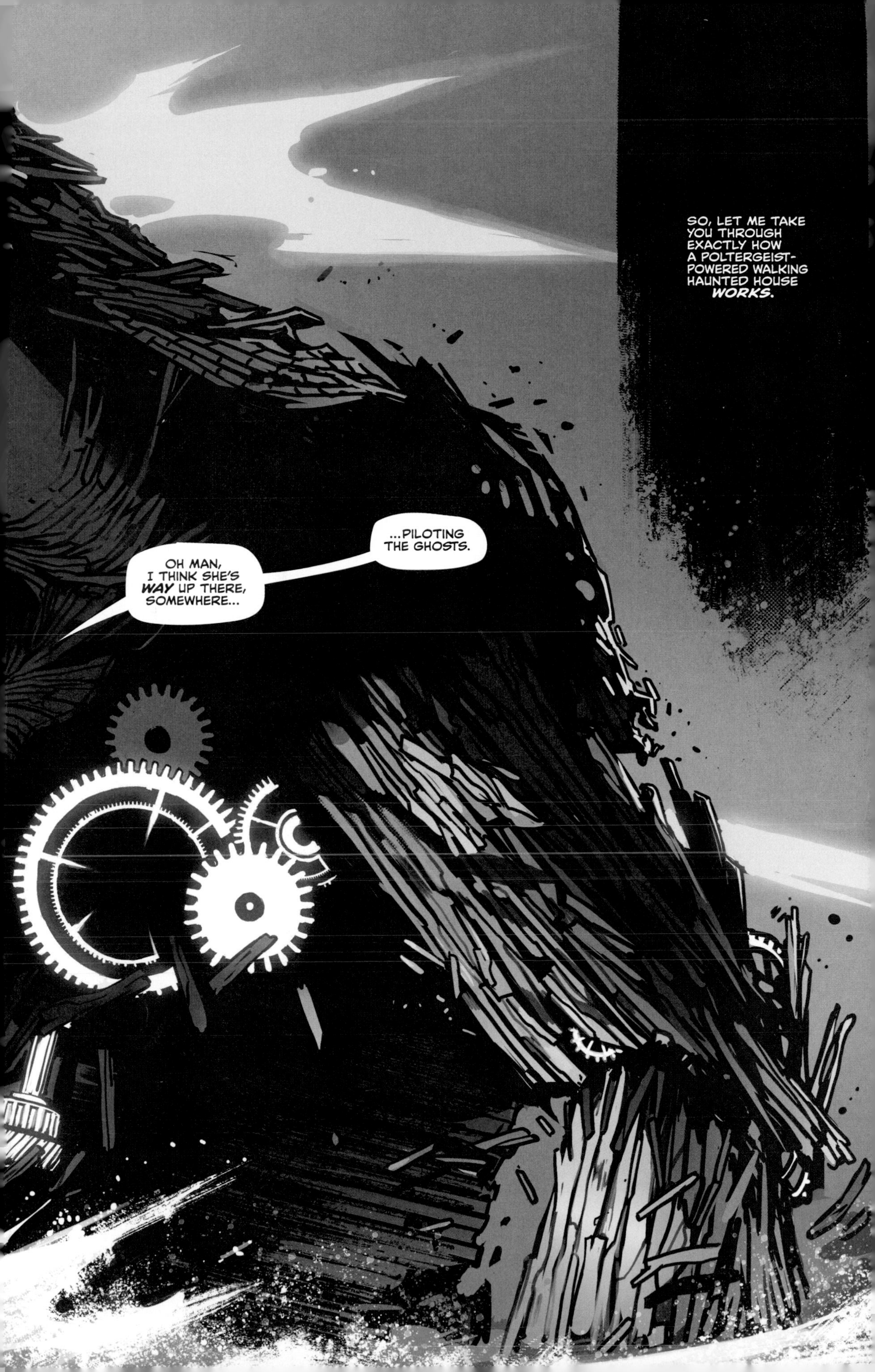
SO, LET ME TAKE YOU THROUGH EXACTLY HOW A POLTERGEIST-POWERED WALKING HAUNTED HOUSE *WORKS.*
OH MAN, I THINK SHE'S *WAY* UP THERE, SOMEWHERE...
...PILOTING THE GHOSTS.

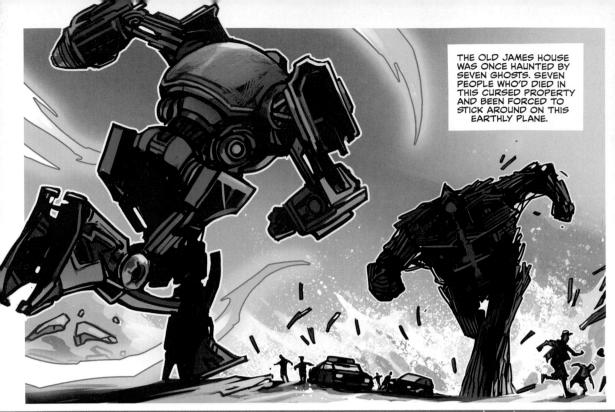

THE OLD JAMES HOUSE WAS ONCE HAUNTED BY SEVEN GHOSTS. SEVEN PEOPLE WHO'D DIED IN THIS CURSED PROPERTY AND BEEN FORCED TO STICK AROUND ON THIS EARTHLY PLANE.

POLTERGEISTS ARE BEST KNOWN FOR KNOCKING CUPS OFF COUNTERS, SHAKING WINDOWPANES IN THE DEAD OF NIGHT.

PERHAPS STACKING THE KITCHEN CHAIRS INTO A PYRAMID IF THEY'RE FEELING REALLY FRISKY.

BUT ALL OF THIS, REALLY, ONLY SPEAKS TO A LACK OF *IMAGINATION*. THEY AREN'T A PART OF THIS WORLD. NOT TRULY.

SO THEY SHOULDN'T BE LIMITED BY *SCALE*. THEY DON'T *HAVE* TO BE.

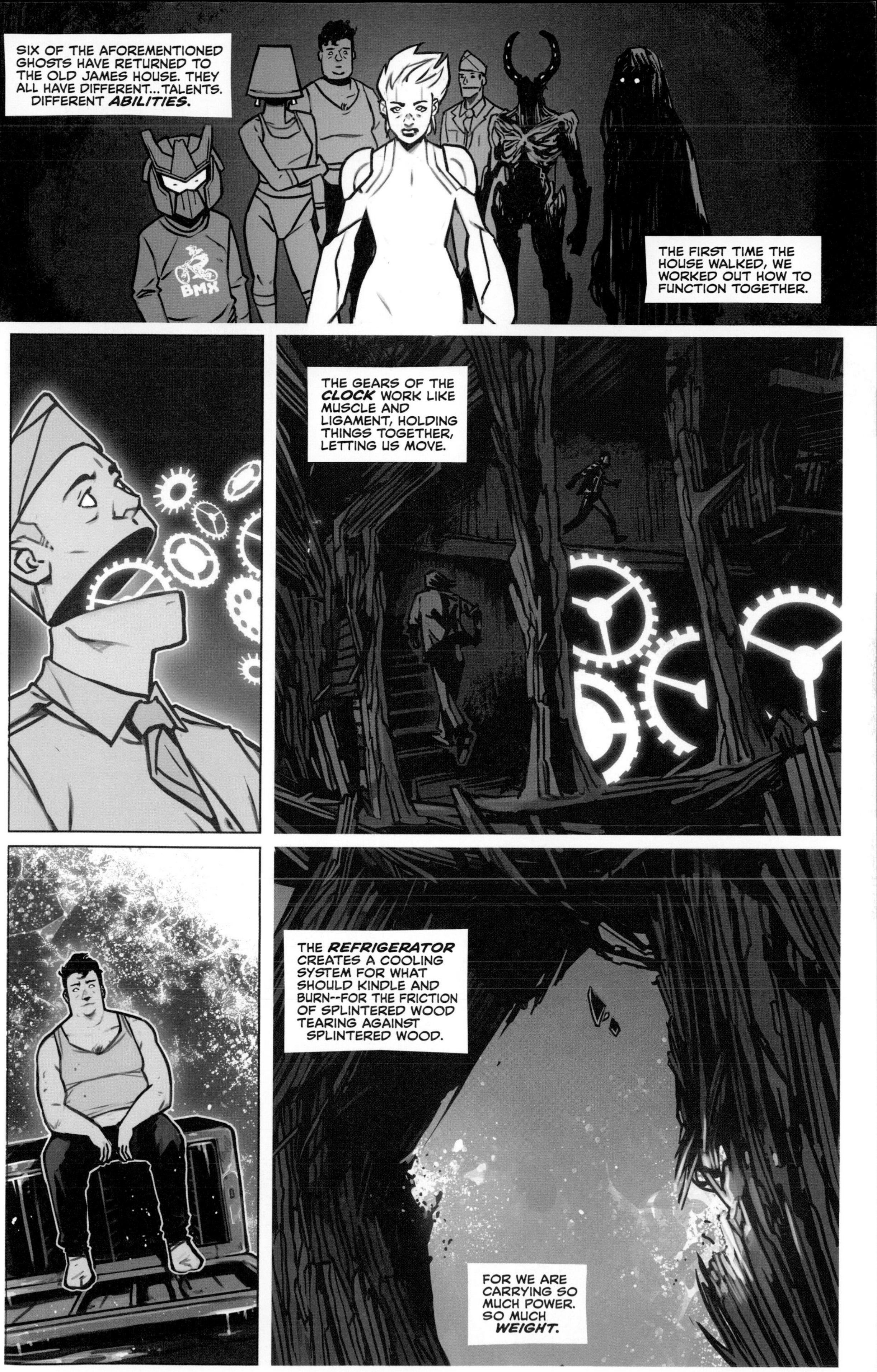
SIX OF THE AFOREMENTIONED GHOSTS HAVE RETURNED TO THE OLD JAMES HOUSE. THEY ALL HAVE DIFFERENT...TALENTS. DIFFERENT *ABILITIES.*
BMX
THE FIRST TIME THE HOUSE WALKED, WE WORKED OUT HOW TO FUNCTION TOGETHER.
THE GEARS OF THE *CLOCK* WORK LIKE MUSCLE AND LIGAMENT, HOLDING THINGS TOGETHER, LETTING US MOVE.
THE *REFRIGERATOR* CREATES A COOLING SYSTEM FOR WHAT SHOULD KINDLE AND BURN--FOR THE FRICTION OF SPLINTERED WOOD TEARING AGAINST SPLINTERED WOOD.
FOR WE ARE CARRYING SO MUCH POWER. SO MUCH *WEIGHT.*

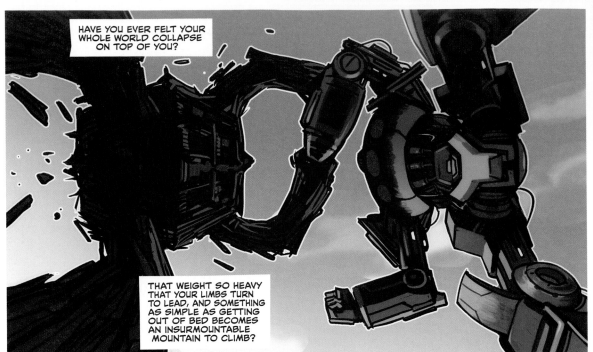

HAVE YOU EVER FELT YOUR WHOLE WORLD COLLAPSE ON TOP OF YOU?

THAT WEIGHT SO HEAVY THAT YOUR LIMBS TURN TO LEAD, AND SOMETHING AS SIMPLE AS GETTING OUT OF BED BECOMES AN INSURMOUNTABLE MOUNTAIN TO CLIMB?

HAVE YOU EVER FELT THE HORRORS OF REAL LIFE BECOME TOO MUCH TO BEAR?

I HOPE YOU HAVEN'T. I HAVE.

SO HAVE EACH OF THE GHOSTS. IT'S WHAT WEIGHS THEM DOWN TO THIS REALM. IT'S WHAT *CONNECTS* THEM TO *ME*.

IT'S THE HEAVINESS WE SWING IN THESE FISTS, AND HOWL FROM OUR CHESTS.

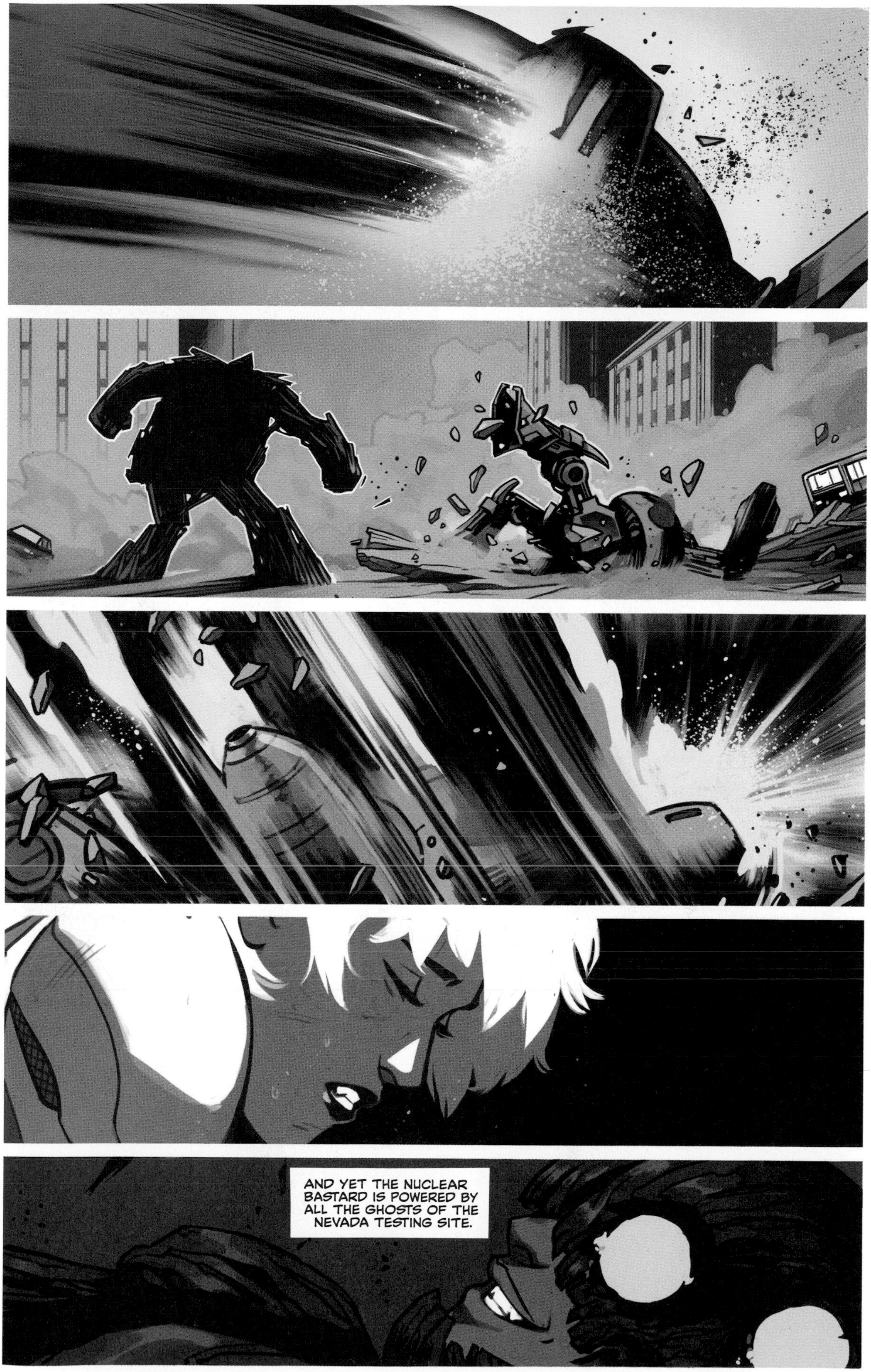
AND YET THE NUCLEAR BASTARD IS POWERED BY ALL THE GHOSTS OF THE NEVADA TESTING SITE.

IT STRIKES BACK WITH THE MIND-SHATTERED AWE OF ALL THOSE WHO HAVE LOOKED FROM THEIR WINDOW TO SEE A MUSHROOM CLOUD PLUME ON THE HORIZON.

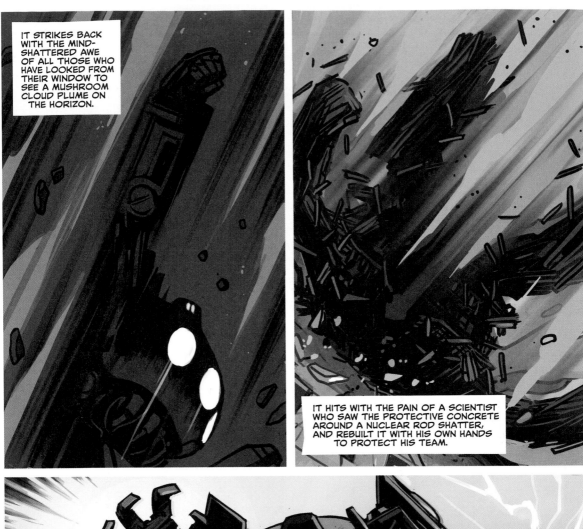

IT HITS WITH THE PAIN OF A SCIENTIST WHO SAW THE PROTECTIVE CONCRETE AROUND A NUCLEAR ROD SHATTER, AND REBUILT IT WITH HIS OWN HANDS TO PROTECT HIS TEAM.

THE OTHER FIST COMES DOWN WITH THE AGONY OF HIS MONTH IN THE HOSPITAL, WAITING TO DIE AS HIS HAIR FELL OUT AND ORGANS LIQUEFIED.

AND IT COMES DOWN AGAIN, WITH THE CRUSHING MISERY OF HIS--FINAL MOMENTS, AS HE REFLECTED THAT--WHAT HE WAS GOING THROUGH THAT DAY, AS EVERY-THING GREW DARK AROUND HIM?

FUOOOM

WELL, THAT WAS WHAT HIS LIFE'S WORK--AND THE WORK OF THE TEAM HE HAD PUT HIMSELF THROUGH THIS TO PROTECT--WAS GOING TO PUT OTHER HUMAN BEINGS THROUGH.

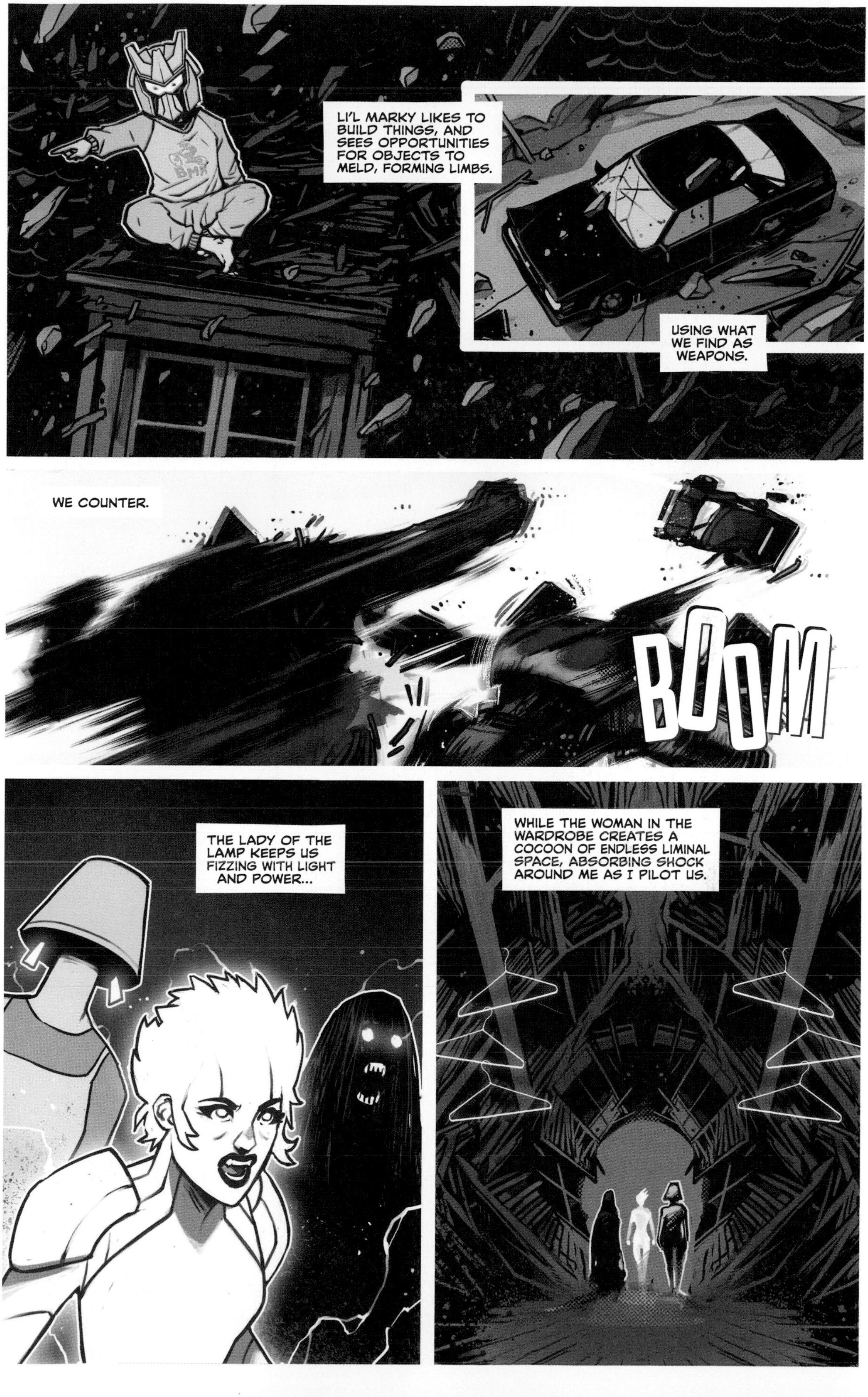
LI'L MARKY LIKES TO BUILD THINGS, AND SEES OPPORTUNITIES FOR OBJECTS TO MELD, FORMING LIMBS.
USING WHAT WE FIND AS WEAPONS.
BMX
WE COUNTER.
BOOM
THE LADY OF THE LAMP KEEPS US FIZZING WITH LIGHT AND POWER...
WHILE THE WOMAN IN THE WARDROBE CREATES A COCOON OF ENDLESS LIMINAL SPACE, ABSORBING SHOCK AROUND ME AS I PILOT US.

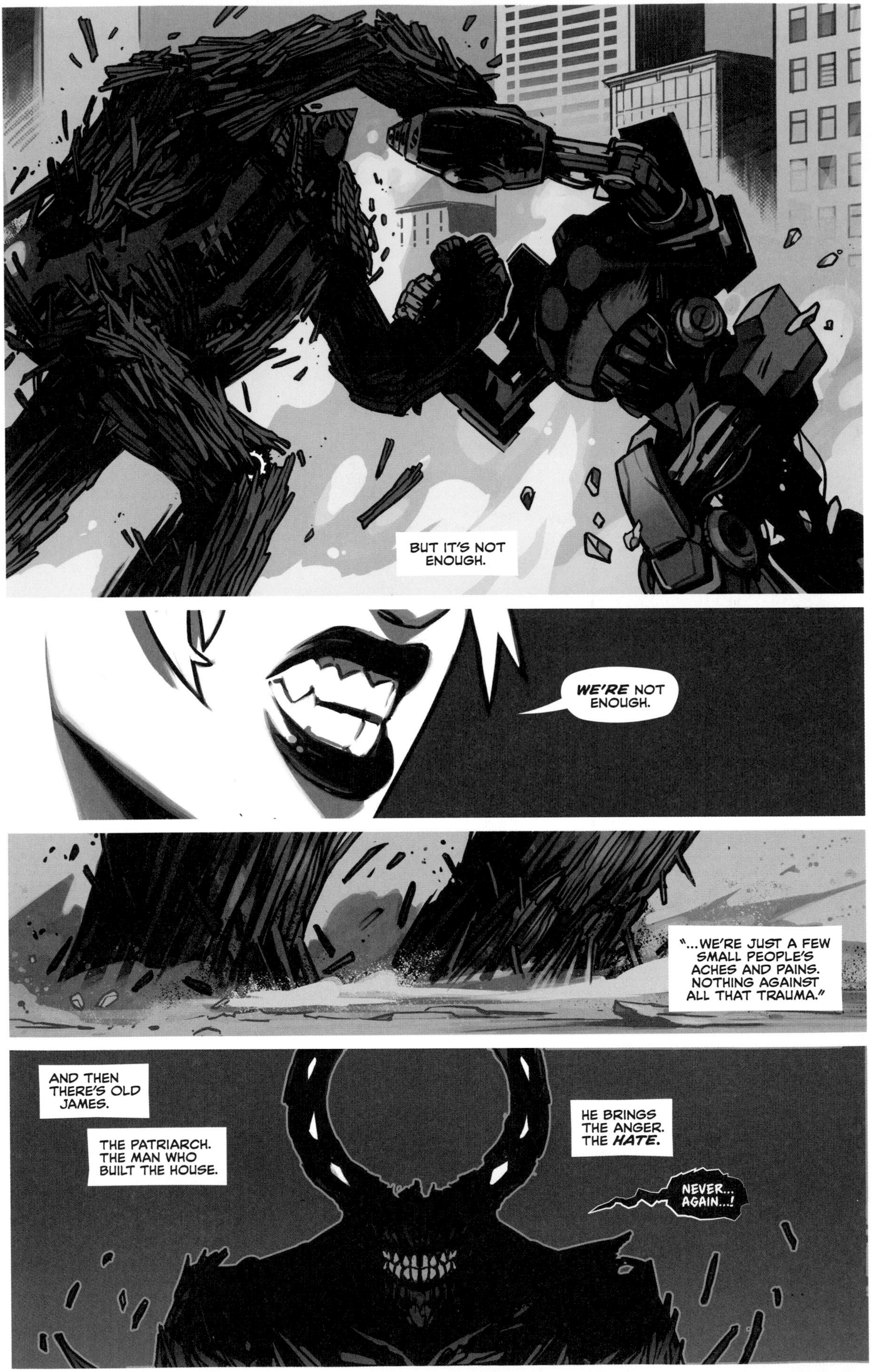
BUT IT'S NOT ENOUGH.
WE'RE NOT ENOUGH.
"...WE'RE JUST A FEW SMALL PEOPLE'S ACHES AND PAINS. NOTHING AGAINST ALL THAT TRAUMA."
AND THEN THERE'S OLD JAMES.
THE PATRIARCH. THE MAN WHO BUILT THE HOUSE.
HE BRINGS THE ANGER. THE *HATE*.
NEVER... AGAIN...!

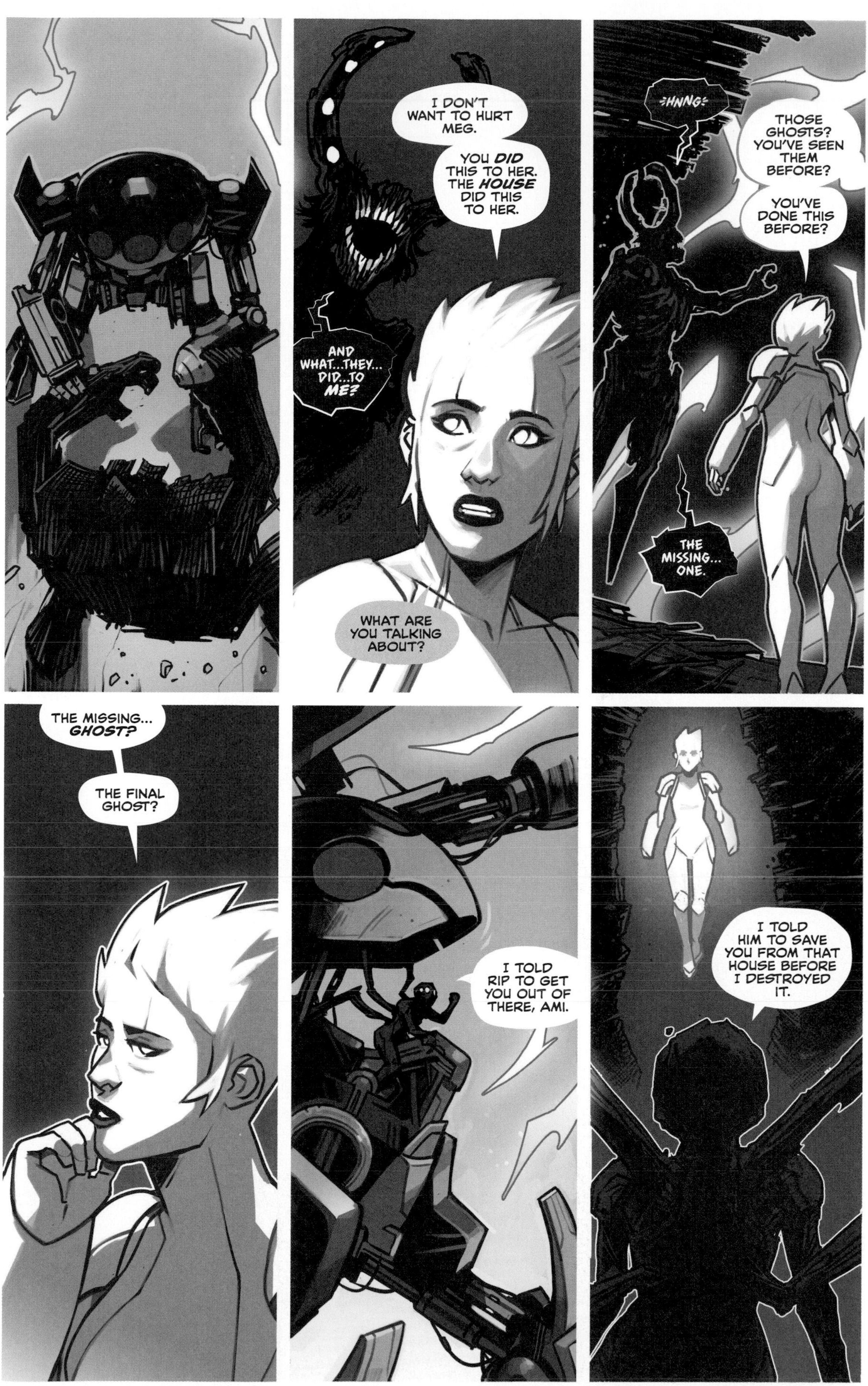

I DON'T WANT TO HURT MEG.
YOU DID THIS TO HER. THE HOUSE DID THIS TO HER.
AND WHAT...THEY... DID...TO ME?
WHAT ARE YOU TALKING ABOUT?
HNNG
THOSE GHOSTS? YOU'VE SEEN THEM BEFORE?
YOU'VE DONE THIS BEFORE?
THE MISSING... ONE.
THE MISSING... GHOST?
THE FINAL GHOST?
I TOLD RIP TO GET YOU OUT OF THERE, AMI.
I TOLD HIM TO SAVE YOU FROM THAT HOUSE BEFORE I DESTROYED IT.

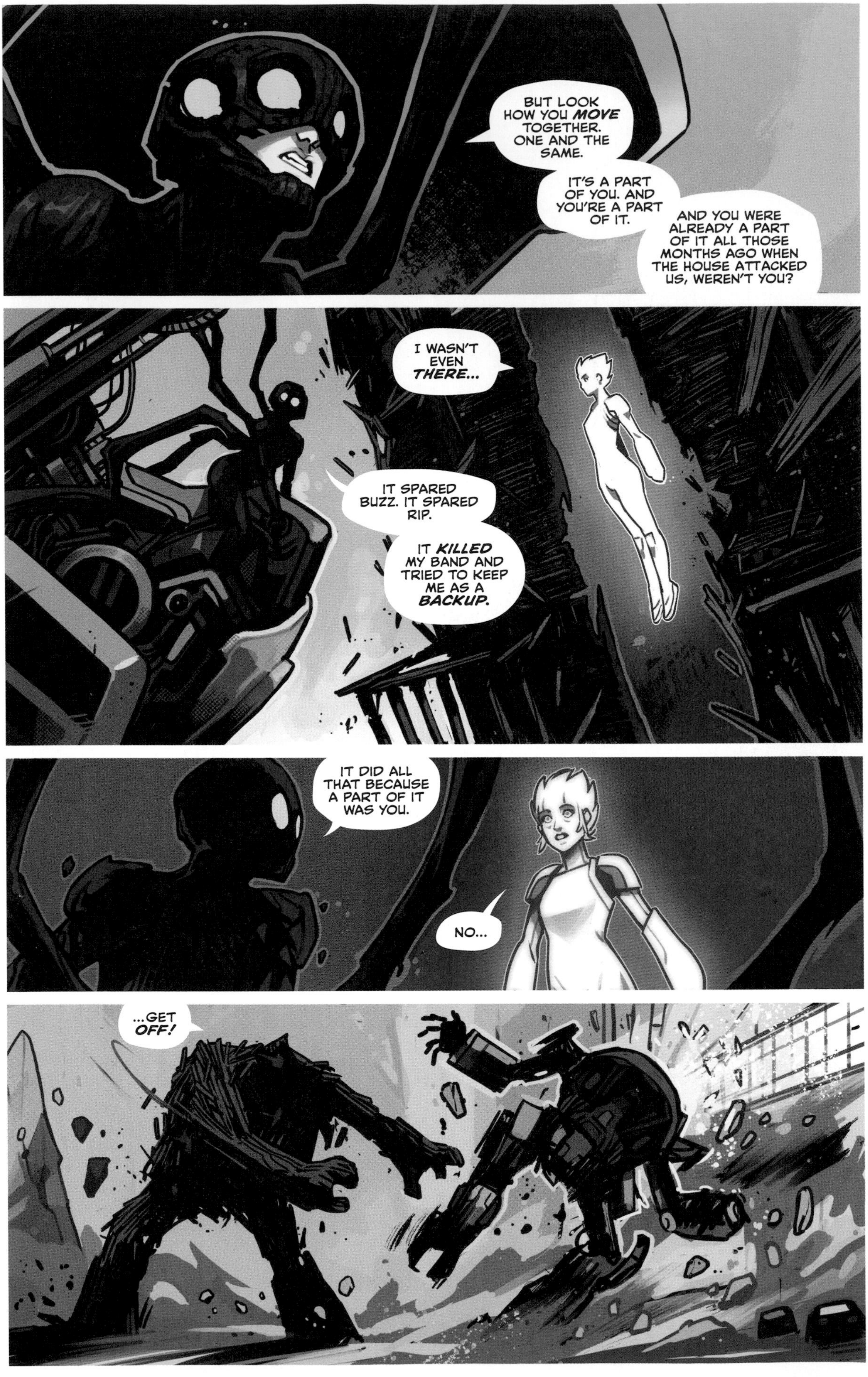
BUT LOOK HOW YOU *MOVE* TOGETHER. ONE AND THE SAME.
IT'S A PART OF YOU. AND YOU'RE A PART OF IT.
AND YOU WERE ALREADY A PART OF IT ALL THOSE MONTHS AGO WHEN THE HOUSE ATTACKED US, WEREN'T YOU?
I WASN'T EVEN *THERE...*
IT SPARED BUZZ. IT SPARED RIP.
IT *KILLED* MY BAND AND TRIED TO KEEP ME AS A *BACKUP.*
IT DID ALL THAT BECAUSE A PART OF IT WAS YOU.
NO...
...GET *OFF!*

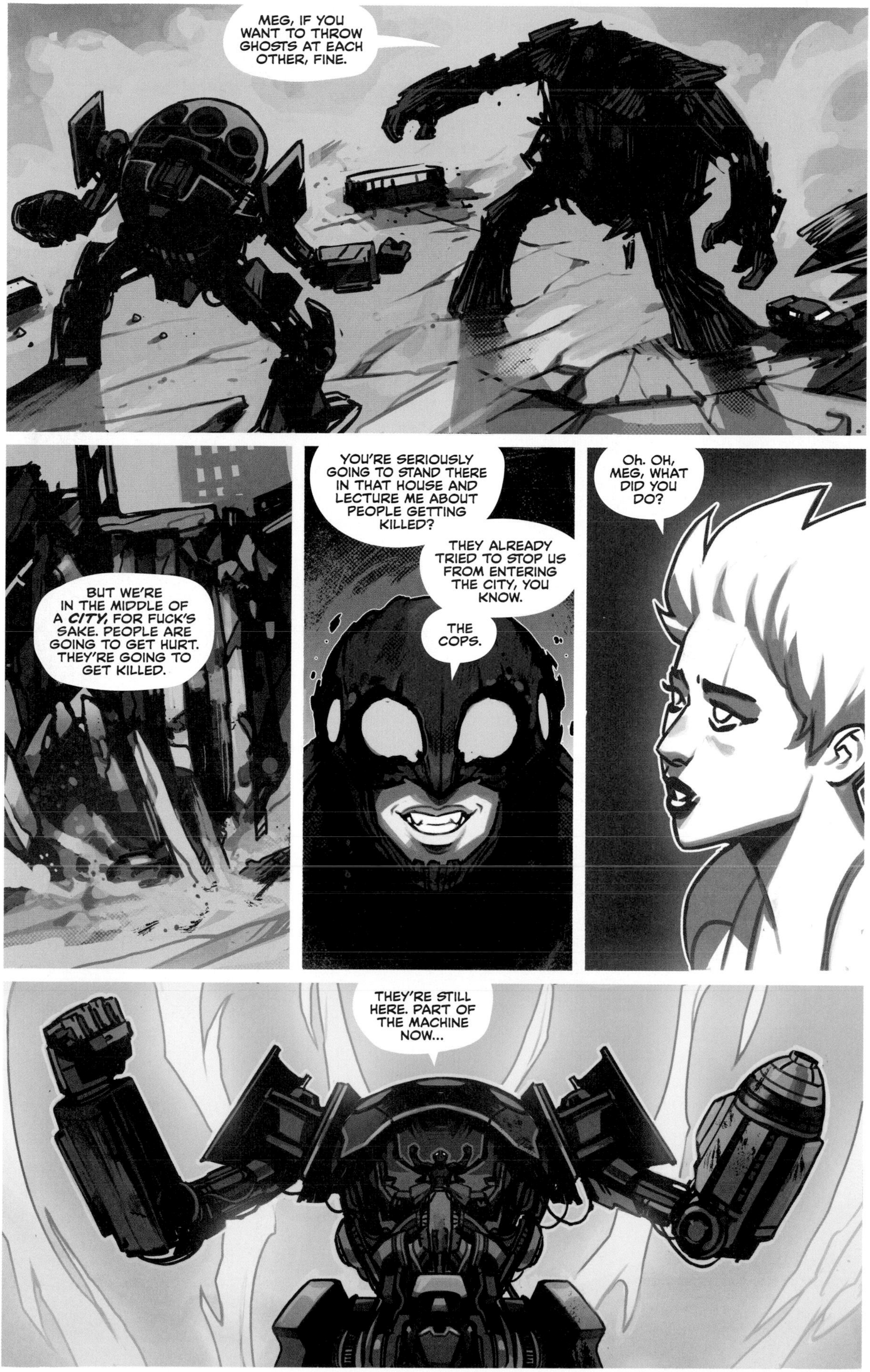
MEG, IF YOU WANT TO THROW GHOSTS AT EACH OTHER, FINE.
BUT WE'RE IN THE MIDDLE OF A *CITY*, FOR FUCK'S SAKE. PEOPLE ARE GOING TO GET HURT. THEY'RE GOING TO GET KILLED.
YOU'RE SERIOUSLY GOING TO STAND THERE IN THAT HOUSE AND LECTURE ME ABOUT PEOPLE GETTING KILLED?
THEY ALREADY TRIED TO STOP US FROM ENTERING THE CITY, YOU KNOW.
THE COPS.
Oh. OH, MEG, WHAT DID YOU DO?
THEY'RE STILL HERE. PART OF THE MACHINE NOW...

LOOK.

PART OF THE TRAUMA OF AMERICA.

OH MY GOD...

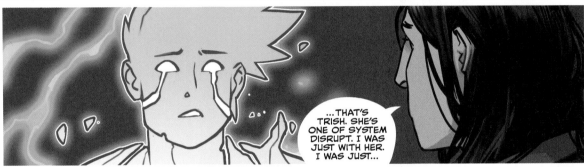

...THAT'S TRISH. SHE'S ONE OF SYSTEM DISRUPT. I WAS JUST WITH HER. I WAS JUST...

MEG WOULDN'T. SHE WOULDN'T...

IT'S NOT HER. NOT REALLY. THE GHOSTS ARE IN CONTROL.

EVERY DEATH HERE IS DOWN TO YOU AND THAT HOUSE. EVERY DEATH AN ACCEPTABLE LOSS.

JUST LIKE WITH THE ATOM.

IF YOU REALLY WANT TO MINIMIZE THE DAMAGE? LIE DOWN, AND LET US TAKE YOU APART, PIECE BY PIECE, UNTIL THERE'S NOTHING LEFT.

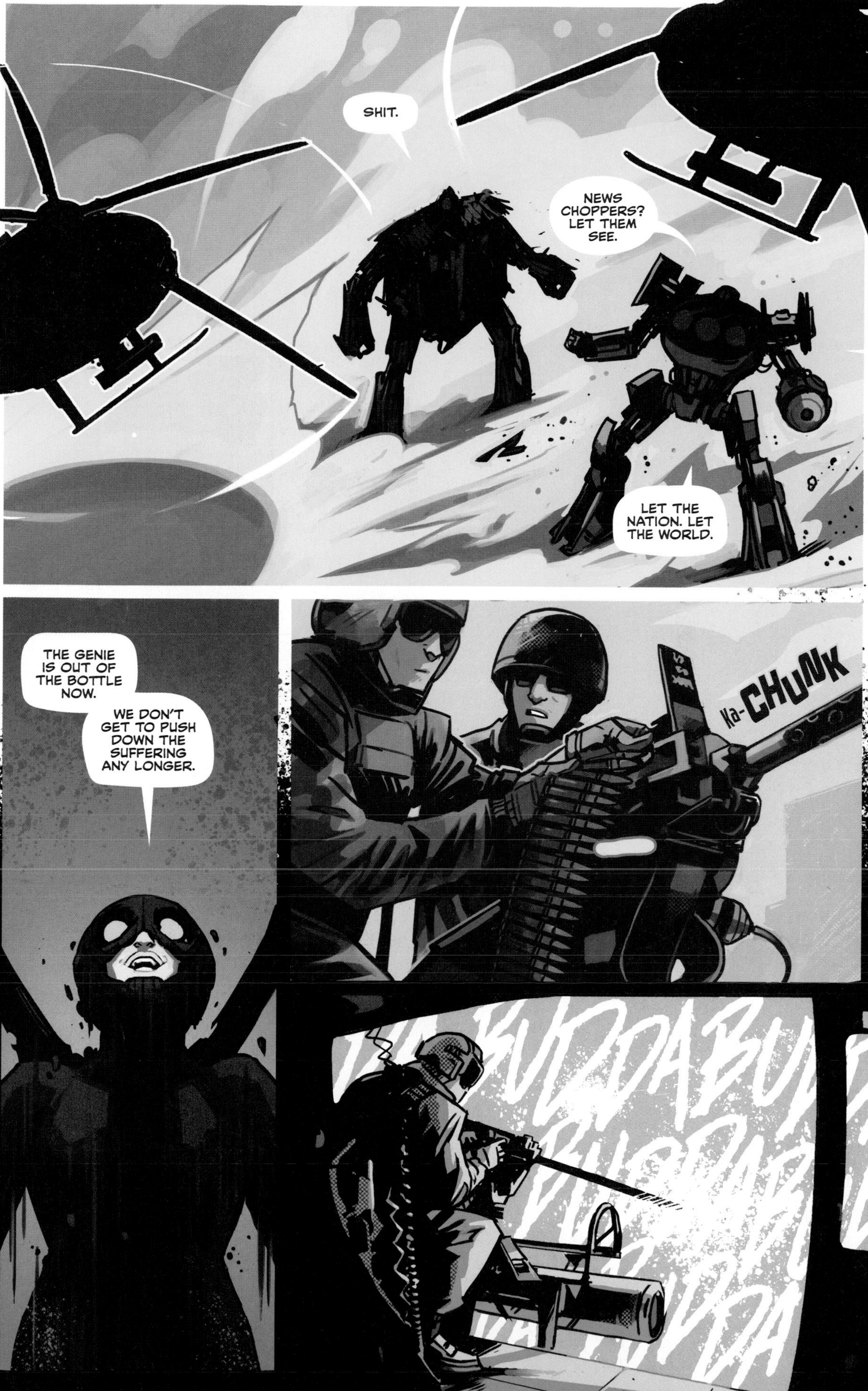
SHIT.
NEWS CHOPPERS? LET THEM SEE.
LET THE NATION. LET THE WORLD.
THE GENIE IS OUT OF THE BOTTLE NOW.
WE DON'T GET TO PUSH DOWN THE SUFFERING ANY LONGER.
Ka-CHUNK

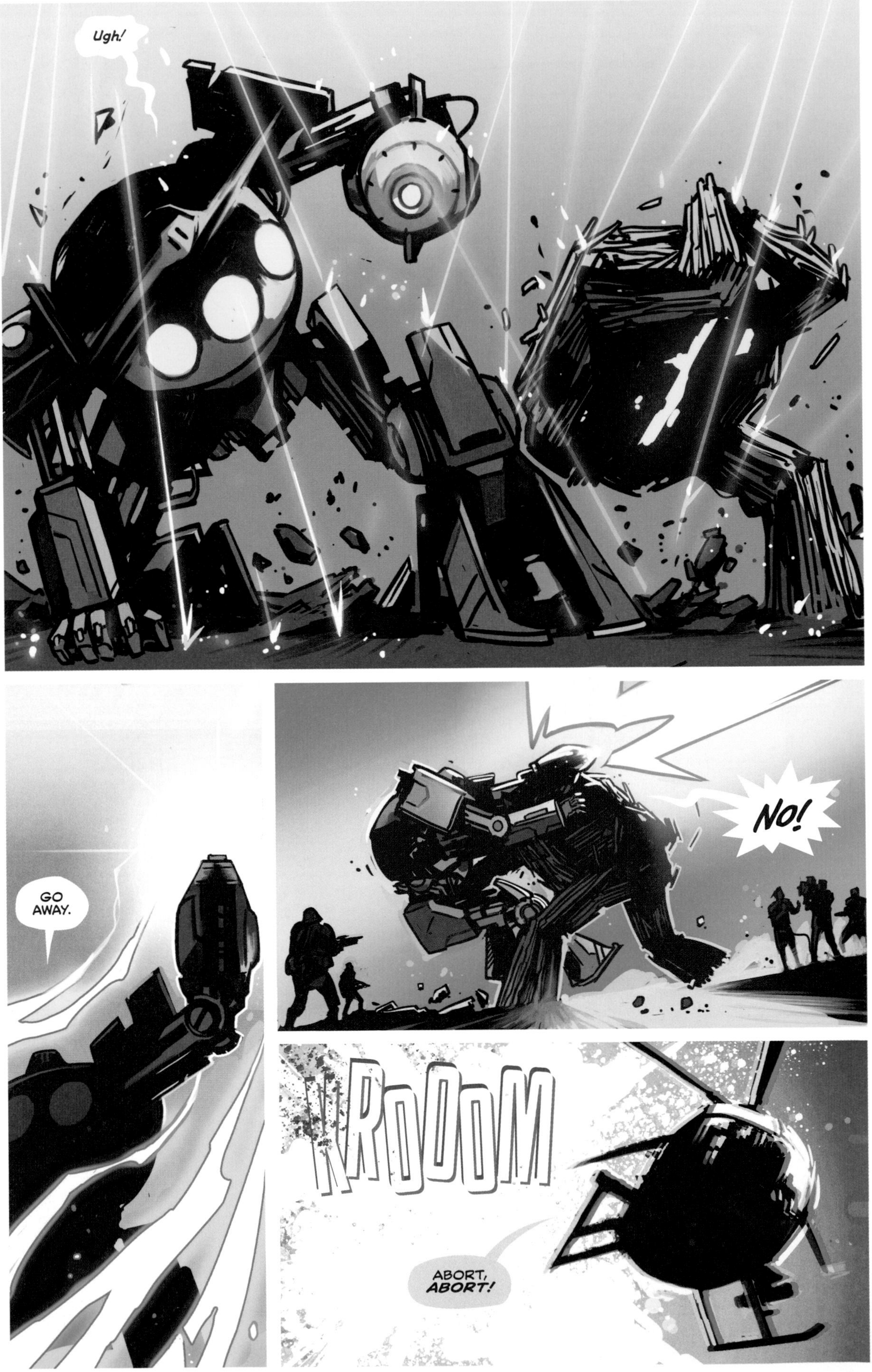
Ugh!
GO AWAY.
NO!
KROOOM
ABORT, ABORT!

WHERE'D SHE *GO?* DID YOU STOP HER?

NO CHANCE. GUYS, SHE'S NOT IN CONTROL. SHE'S NOT *GOING* TO STOP.

THAT MACHINE... IT'S *AMERICA INCARNATE.* IT BEGAN WITH AN ACTUAL GOAL...BUT NOW IT'S GOT A TASTE, IT'S GOING TO FEAST AND FEAST AND IT'S NOT GOING TO STOP.

AND IT'S WAY TOO MUCH FOR THIS HOUSE TO HANDLE. I DON'T KNOW WHAT TO--

THE MISSING... ONE...

YOU'RE SURE?

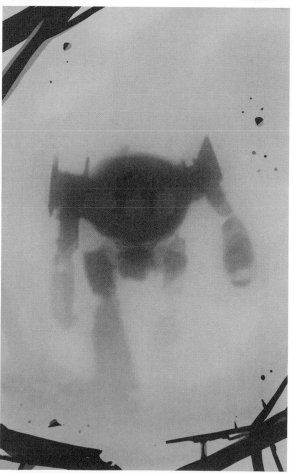

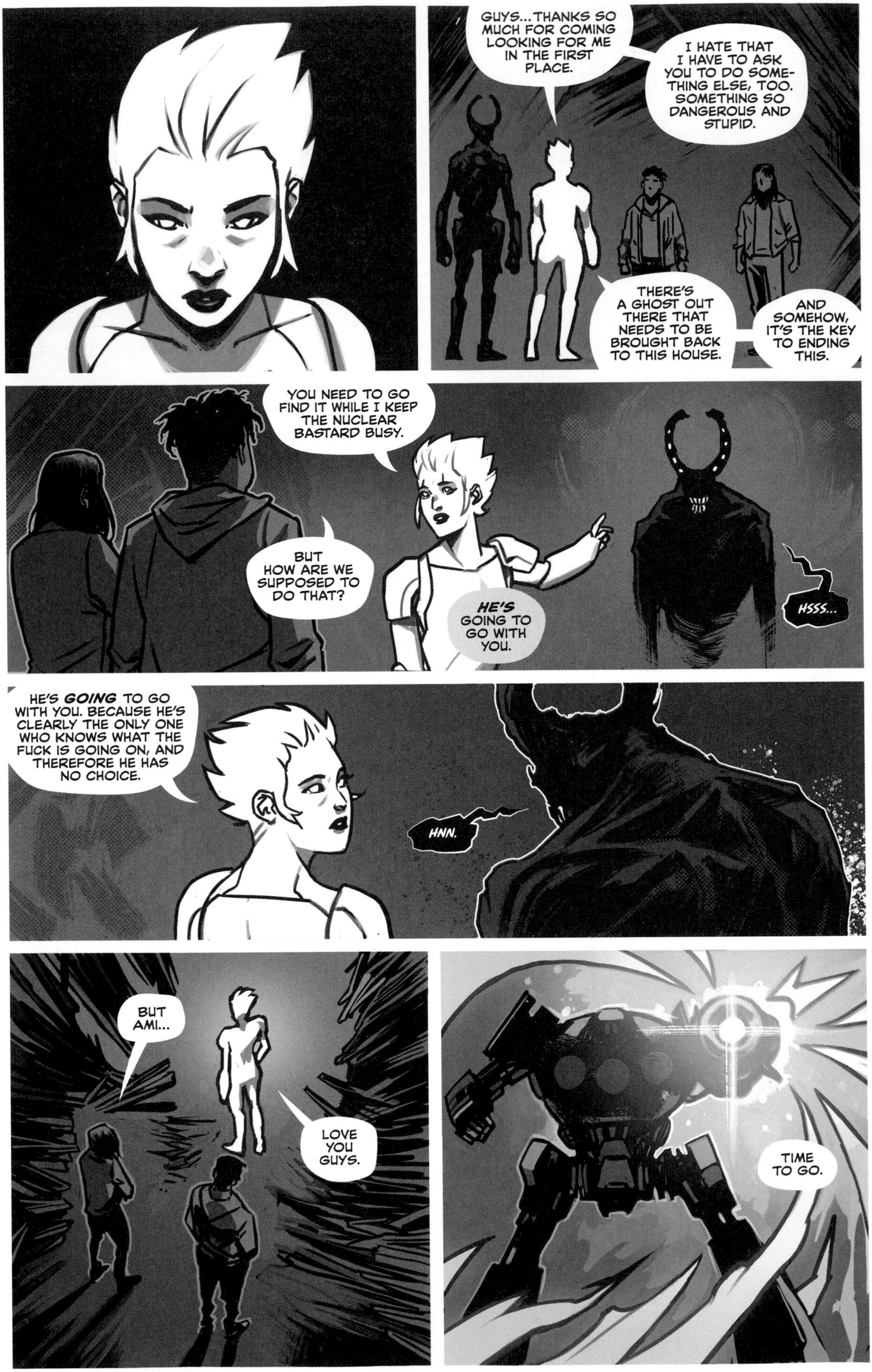
GUYS...THANKS SO MUCH FOR COMING LOOKING FOR ME IN THE FIRST PLACE.
I HATE THAT I HAVE TO ASK YOU TO DO SOMETHING ELSE, TOO. SOMETHING SO DANGEROUS AND STUPID.
THERE'S A GHOST OUT THERE THAT NEEDS TO BE BROUGHT BACK TO THIS HOUSE.
AND SOMEHOW, IT'S THE KEY TO ENDING THIS.
YOU NEED TO GO FIND IT WHILE I KEEP THE NUCLEAR BASTARD BUSY.
BUT HOW ARE WE SUPPOSED TO DO THAT?
HE'S GOING TO GO WITH YOU.
HSSS...
HE'S GOING TO GO WITH YOU. BECAUSE HE'S CLEARLY THE ONLY ONE WHO KNOWS WHAT THE FUCK IS GOING ON, AND THEREFORE HE HAS NO CHOICE.
HNN.
BUT AMI...
LOVE YOU GUYS.
TIME TO GO.

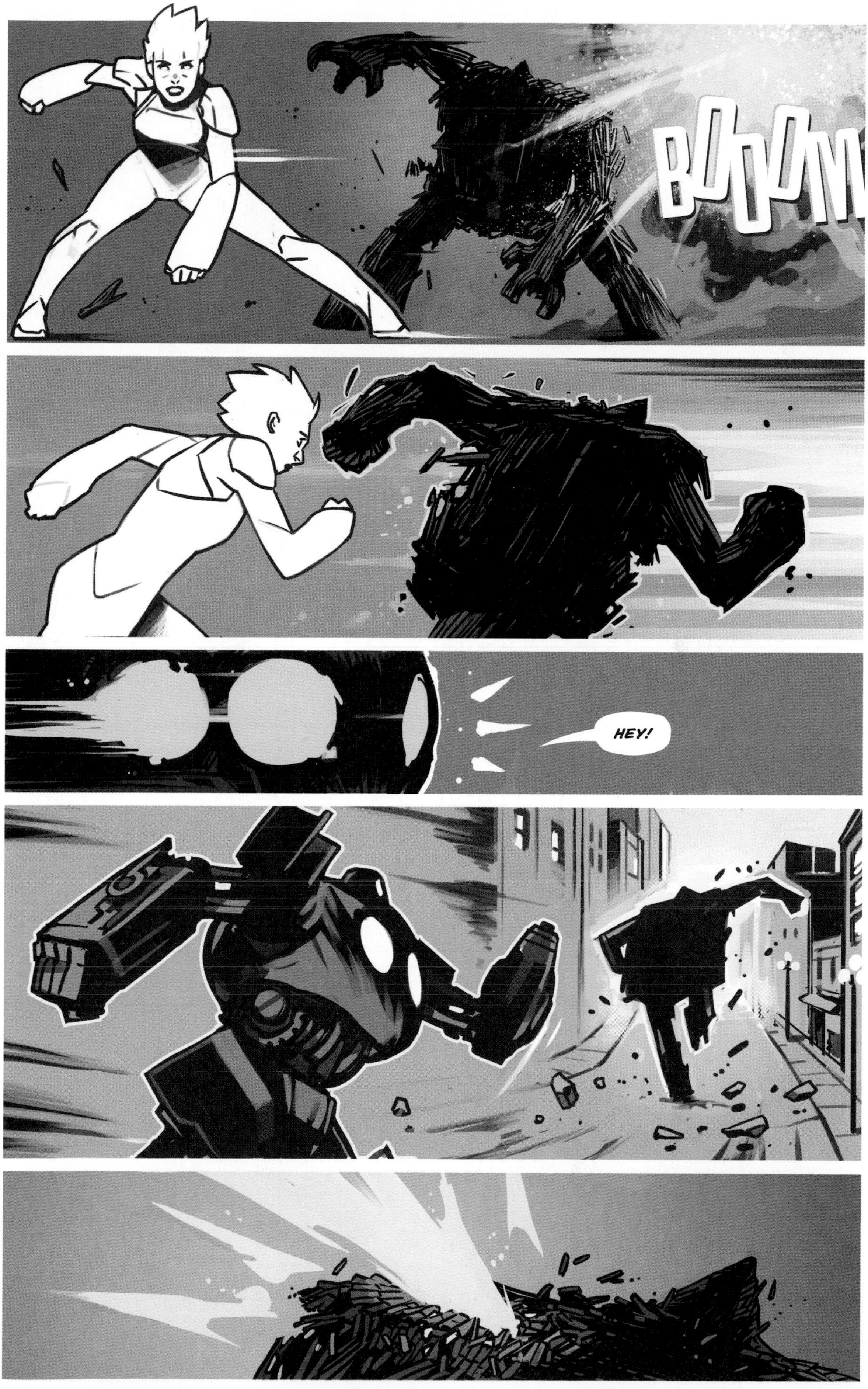
BOOOM
HEY!

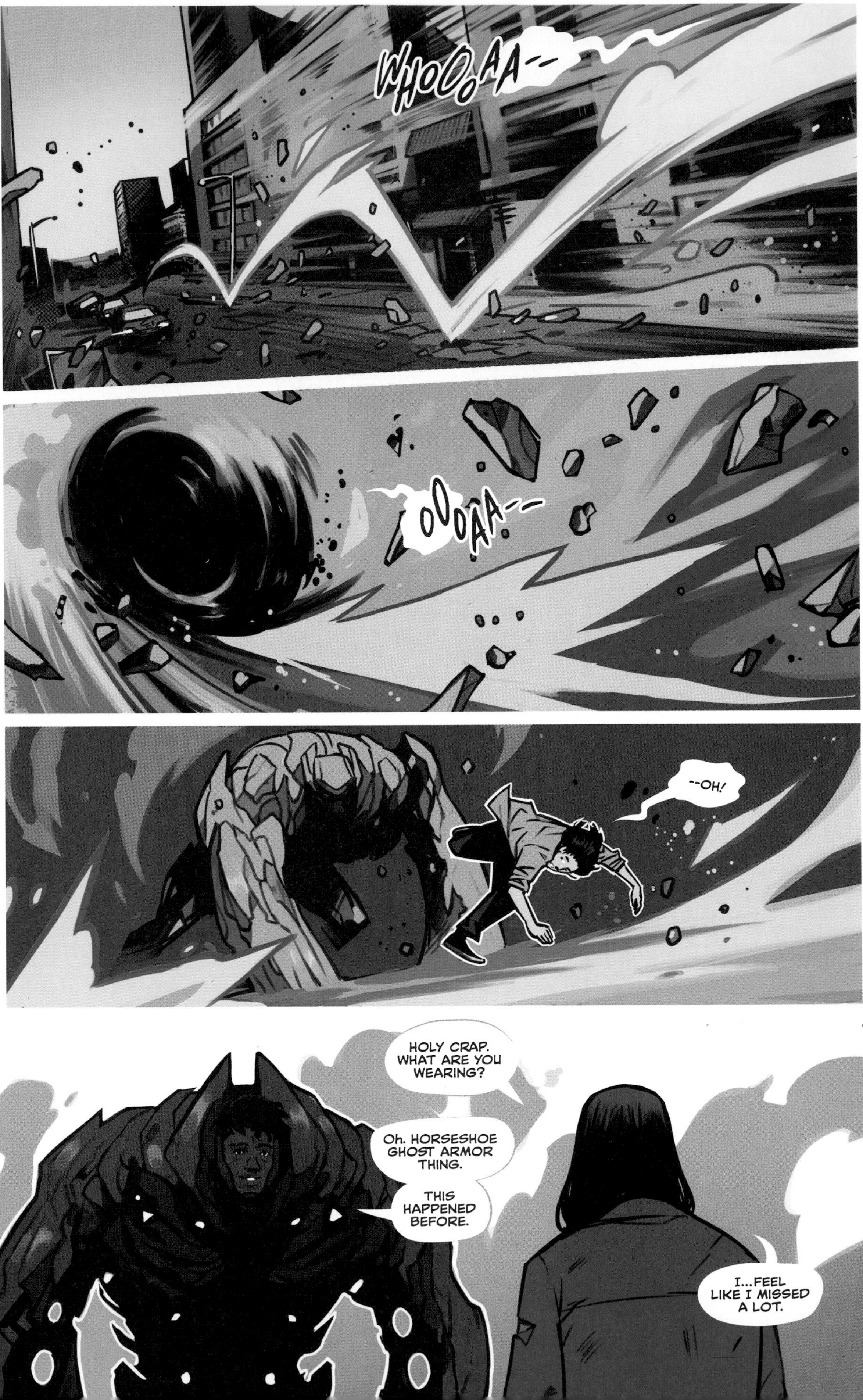
WHOOOoAA--
OOOAA--
--OH!
HOLY CRAP. WHAT ARE YOU WEARING?
Oh. HORSESHOE GHOST ARMOR THING.
THIS HAPPENED BEFORE.
I...FEEL LIKE I MISSED A LOT.

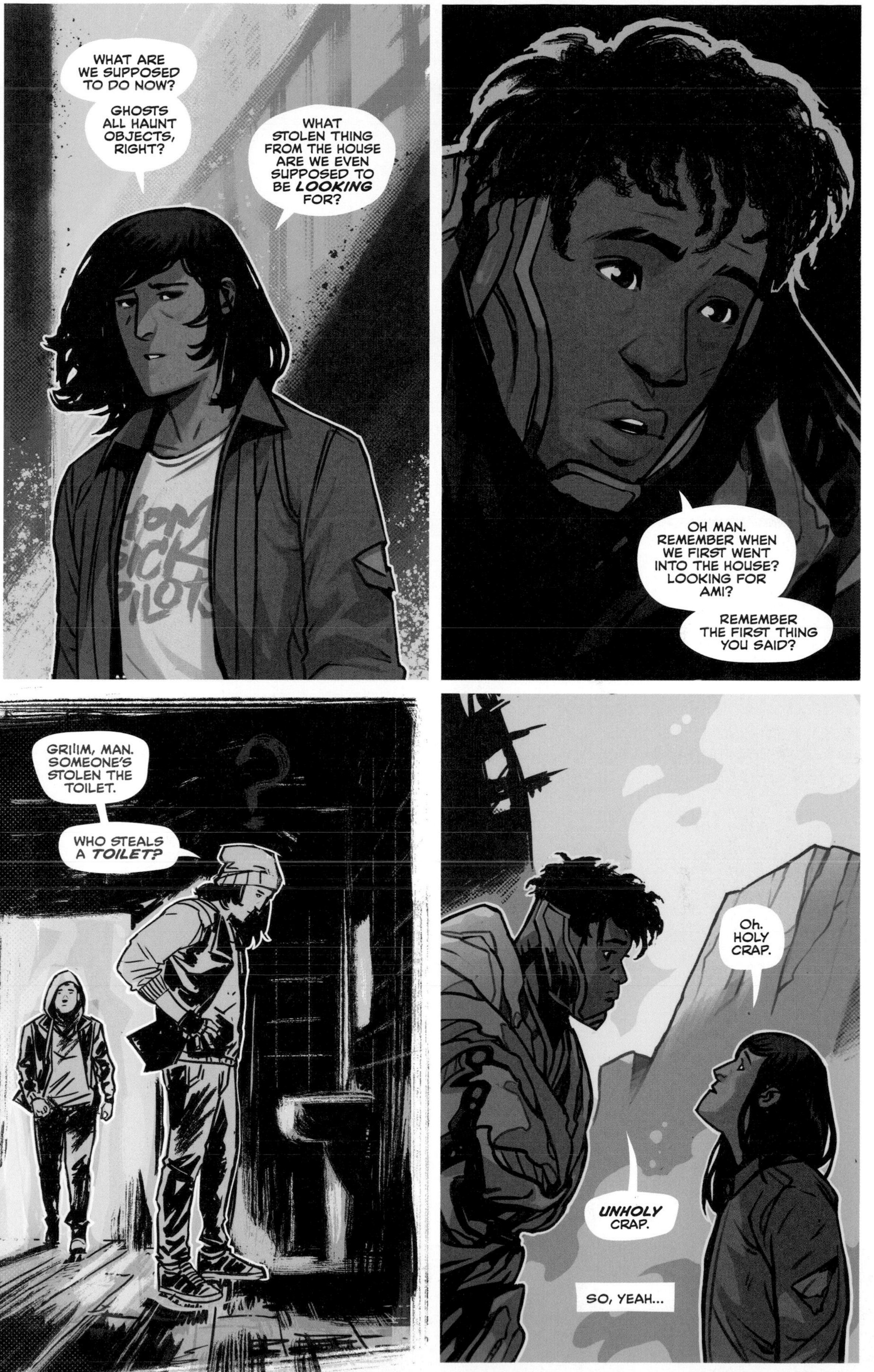
WHAT ARE WE SUPPOSED TO DO NOW?
GHOSTS ALL HAUNT OBJECTS, RIGHT?
WHAT STOLEN THING FROM THE HOUSE ARE WE EVEN SUPPOSED TO BE ***LOOKING*** FOR?
OH MAN. REMEMBER WHEN WE FIRST WENT INTO THE HOUSE? LOOKING FOR AMI?
REMEMBER THE FIRST THING YOU SAID?
GRIIIM, MAN. SOMEONE'S STOLEN THE TOILET.
WHO STEALS A ***TOILET?***
Oh. HOLY CRAP.
UNHOLY CRAP.
SO, YEAH...

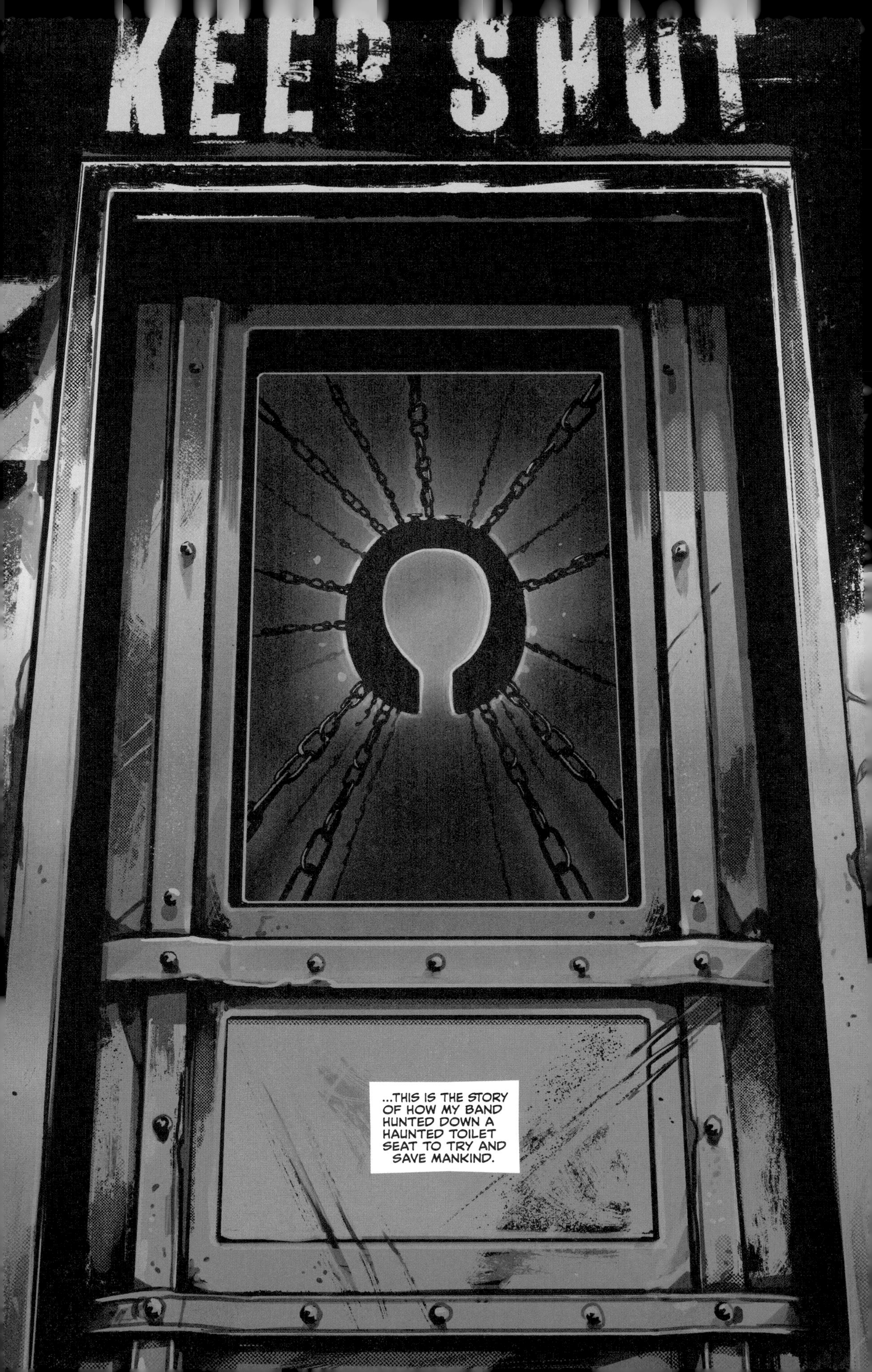
KEEP SHUT
...THIS IS THE STORY OF HOW MY BAND HUNTED DOWN A HAUNTED TOILET SEAT TO TRY AND SAVE MANKIND.

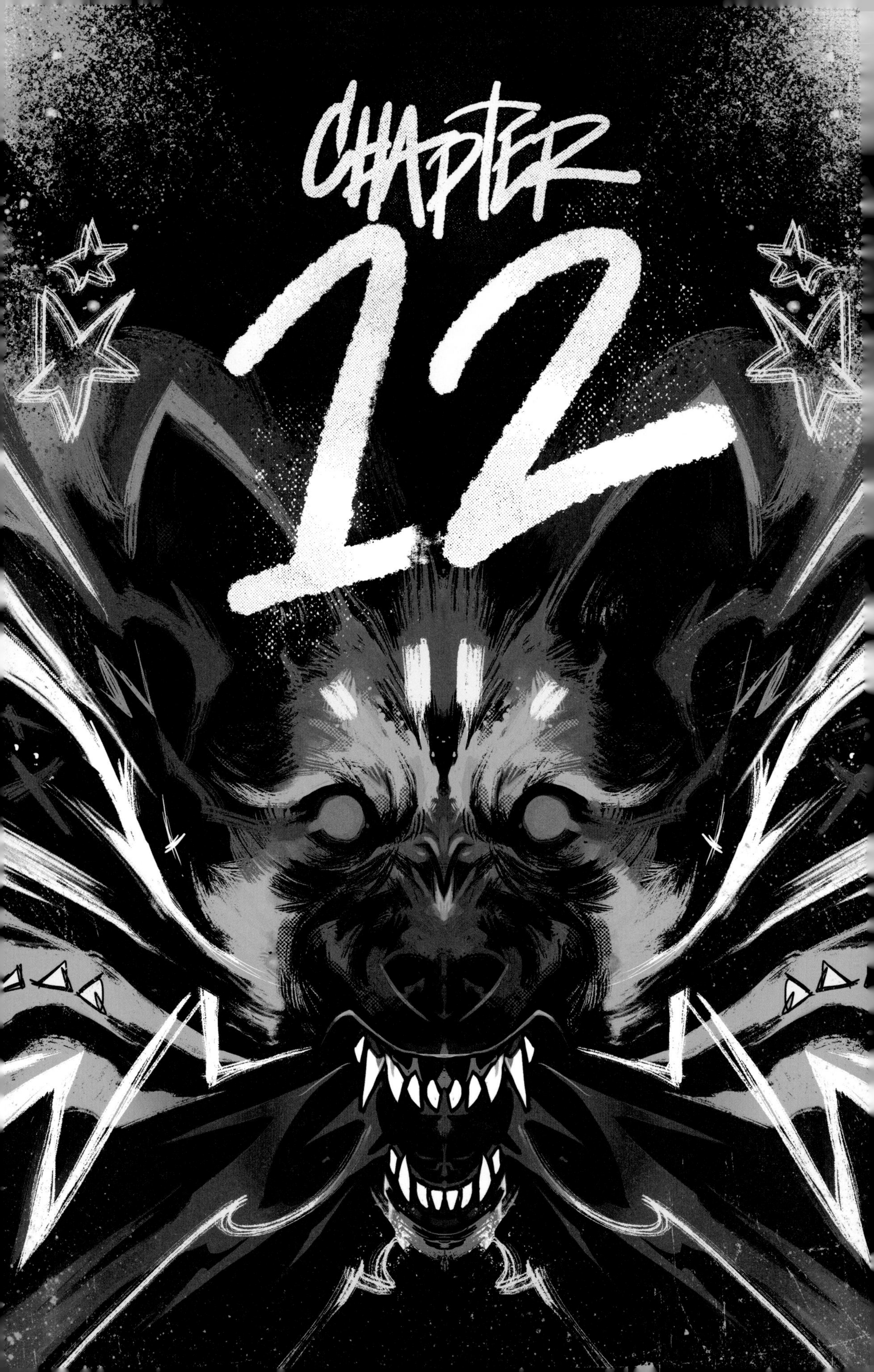
CHAPTER
22

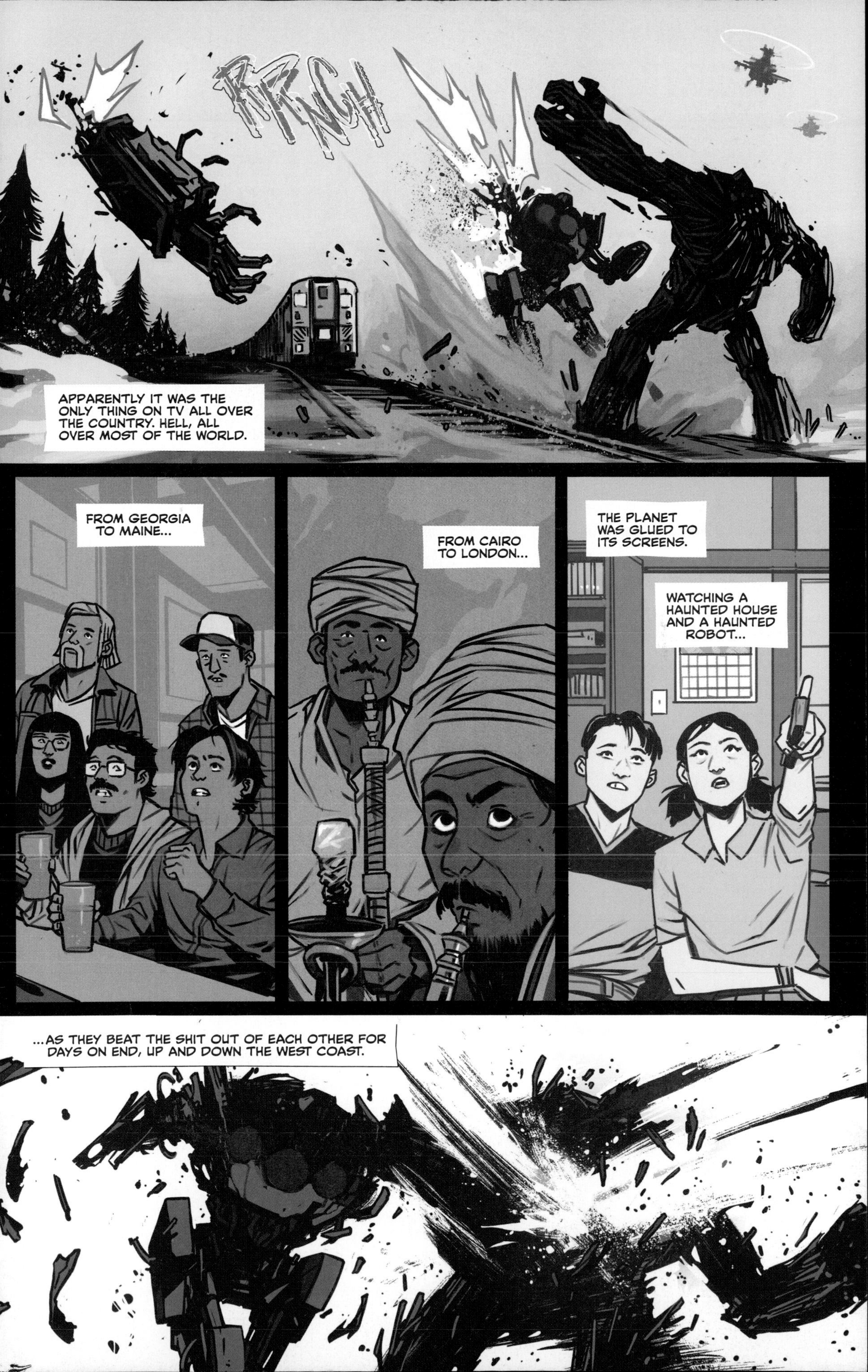
RRRNCH
APPARENTLY IT WAS THE ONLY THING ON TV ALL OVER THE COUNTRY. HELL, ALL OVER MOST OF THE WORLD.
FROM GEORGIA TO MAINE...
FROM CAIRO TO LONDON...
THE PLANET WAS GLUED TO ITS SCREENS.
WATCHING A HAUNTED HOUSE AND A HAUNTED ROBOT...
...AS THEY BEAT THE SHIT OUT OF EACH OTHER FOR DAYS ON END, UP AND DOWN THE WEST COAST.

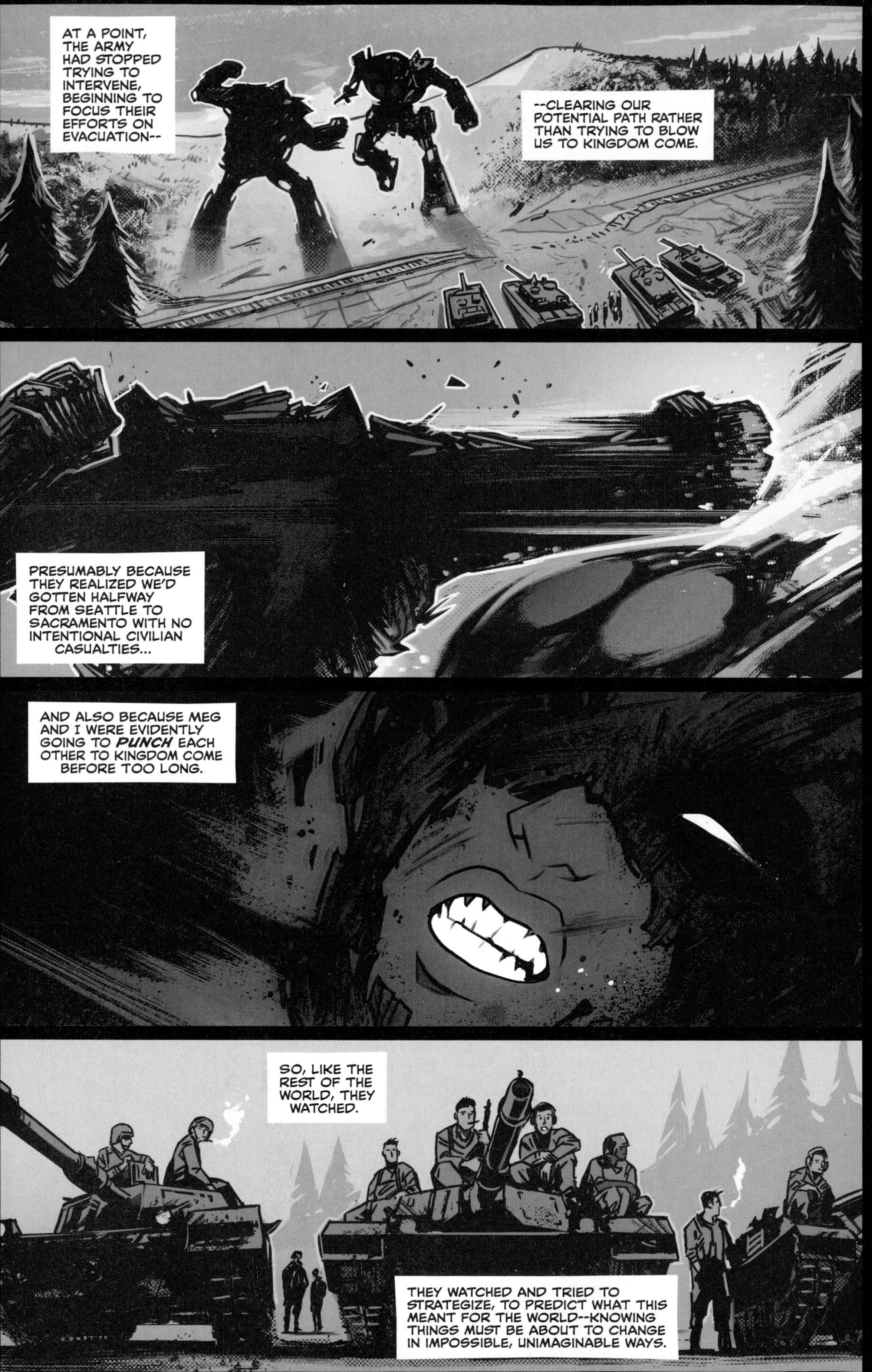
AT A POINT, THE ARMY HAD STOPPED TRYING TO INTERVENE, BEGINNING TO FOCUS THEIR EFFORTS ON EVACUATION--
--CLEARING OUR POTENTIAL PATH RATHER THAN TRYING TO BLOW US TO KINGDOM COME.
PRESUMABLY BECAUSE THEY REALIZED WE'D GOTTEN HALFWAY FROM SEATTLE TO SACRAMENTO WITH NO INTENTIONAL CIVILIAN CASUALTIES...
AND ALSO BECAUSE MEG AND I WERE EVIDENTLY GOING TO PUNCH EACH OTHER TO KINGDOM COME BEFORE TOO LONG.
SO, LIKE THE REST OF THE WORLD, THEY WATCHED.
THEY WATCHED AND TRIED TO STRATEGIZE, TO PREDICT WHAT THIS MEANT FOR THE WORLD--KNOWING THINGS MUST BE ABOUT TO CHANGE IN IMPOSSIBLE, UNIMAGINABLE WAYS.

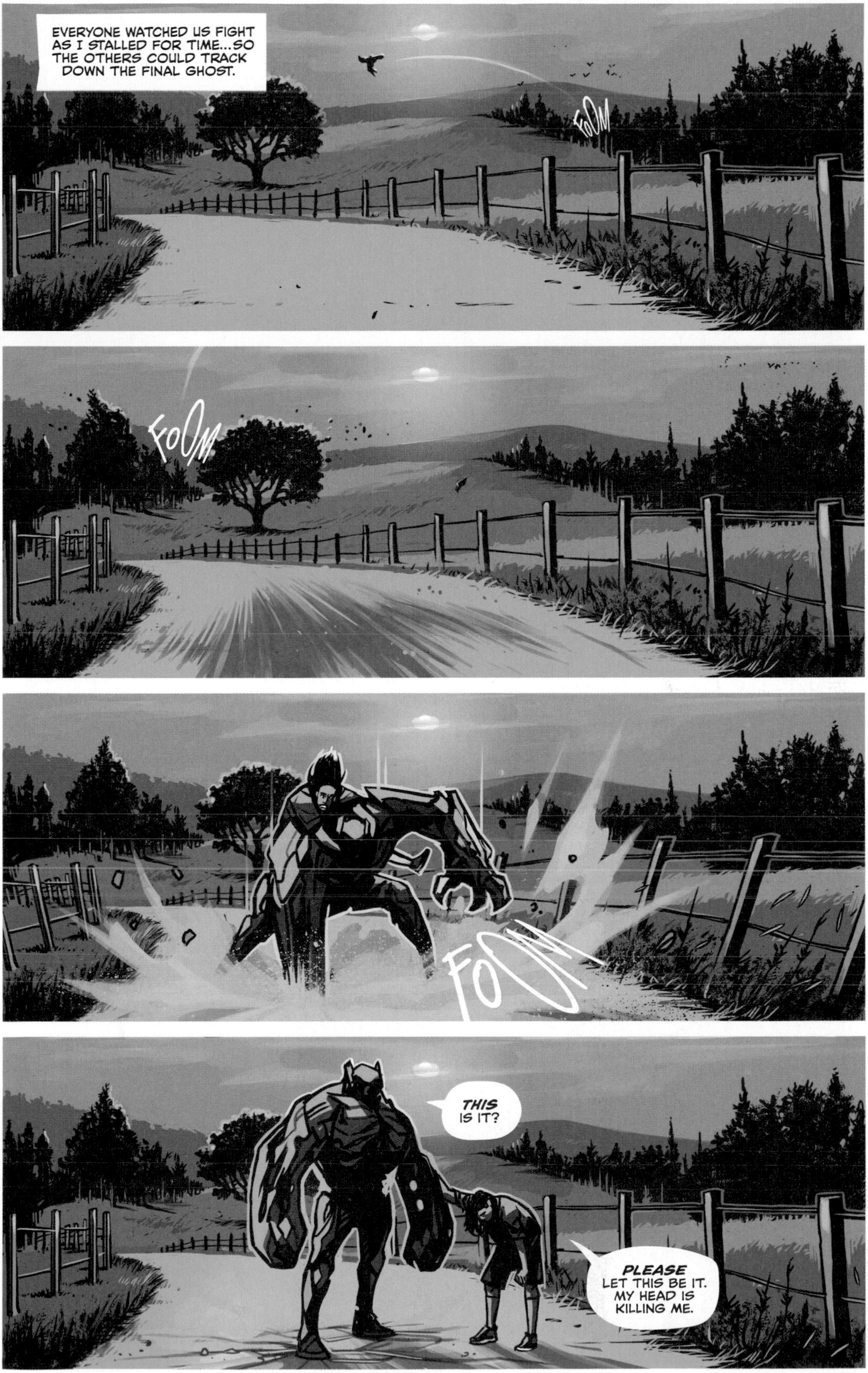
EVERYONE WATCHED US FIGHT AS I STALLED FOR TIME...SO THE OTHERS COULD TRACK DOWN THE FINAL GHOST.
FOOM
FOOM
FOOM
THIS IS IT?
PLEASE LET THIS BE IT. MY HEAD IS KILLING ME.

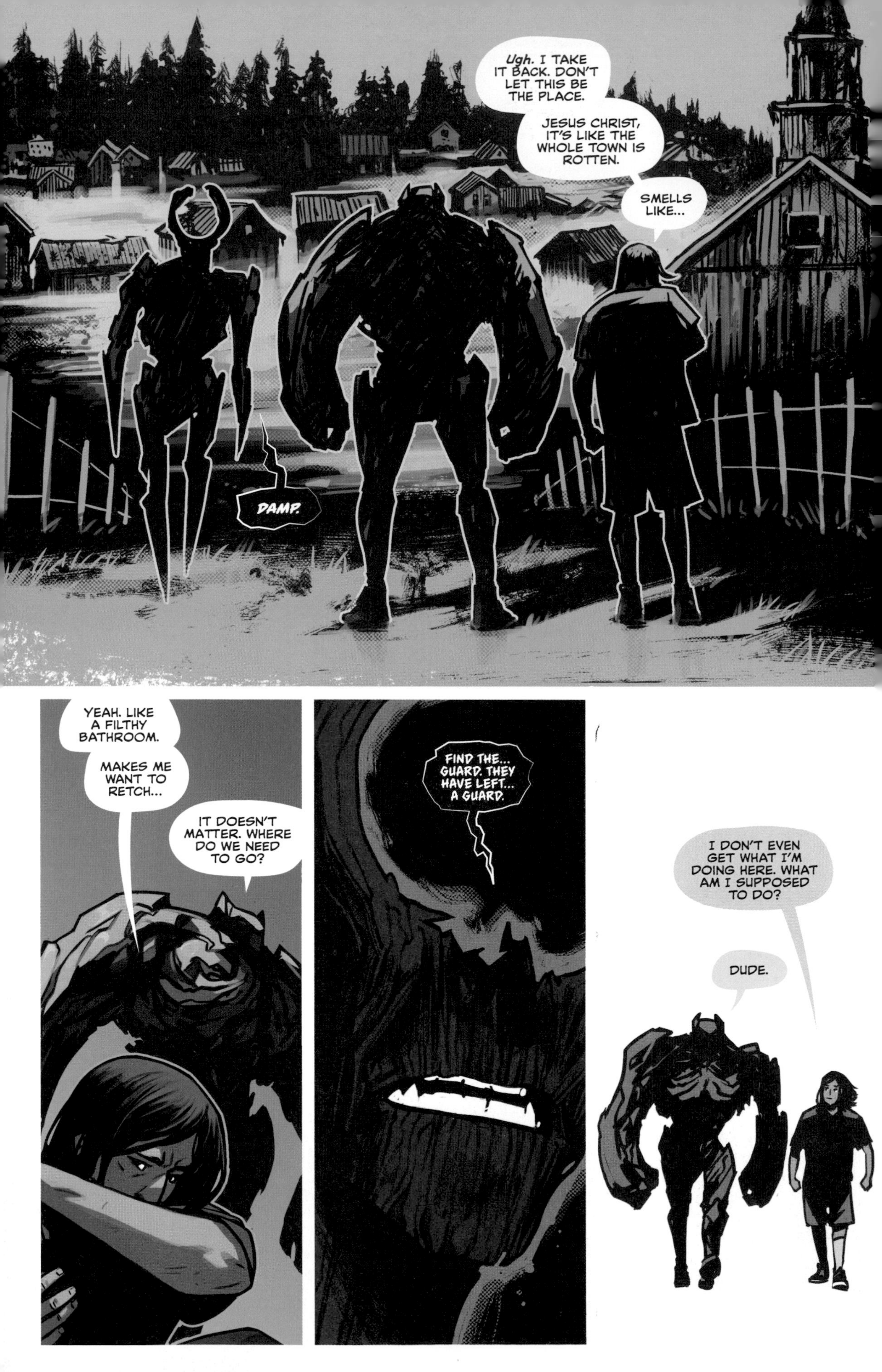
Ugh. I TAKE IT BACK. DON'T LET THIS BE THE PLACE.
JESUS CHRIST, IT'S LIKE THE WHOLE TOWN IS ROTTEN.
SMELLS LIKE...
DAMP.
YEAH. LIKE A FILTHY BATHROOM.
MAKES ME WANT TO RETCH...
IT DOESN'T MATTER. WHERE DO WE NEED TO GO?
FIND THE... GUARD. THEY HAVE LEFT... A GUARD.
I DON'T EVEN GET WHAT I'M DOING HERE. WHAT AM I SUPPOSED TO DO?
DUDE.

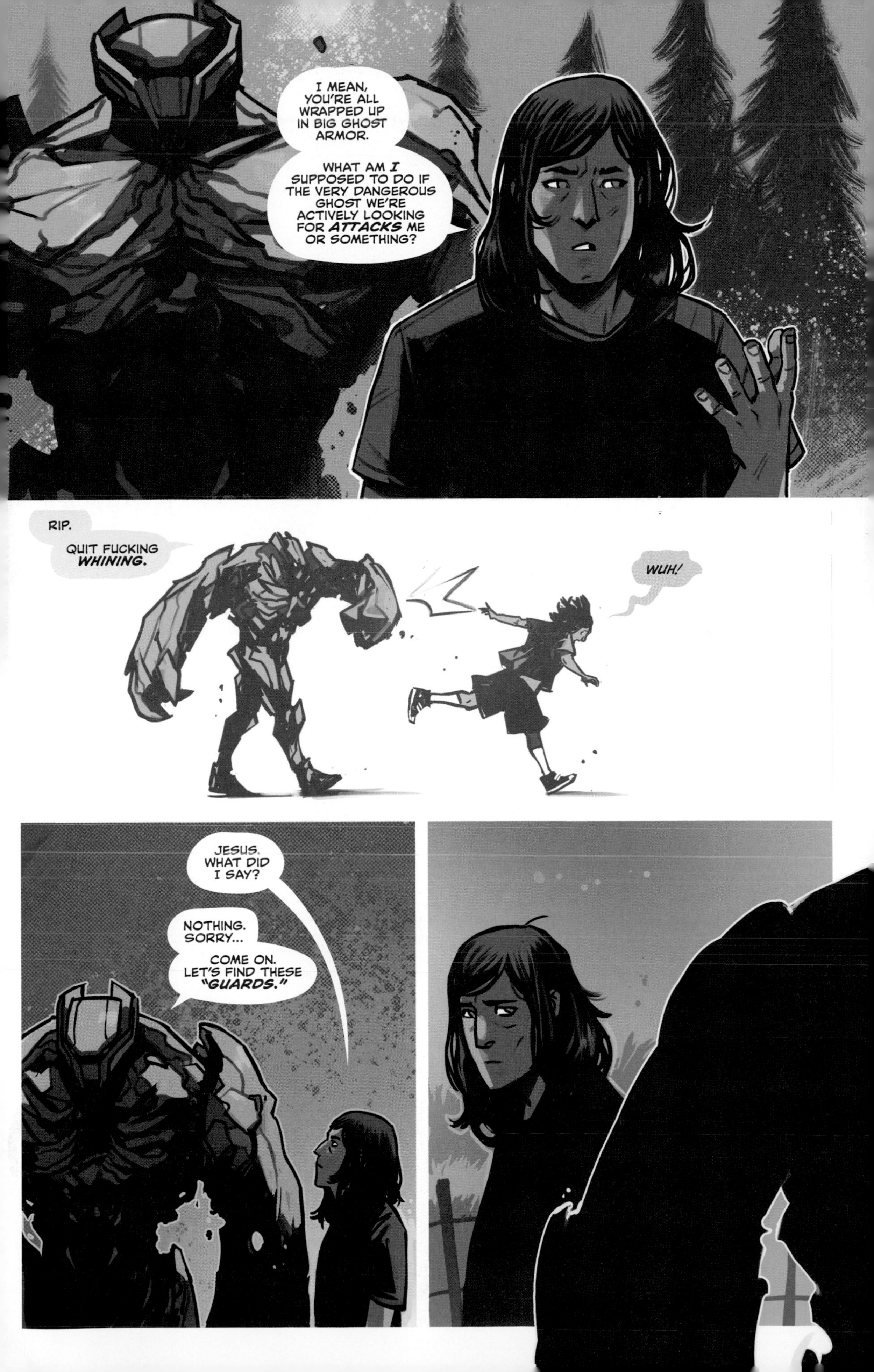
I MEAN, YOU'RE ALL WRAPPED UP IN BIG GHOST ARMOR.
WHAT AM *I* SUPPOSED TO DO IF THE VERY DANGEROUS GHOST WE'RE ACTIVELY LOOKING FOR *ATTACKS* ME OR SOMETHING?
RIP.
QUIT FUCKING *WHINING.*
WUH!
JESUS. WHAT DID I SAY?
NOTHING. SORRY...
COME ON. LET'S FIND THESE *"GUARDS."*

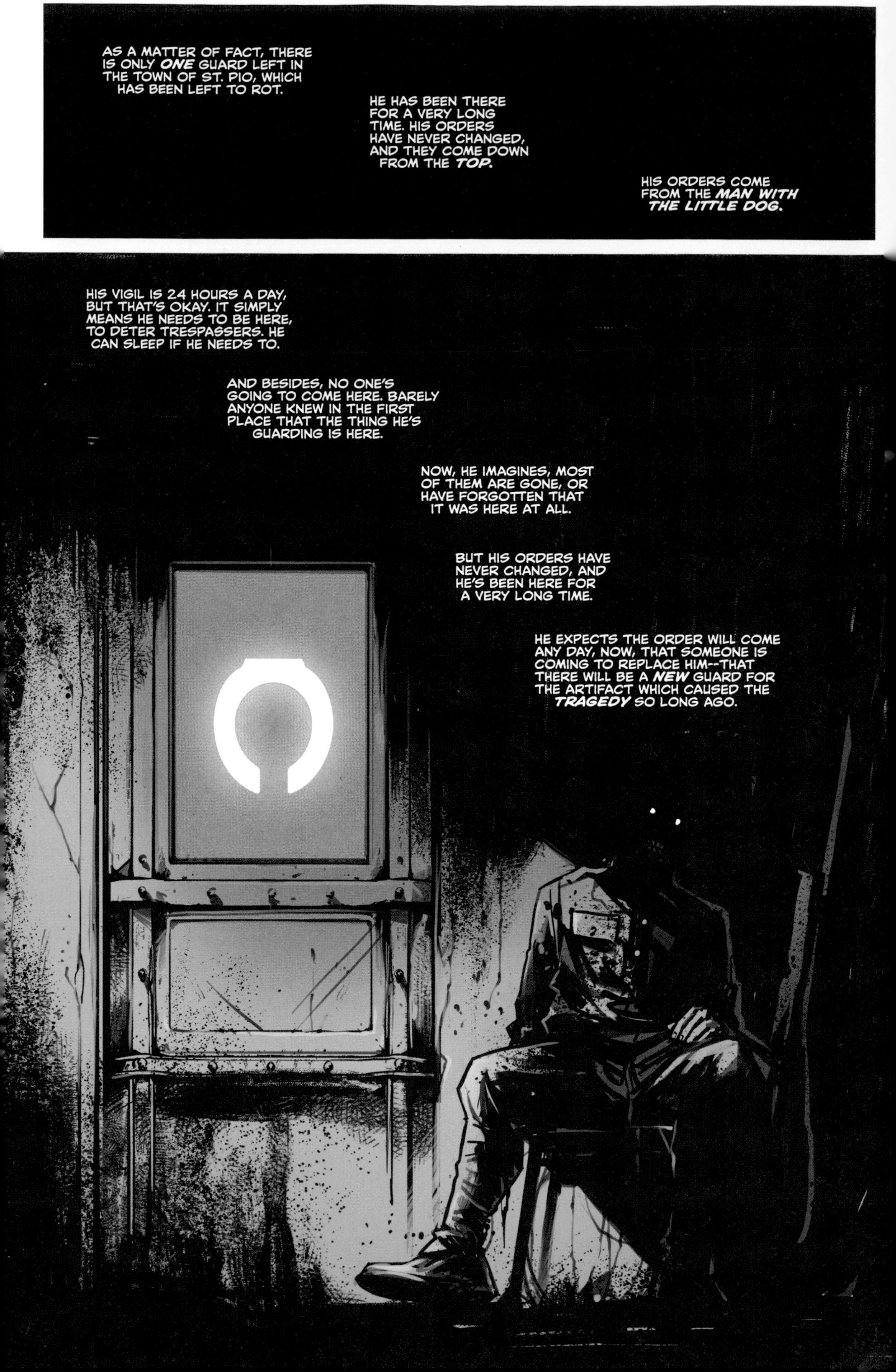
AS A MATTER OF FACT, THERE IS ONLY ***ONE*** GUARD LEFT IN THE TOWN OF ST. PIO, WHICH HAS BEEN LEFT TO ROT.
HE HAS BEEN THERE FOR A VERY LONG TIME. HIS ORDERS HAVE NEVER CHANGED, AND THEY COME DOWN FROM THE ***TOP***.
HIS ORDERS COME FROM THE ***MAN WITH THE LITTLE DOG***.
HIS VIGIL IS 24 HOURS A DAY, BUT THAT'S OKAY. IT SIMPLY MEANS HE NEEDS TO BE HERE, TO DETER TRESPASSERS. HE CAN SLEEP IF HE NEEDS TO.
AND BESIDES, NO ONE'S GOING TO COME HERE. BARELY ANYONE KNEW IN THE FIRST PLACE THAT THE THING HE'S GUARDING IS HERE.
NOW, HE IMAGINES, MOST OF THEM ARE GONE, OR HAVE FORGOTTEN THAT IT WAS HERE AT ALL.
BUT HIS ORDERS HAVE NEVER CHANGED, AND HE'S BEEN HERE FOR A VERY LONG TIME.
HE EXPECTS THE ORDER WILL COME ANY DAY, NOW, THAT SOMEONE IS COMING TO REPLACE HIM--THAT THERE WILL BE A ***NEW*** GUARD FOR THE ARTIFACT WHICH CAUSED THE ***TRAGEDY*** SO LONG AGO.

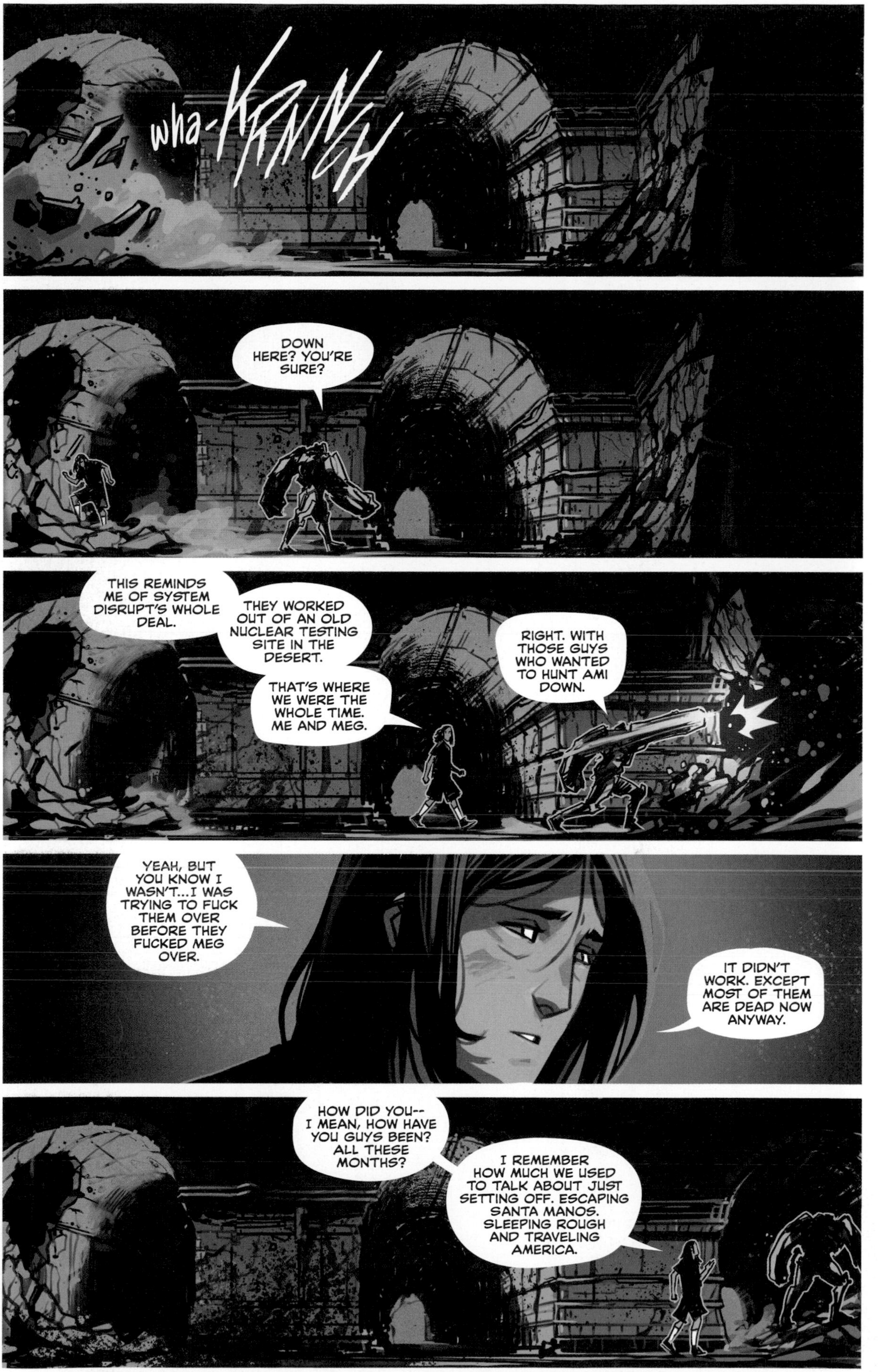
wha-KRNNCH
DOWN HERE? YOU'RE SURE?
THIS REMINDS ME OF SYSTEM DISRUPT'S WHOLE DEAL.
THEY WORKED OUT OF AN OLD NUCLEAR TESTING SITE IN THE DESERT.
THAT'S WHERE WE WERE THE WHOLE TIME. ME AND MEG.
RIGHT. WITH THOSE GUYS WHO WANTED TO HUNT AMI DOWN.
YEAH, BUT YOU KNOW I WASN'T...I WAS TRYING TO FUCK THEM OVER BEFORE THEY FUCKED MEG OVER.
IT DIDN'T WORK. EXCEPT MOST OF THEM ARE DEAD NOW ANYWAY.
HOW DID YOU-- I MEAN, HOW HAVE YOU GUYS BEEN? ALL THESE MONTHS?
I REMEMBER HOW MUCH WE USED TO TALK ABOUT JUST SETTING OFF. ESCAPING SANTA MANOS. SLEEPING ROUGH AND TRAVELING AMERICA.

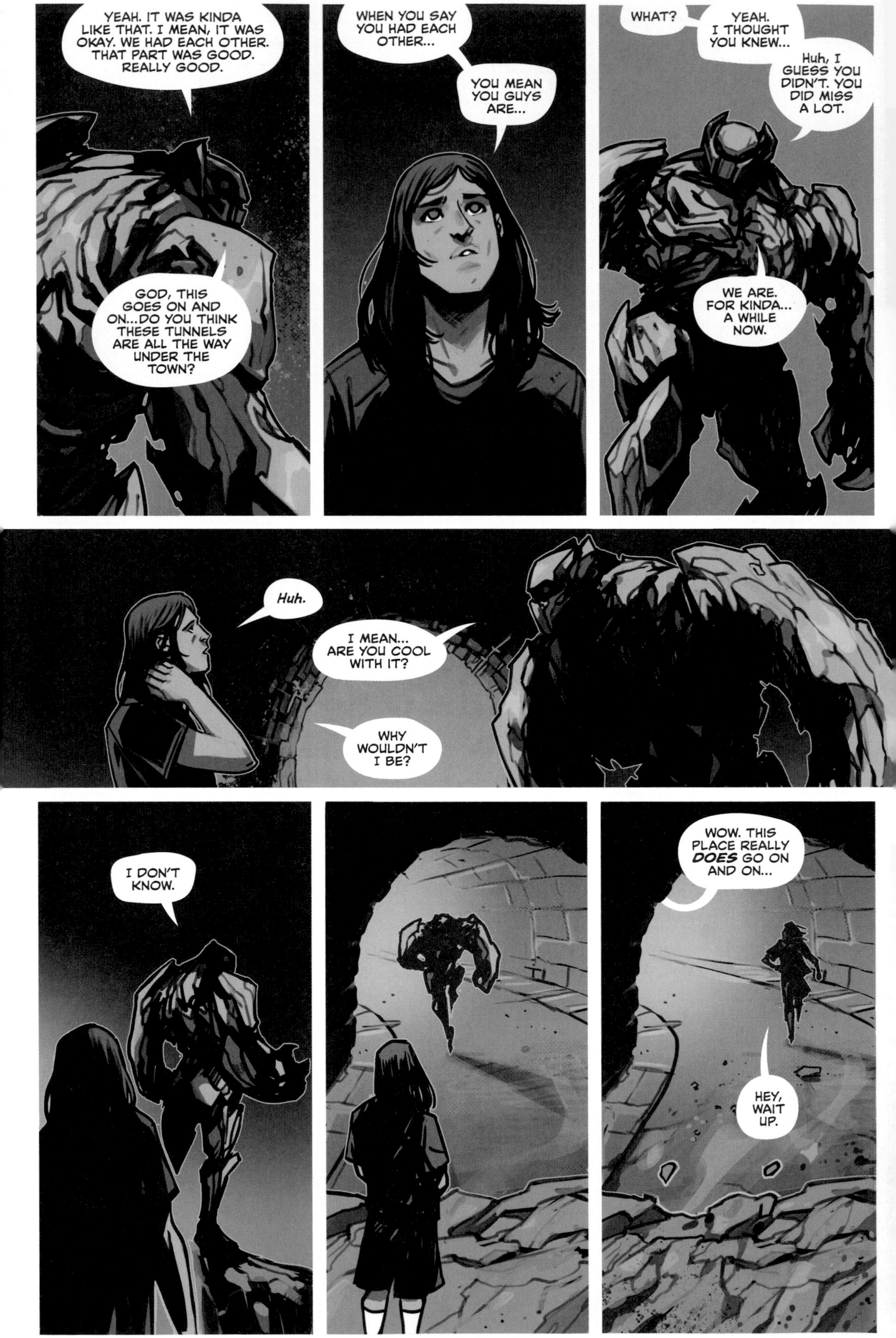
YEAH. IT WAS KINDA LIKE THAT. I MEAN, IT WAS OKAY. WE HAD EACH OTHER. THAT PART WAS GOOD. REALLY GOOD.
GOD, THIS GOES ON AND ON...DO YOU THINK THESE TUNNELS ARE ALL THE WAY UNDER THE TOWN?
WHEN YOU SAY YOU HAD EACH OTHER...
YOU MEAN YOU GUYS ARE...
WHAT?
YEAH. I THOUGHT YOU KNEW...
Huh, I GUESS YOU DIDN'T. YOU DID MISS A LOT.
WE ARE. FOR KINDA... A WHILE NOW.
Huh.
I MEAN... ARE YOU COOL WITH IT?
WHY WOULDN'T I BE?
I DON'T KNOW.
WOW. THIS PLACE REALLY ***DOES*** GO ON AND ON...
HEY, WAIT UP.

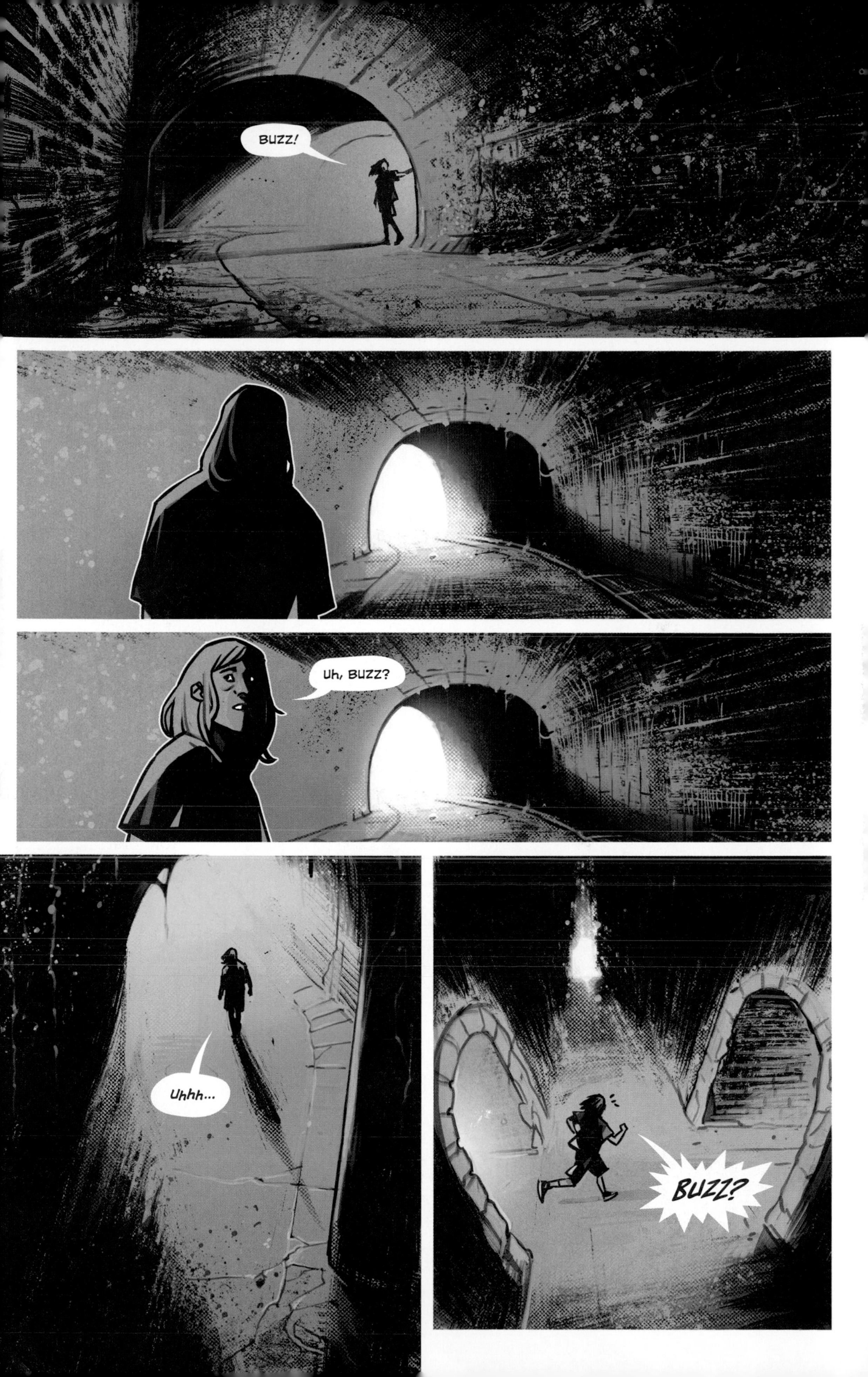
BUZZ!
Uh, BUZZ?
Uhhh...
BUZZ?

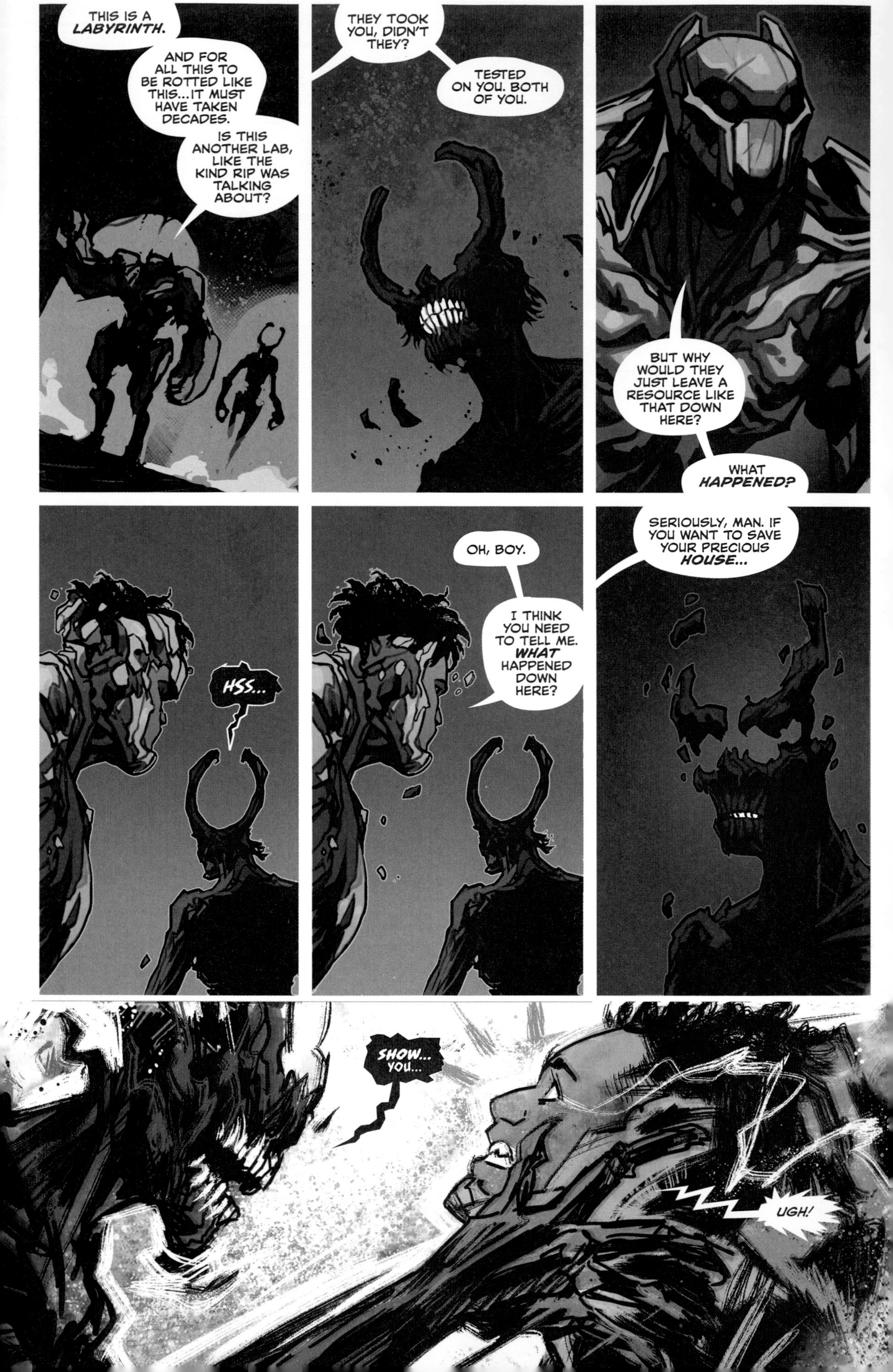

THIS IS A *LABYRINTH*.
AND FOR ALL THIS TO BE ROTTED LIKE THIS...IT MUST HAVE TAKEN DECADES.
IS THIS ANOTHER LAB, LIKE THE KIND RIP WAS TALKING ABOUT?
THEY TOOK YOU, DIDN'T THEY?
TESTED ON YOU. BOTH OF YOU.
BUT WHY WOULD THEY JUST LEAVE A RESOURCE LIKE THAT DOWN HERE?
WHAT *HAPPENED?*
HSS...
OH, BOY.
I THINK YOU NEED TO TELL ME. *WHAT* HAPPENED DOWN HERE?
SERIOUSLY, MAN. IF YOU WANT TO SAVE YOUR PRECIOUS *HOUSE...*
SHOW... YOU...
UGH!

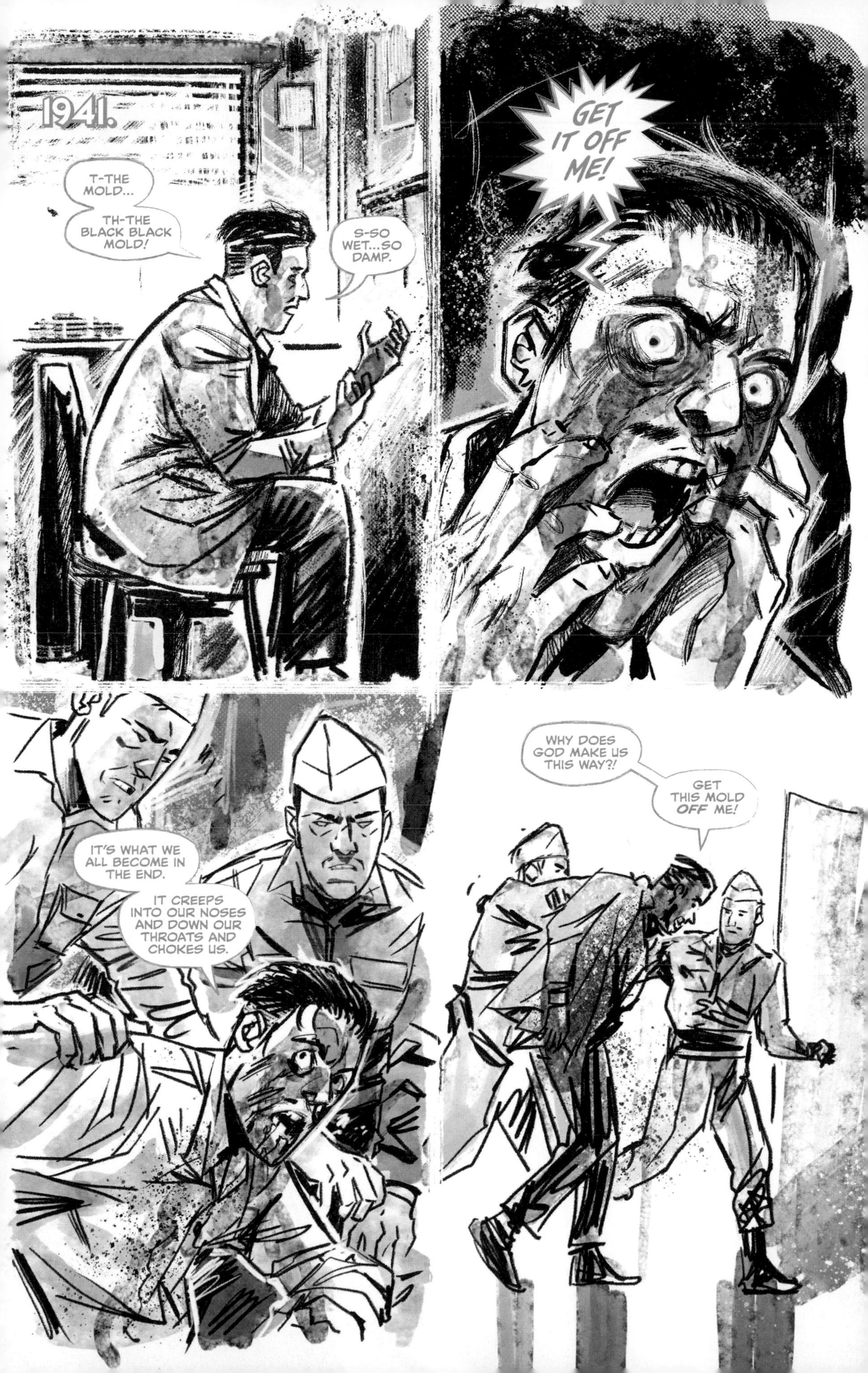
1941.
T-THE MOLD...
TH-THE BLACK BLACK MOLD!
S-SO WET...SO DAMP.
GET IT OFF ME!
IT'S WHAT WE ALL BECOME IN THE END.
IT CREEPS INTO OUR NOSES AND DOWN OUR THROATS AND CHOKES US.
WHY DOES GOD MAKE US THIS WAY?!
GET THIS MOLD OFF ME!

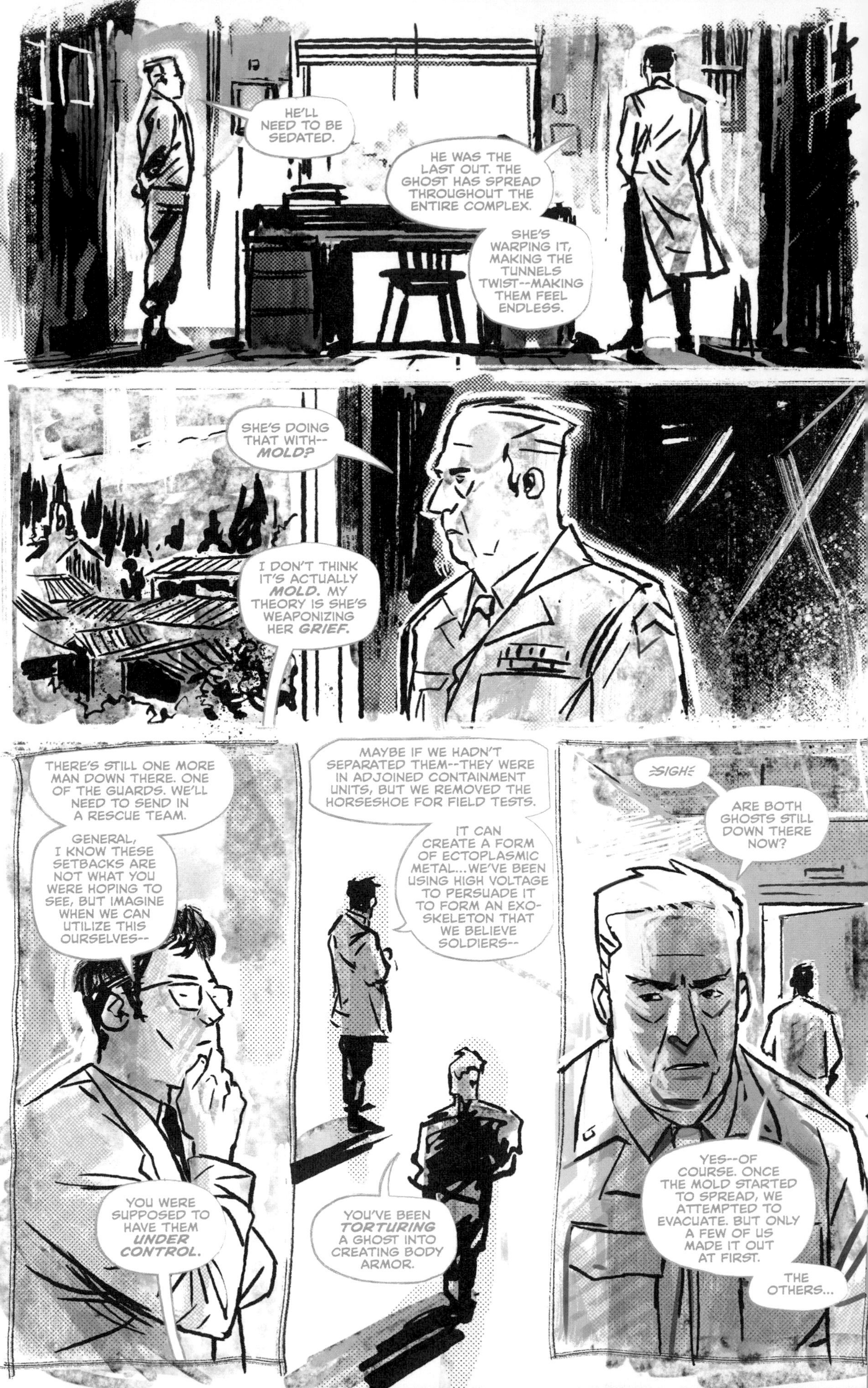
HE'LL NEED TO BE SEDATED.
HE WAS THE LAST OUT. THE GHOST HAS SPREAD THROUGHOUT THE ENTIRE COMPLEX.
SHE'S WARPING IT, MAKING THE TUNNELS TWIST--MAKING THEM FEEL ENDLESS.
SHE'S DOING THAT WITH-- MOLD?
I DON'T THINK IT'S ACTUALLY MOLD. MY THEORY IS SHE'S WEAPONIZING HER GRIEF.
THERE'S STILL ONE MORE MAN DOWN THERE. ONE OF THE GUARDS. WE'LL NEED TO SEND IN A RESCUE TEAM.
GENERAL, I KNOW THESE SETBACKS ARE NOT WHAT YOU WERE HOPING TO SEE, BUT IMAGINE WHEN WE CAN UTILIZE THIS OURSELVES--
YOU WERE SUPPOSED TO HAVE THEM UNDER CONTROL.
MAYBE IF WE HADN'T SEPARATED THEM--THEY WERE IN ADJOINED CONTAINMENT UNITS, BUT WE REMOVED THE HORSESHOE FOR FIELD TESTS.
IT CAN CREATE A FORM OF ECTOPLASMIC METAL...WE'VE BEEN USING HIGH VOLTAGE TO PERSUADE IT TO FORM AN EXO-SKELETON THAT WE BELIEVE SOLDIERS--
YOU'VE BEEN TORTURING A GHOST INTO CREATING BODY ARMOR.
SIGH
ARE BOTH GHOSTS STILL DOWN THERE NOW?
YES--OF COURSE. ONCE THE MOLD STARTED TO SPREAD, WE ATTEMPTED TO EVACUATE. BUT ONLY A FEW OF US MADE IT OUT AT FIRST.
THE OTHERS...

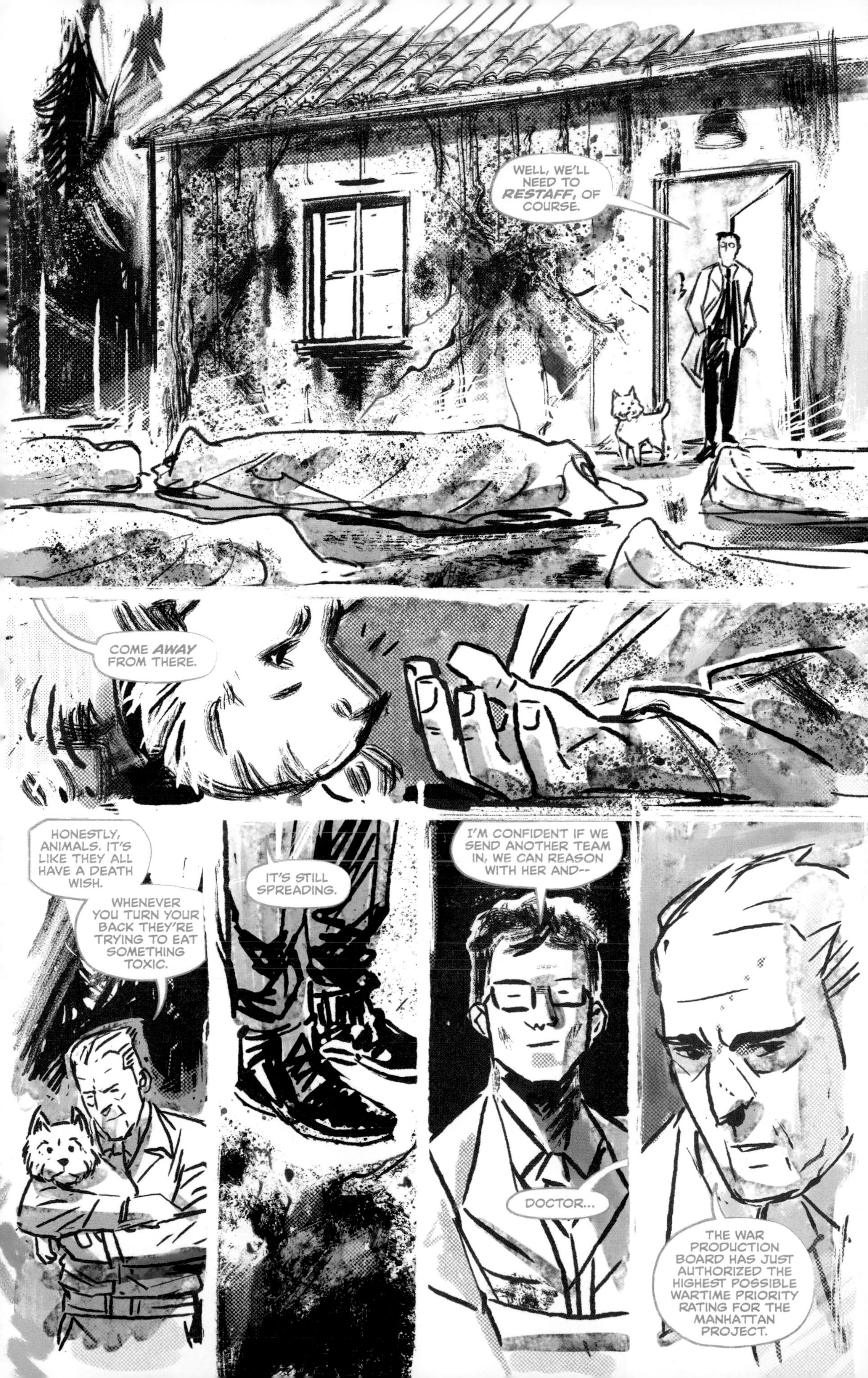
WELL, WE'LL NEED TO RESTAFF, OF COURSE.
COME AWAY FROM THERE.
HONESTLY, ANIMALS. IT'S LIKE THEY ALL HAVE A DEATH WISH.
WHENEVER YOU TURN YOUR BACK THEY'RE TRYING TO EAT SOMETHING TOXIC.
IT'S STILL SPREADING.
I'M CONFIDENT IF WE SEND ANOTHER TEAM IN, WE CAN REASON WITH HER AND--
DOCTOR...
THE WAR PRODUCTION BOARD HAS JUST AUTHORIZED THE HIGHEST POSSIBLE WARTIME PRIORITY RATING FOR THE MANHATTAN PROJECT.

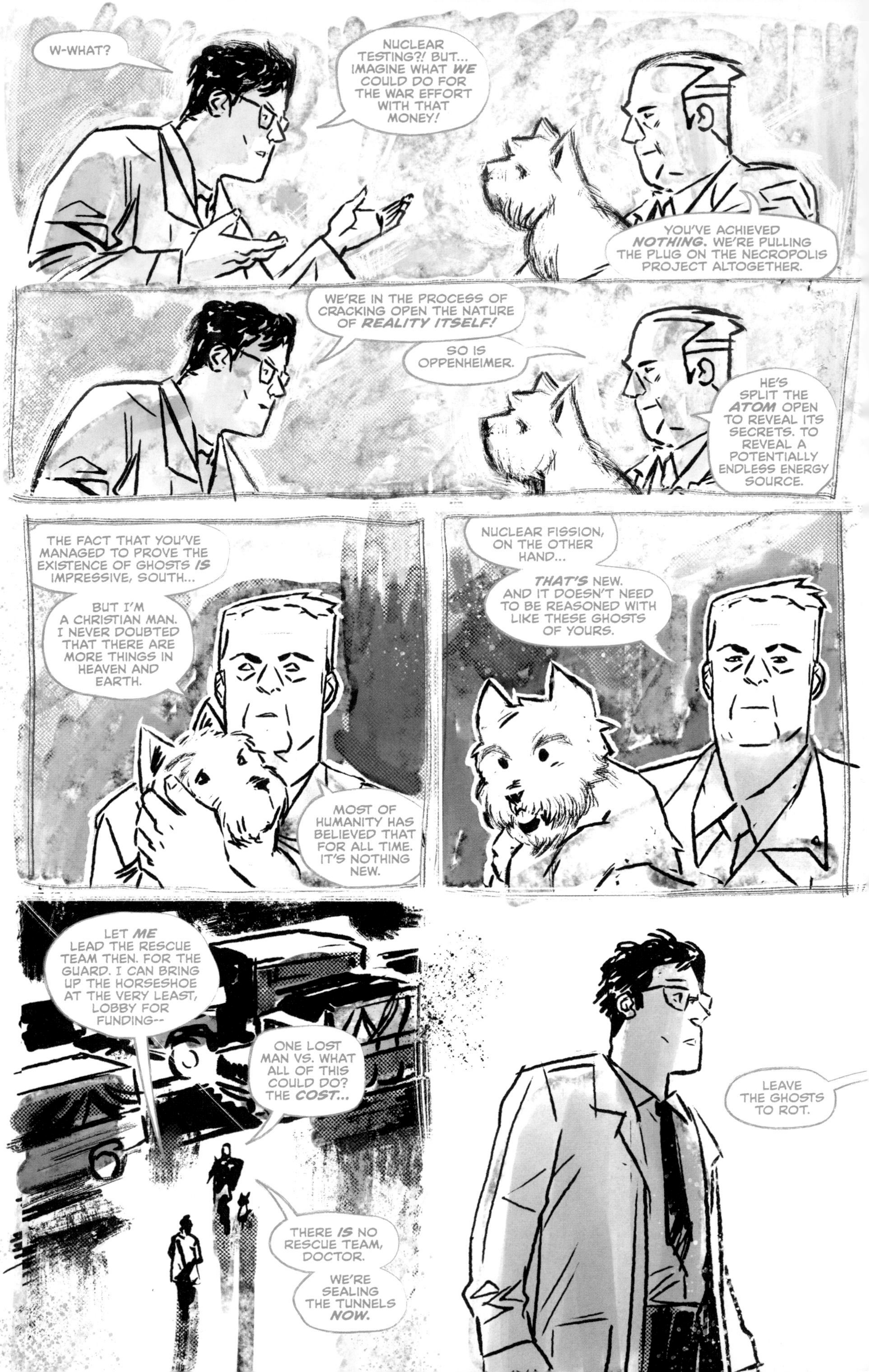
W-WHAT?
NUCLEAR TESTING?! BUT... IMAGINE WHAT WE COULD DO FOR THE WAR EFFORT WITH THAT MONEY!
YOU'VE ACHIEVED NOTHING. WE'RE PULLING THE PLUG ON THE NECROPOLIS PROJECT ALTOGETHER.
WE'RE IN THE PROCESS OF CRACKING OPEN THE NATURE OF REALITY ITSELF!
SO IS OPPENHEIMER.
HE'S SPLIT THE ATOM OPEN TO REVEAL ITS SECRETS. TO REVEAL A POTENTIALLY ENDLESS ENERGY SOURCE.
THE FACT THAT YOU'VE MANAGED TO PROVE THE EXISTENCE OF GHOSTS IS IMPRESSIVE, SOUTH...
BUT I'M A CHRISTIAN MAN. I NEVER DOUBTED THAT THERE ARE MORE THINGS IN HEAVEN AND EARTH.
MOST OF HUMANITY HAS BELIEVED THAT FOR ALL TIME. IT'S NOTHING NEW.
NUCLEAR FISSION, ON THE OTHER HAND...
THAT'S NEW. AND IT DOESN'T NEED TO BE REASONED WITH LIKE THESE GHOSTS OF YOURS.
LET ME LEAD THE RESCUE TEAM THEN. FOR THE GUARD. I CAN BRING UP THE HORSESHOE AT THE VERY LEAST, LOBBY FOR FUNDING--
ONE LOST MAN VS. WHAT ALL OF THIS COULD DO? THE COST...
THERE IS NO RESCUE TEAM, DOCTOR.
WE'RE SEALING THE TUNNELS NOW.
LEAVE THE GHOSTS TO ROT.

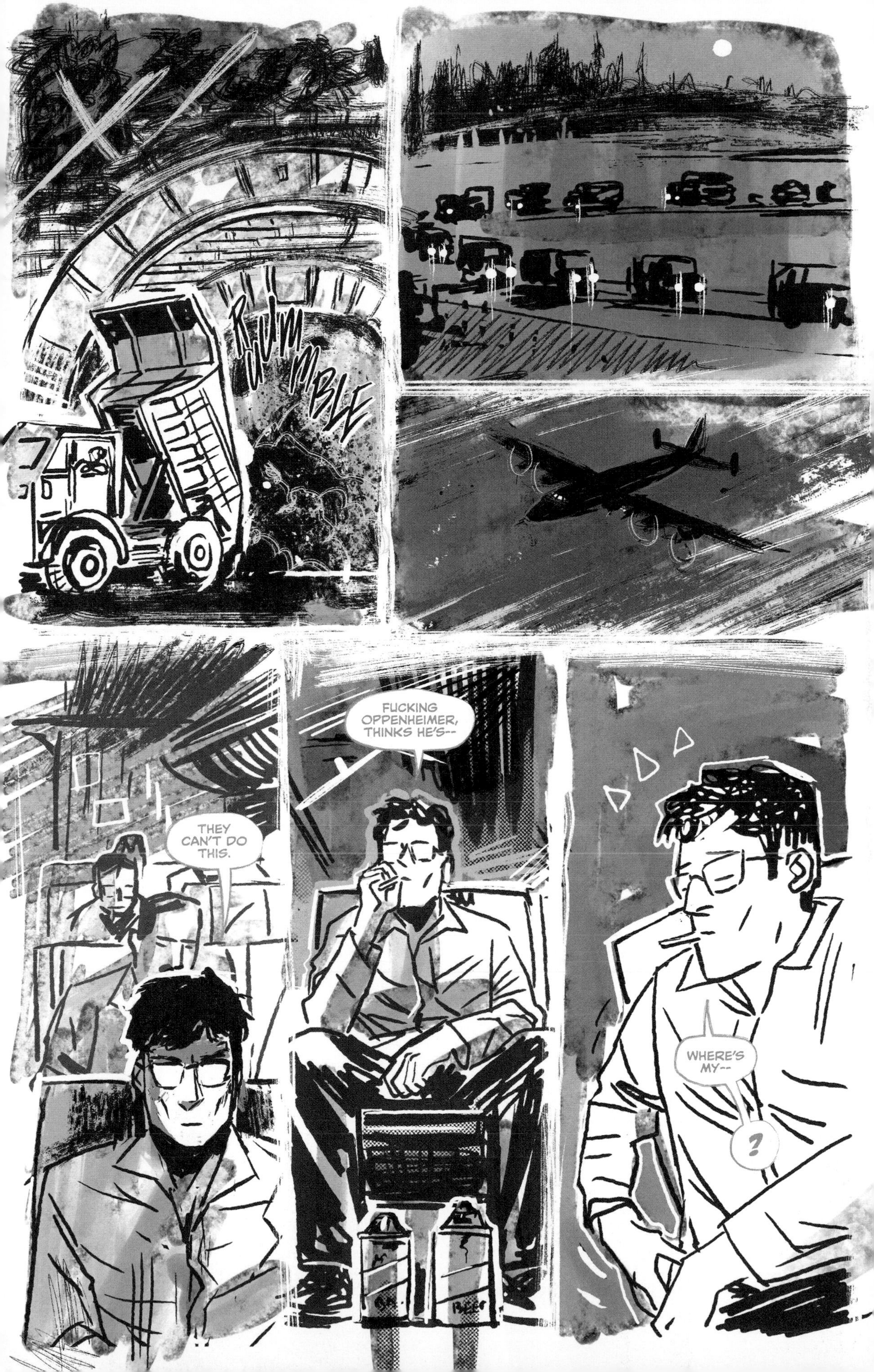
RUUMMBLE
THEY CAN'T DO THIS.
FUCKING OPPENHEIMER, THINKS HE'S--
WHERE'S MY--
?

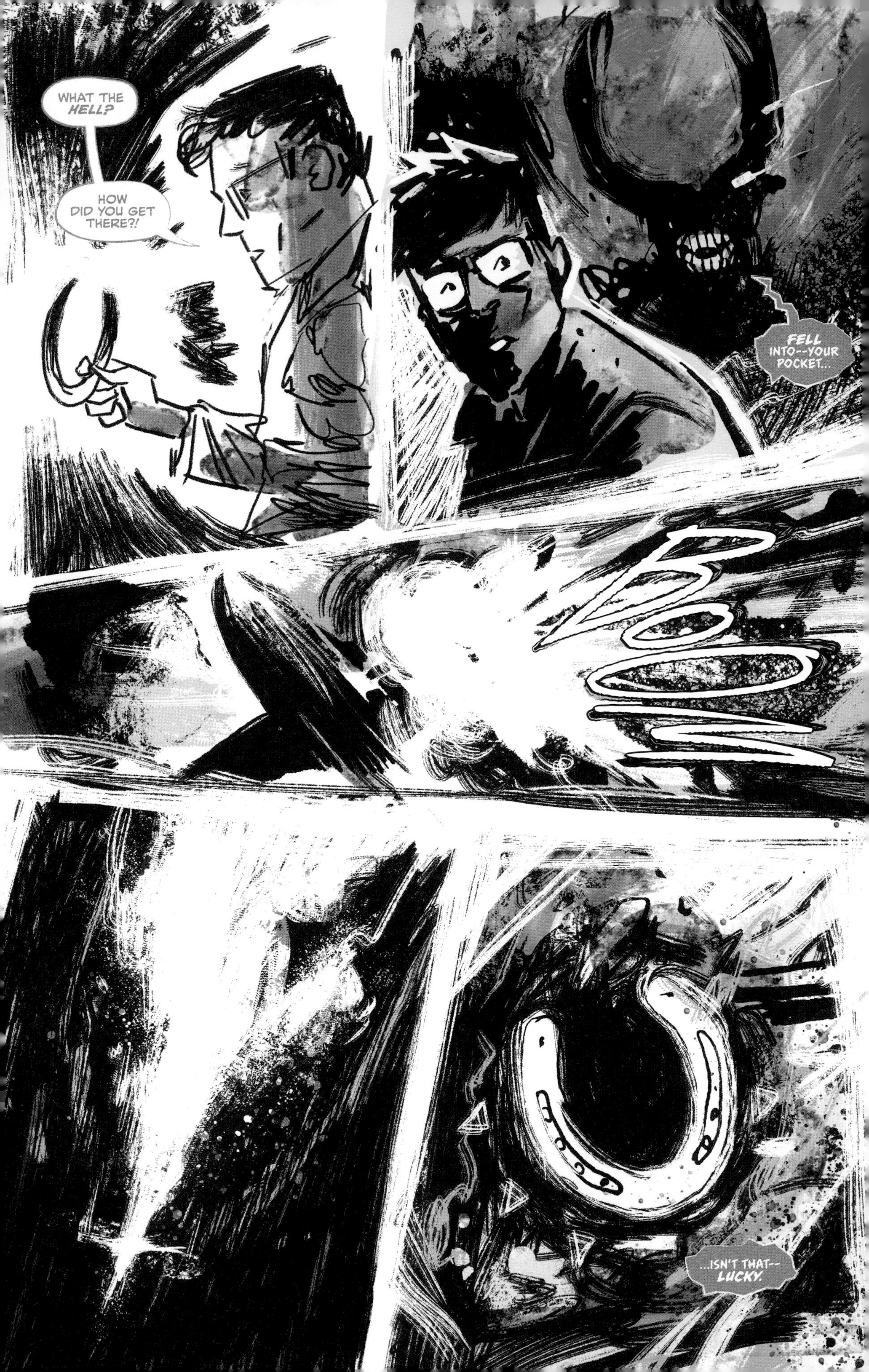
WHAT THE *HELL?*
HOW DID YOU GET THERE?!
FELL INTO--YOUR POCKET...
BOOM
...ISN'T THAT-- *LUCKY.*

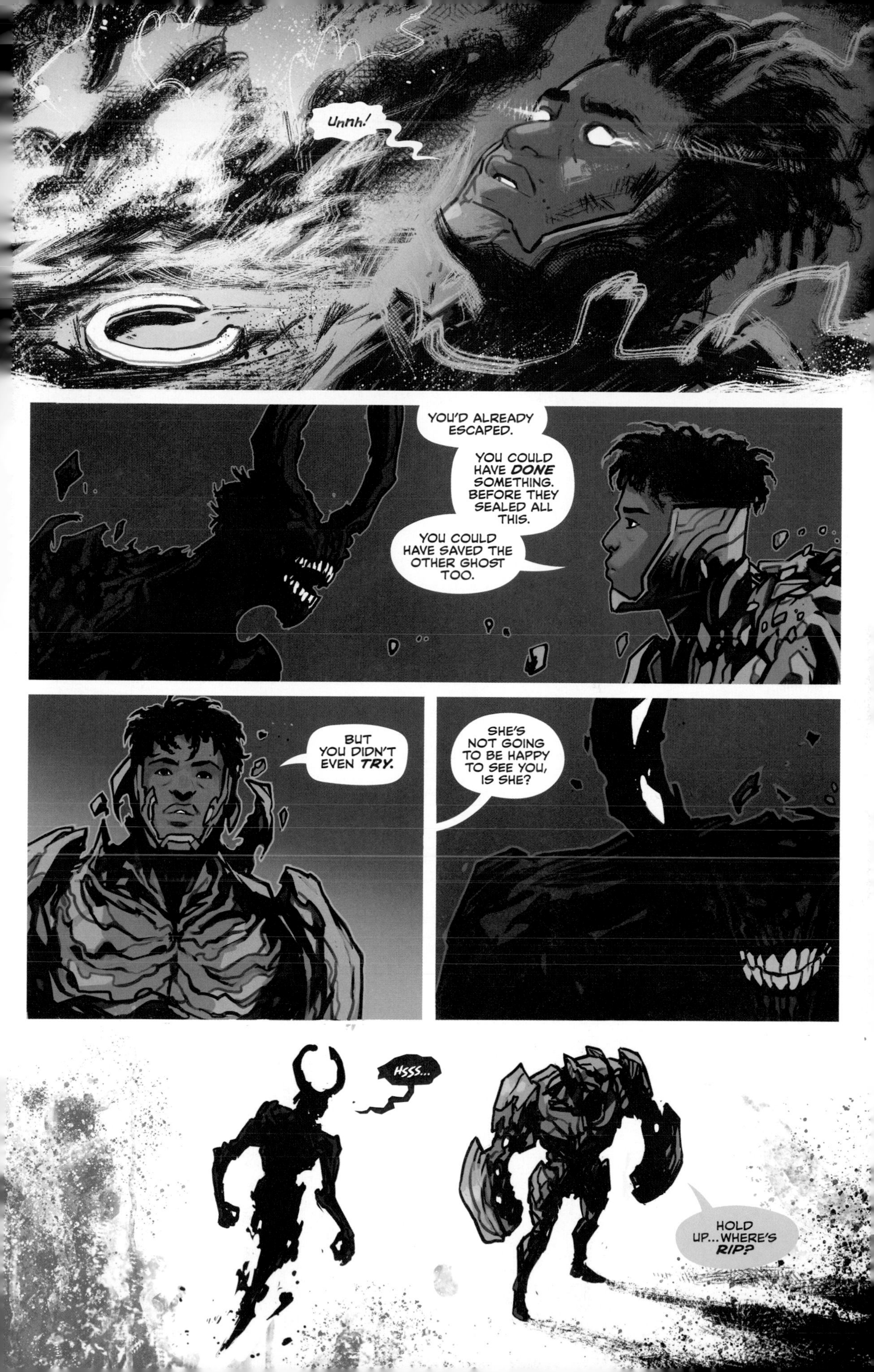
Unnh!
YOU'D ALREADY ESCAPED.
YOU COULD HAVE DONE SOMETHING. BEFORE THEY SEALED ALL THIS.
YOU COULD HAVE SAVED THE OTHER GHOST TOO.
BUT YOU DIDN'T EVEN TRY.
SHE'S NOT GOING TO BE HAPPY TO SEE YOU, IS SHE?
HSSS...
HOLD UP...WHERE'S RIP?

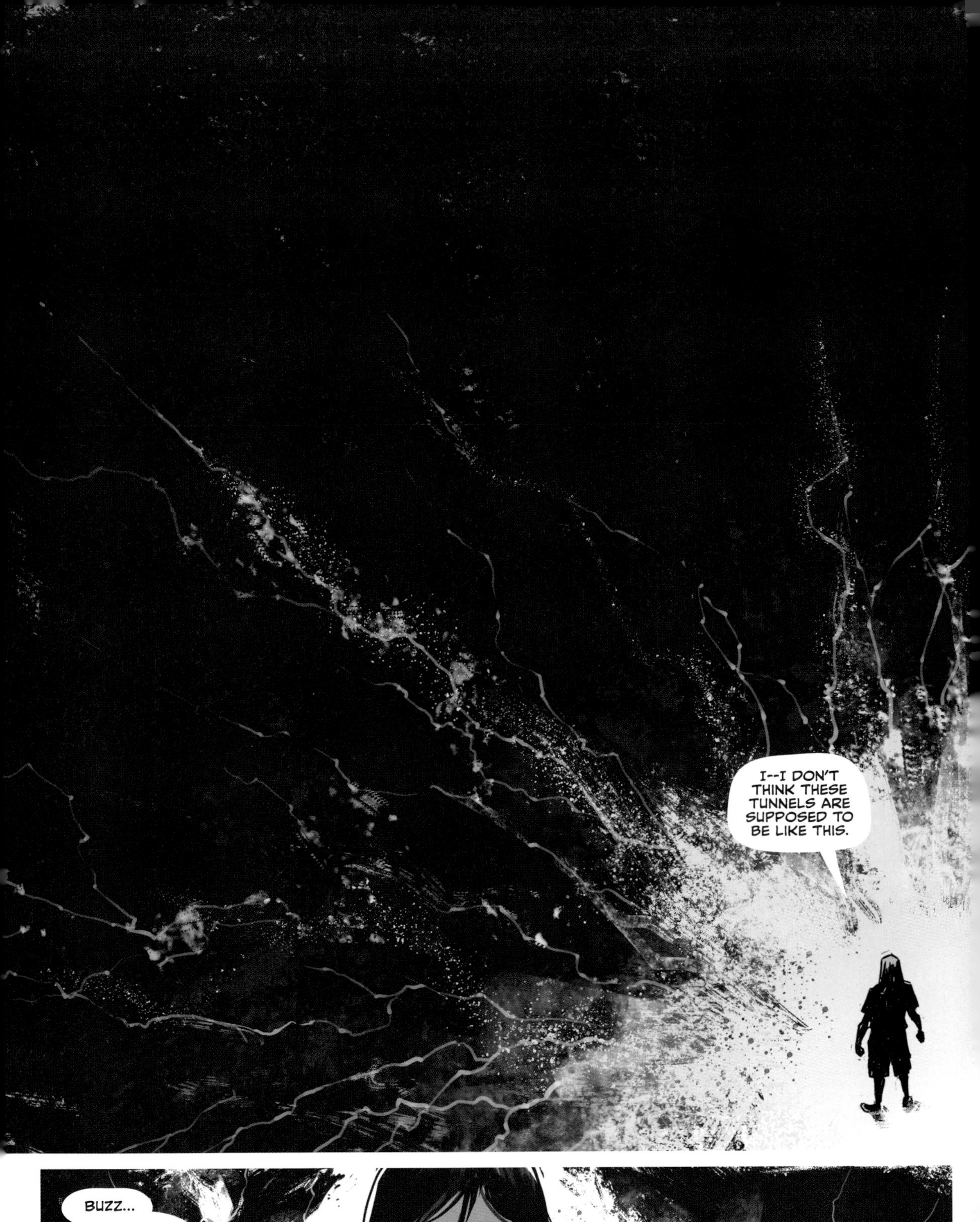
I--I DON'T THINK THESE TUNNELS ARE SUPPOSED TO BE LIKE THIS.
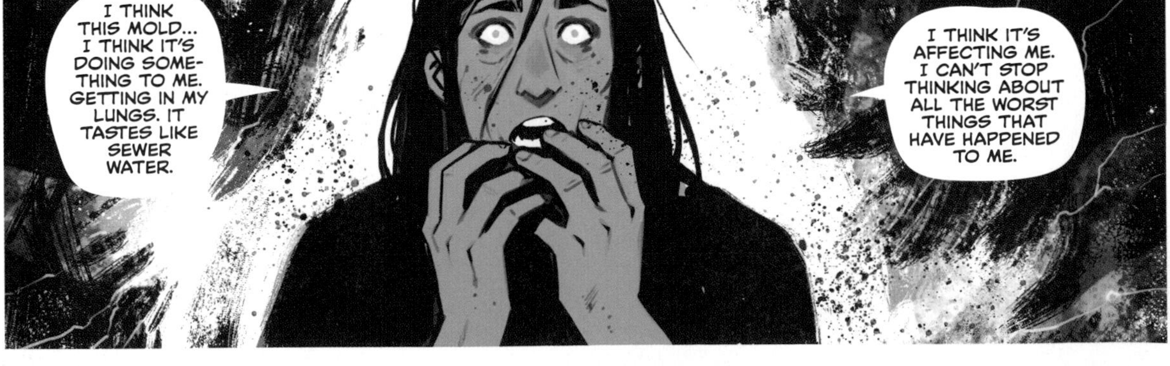
BUZZ...
I THINK THIS MOLD... I THINK IT'S DOING SOME-THING TO ME. GETTING IN MY LUNGS. IT TASTES LIKE SEWER WATER.
I THINK IT'S AFFECTING ME. I CAN'T STOP THINKING ABOUT ALL THE WORST THINGS THAT HAVE HAPPENED TO ME.

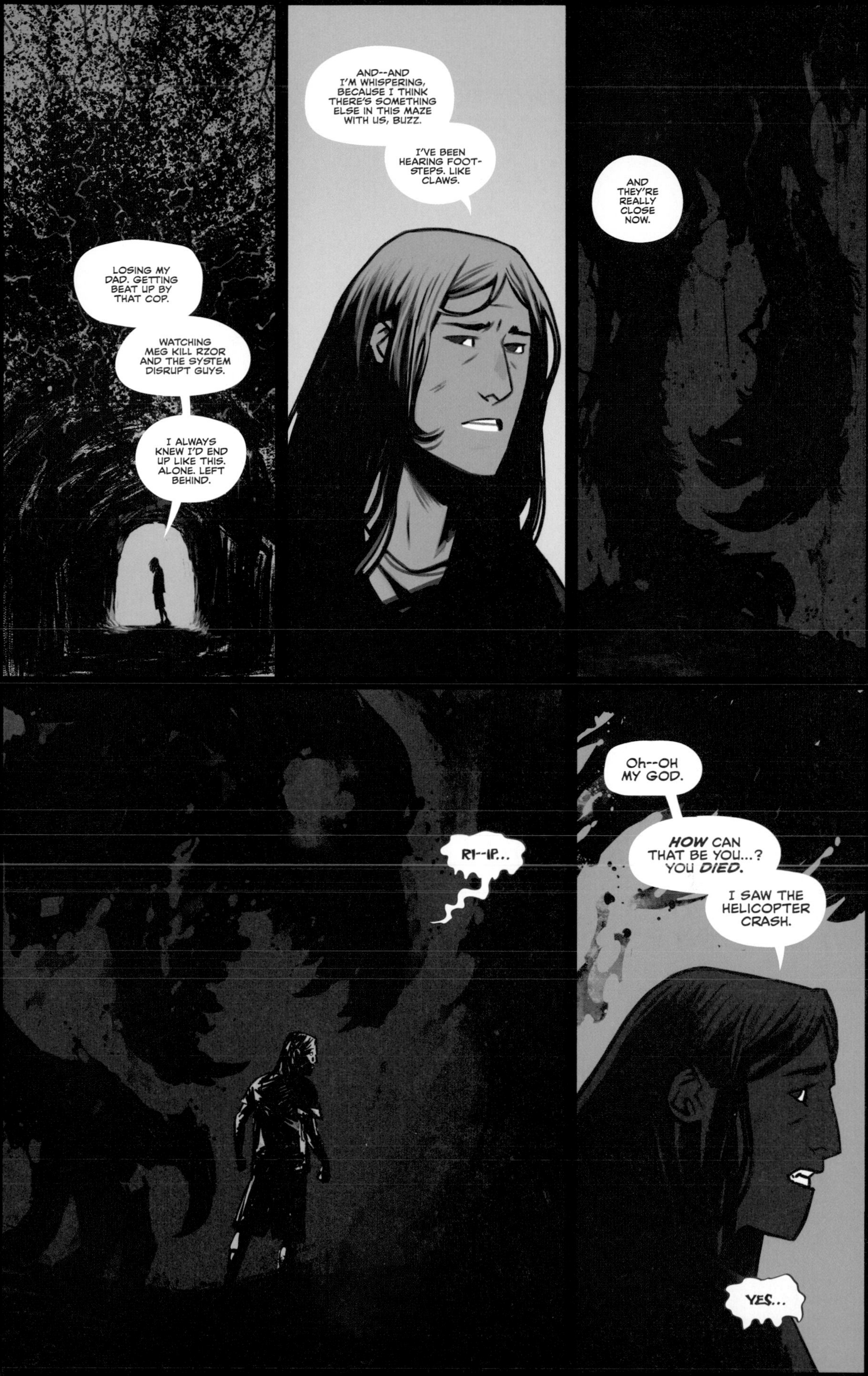
LOSING MY DAD. GETTING BEAT UP BY THAT COP.
WATCHING MEG KILL RZOR AND THE SYSTEM DISRUPT GUYS.
I ALWAYS KNEW I'D END UP LIKE THIS. ALONE. LEFT BEHIND.
AND--AND I'M WHISPERING, BECAUSE I THINK THERE'S SOMETHING ELSE IN THIS MAZE WITH US, BUZZ.
I'VE BEEN HEARING FOOT-STEPS. LIKE CLAWS.
AND THEY'RE REALLY CLOSE NOW.
RI--IP...
Oh--OH MY GOD.
HOW CAN THAT BE YOU...? YOU DIED.
I SAW THE HELICOPTER CRASH.
YES...

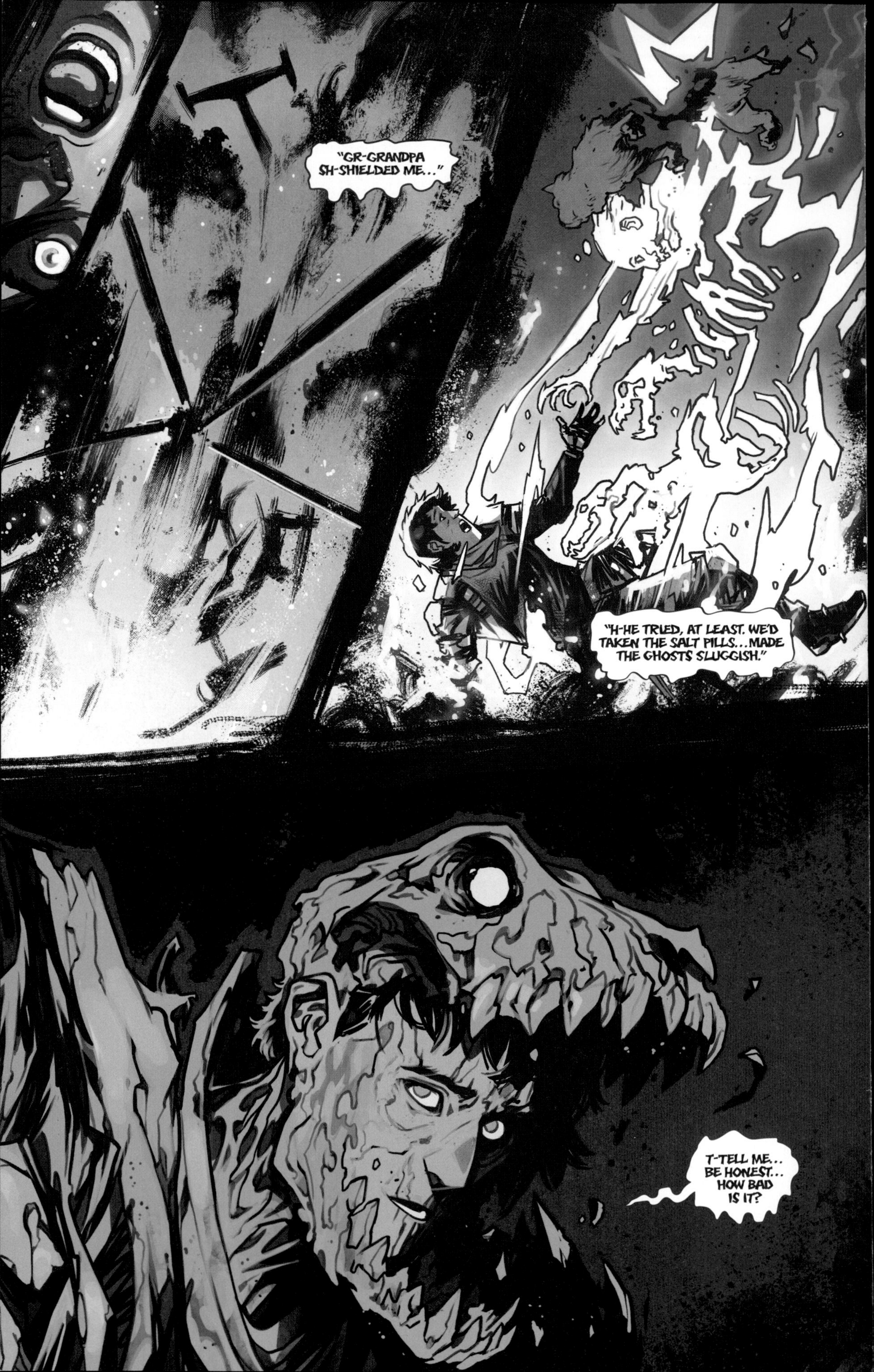
"GR-GRANDPA SH-SHIELDED ME..."
"H-HE TRIED, AT LEAST. WE'D TAKEN THE SALT PILLS...MADE THE GHOSTS SLUGGISH."
T-TELL ME... BE HONEST... HOW BAD IS IT?

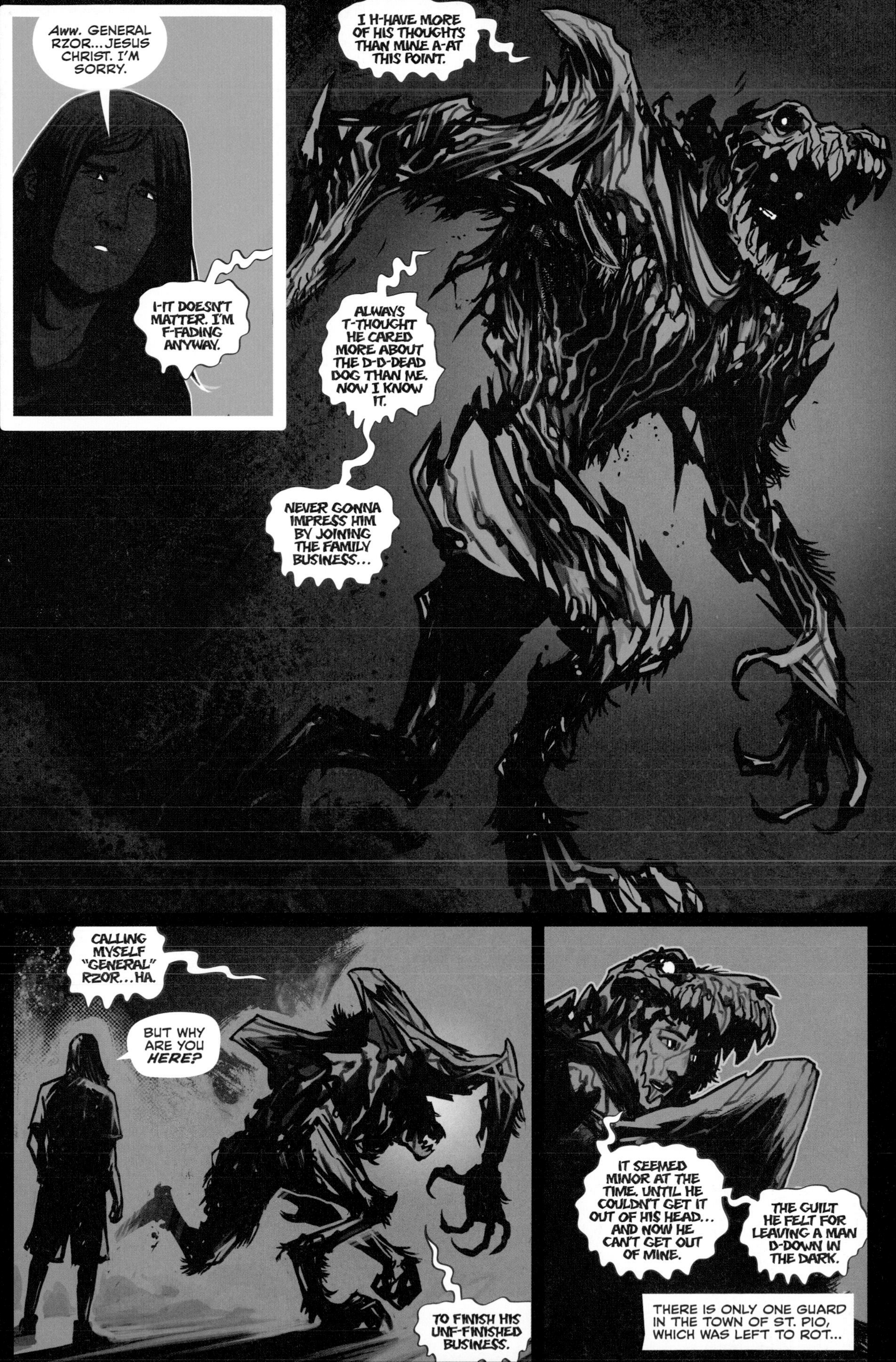
Aww. GENERAL RZOR...JESUS CHRIST. I'M SORRY.
I-IT DOESN'T MATTER. I'M F-FADING ANYWAY.
I H-HAVE MORE OF HIS THOUGHTS THAN MINE A-AT THIS POINT.
ALWAYS T-THOUGHT HE CARED MORE ABOUT THE D-D-DEAD DOG THAN ME. NOW I KNOW IT.
NEVER GONNA IMPRESS HIM BY JOINING THE FAMILY BUSINESS...
CALLING MYSELF "GENERAL" RZOR...HA.
BUT WHY ARE YOU HERE?
TO FINISH HIS UNF-FINISHED BUSINESS.
IT SEEMED MINOR AT THE TIME. UNTIL HE COULDN'T GET IT OUT OF HIS HEAD... AND NOW HE CAN'T GET OUT OF MINE.
THE GUILT HE FELT FOR LEAVING A MAN D-DOWN IN THE DARK.
THERE IS ONLY ONE GUARD IN THE TOWN OF ST. PIO, WHICH WAS LEFT TO ROT...

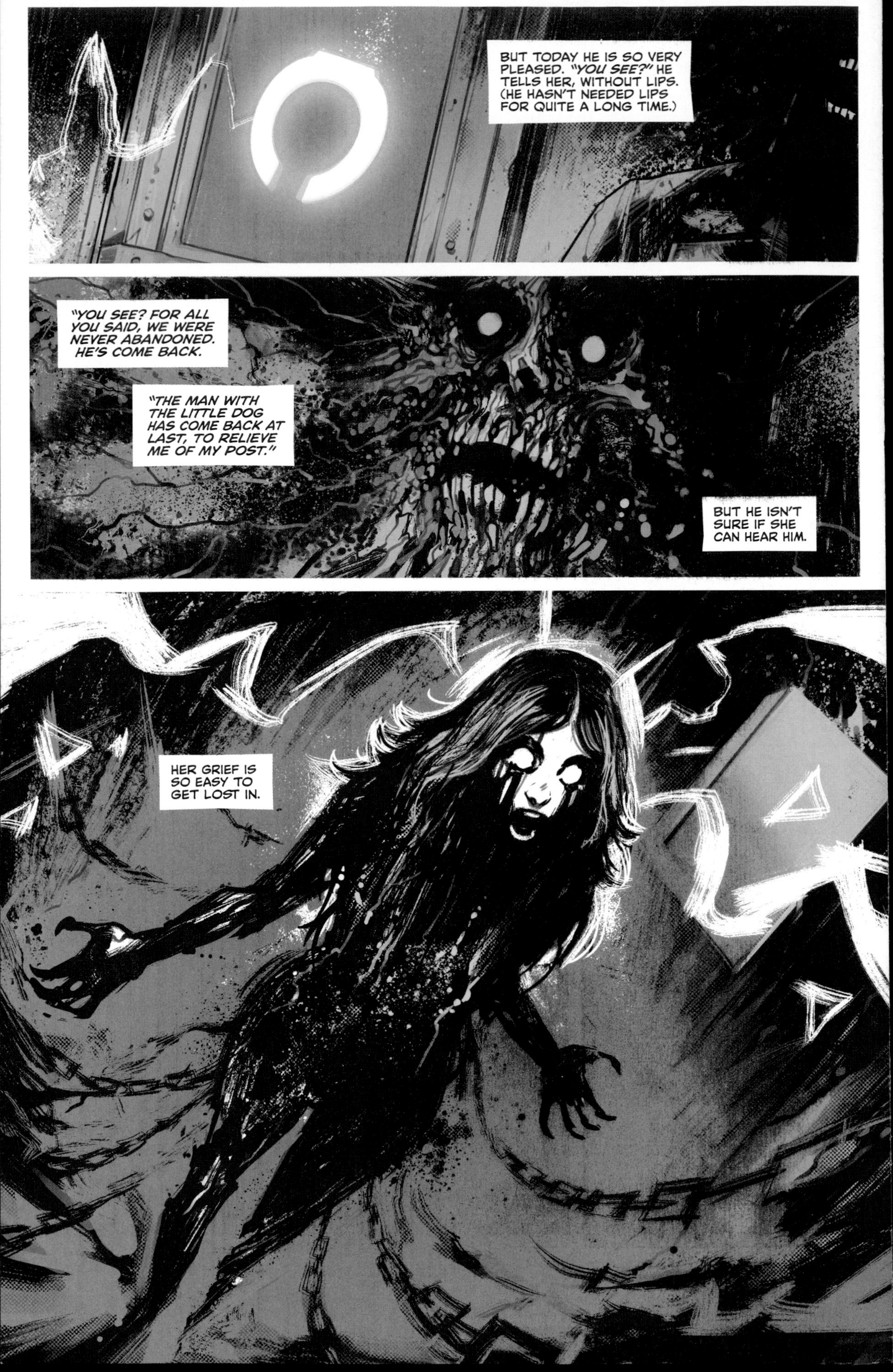
BUT TODAY HE IS SO VERY PLEASED. "YOU SEE?" HE TELLS HER, WITHOUT LIPS. (HE HASN'T NEEDED LIPS FOR QUITE A LONG TIME.)
"YOU SEE? FOR ALL YOU SAID, WE WERE NEVER ABANDONED. HE'S COME BACK.
"THE MAN WITH THE LITTLE DOG HAS COME BACK AT LAST, TO RELIEVE ME OF MY POST."
BUT HE ISN'T SURE IF SHE CAN HEAR HIM.
HER GRIEF IS SO EASY TO GET LOST IN.

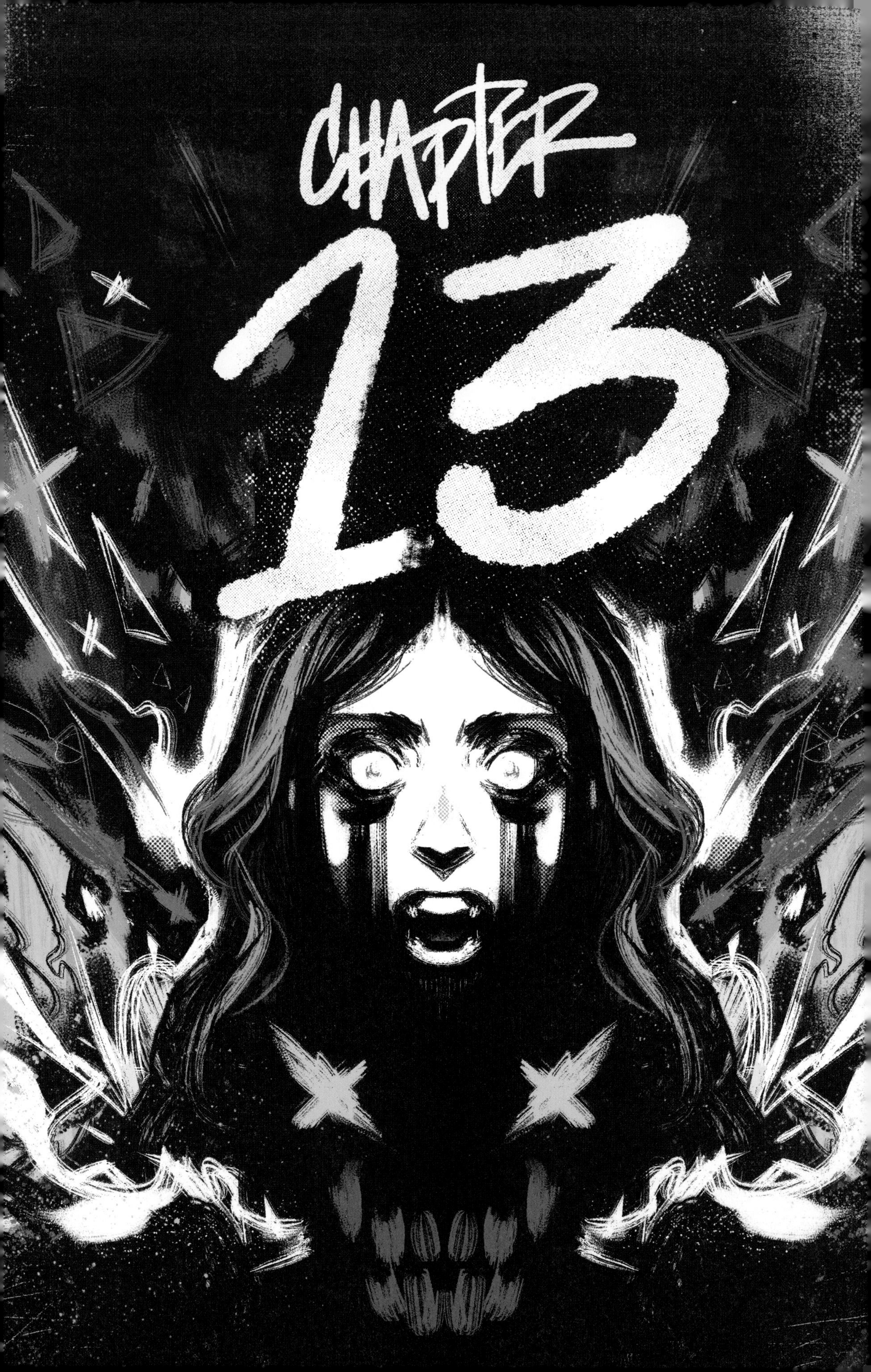
CHAPTER
13

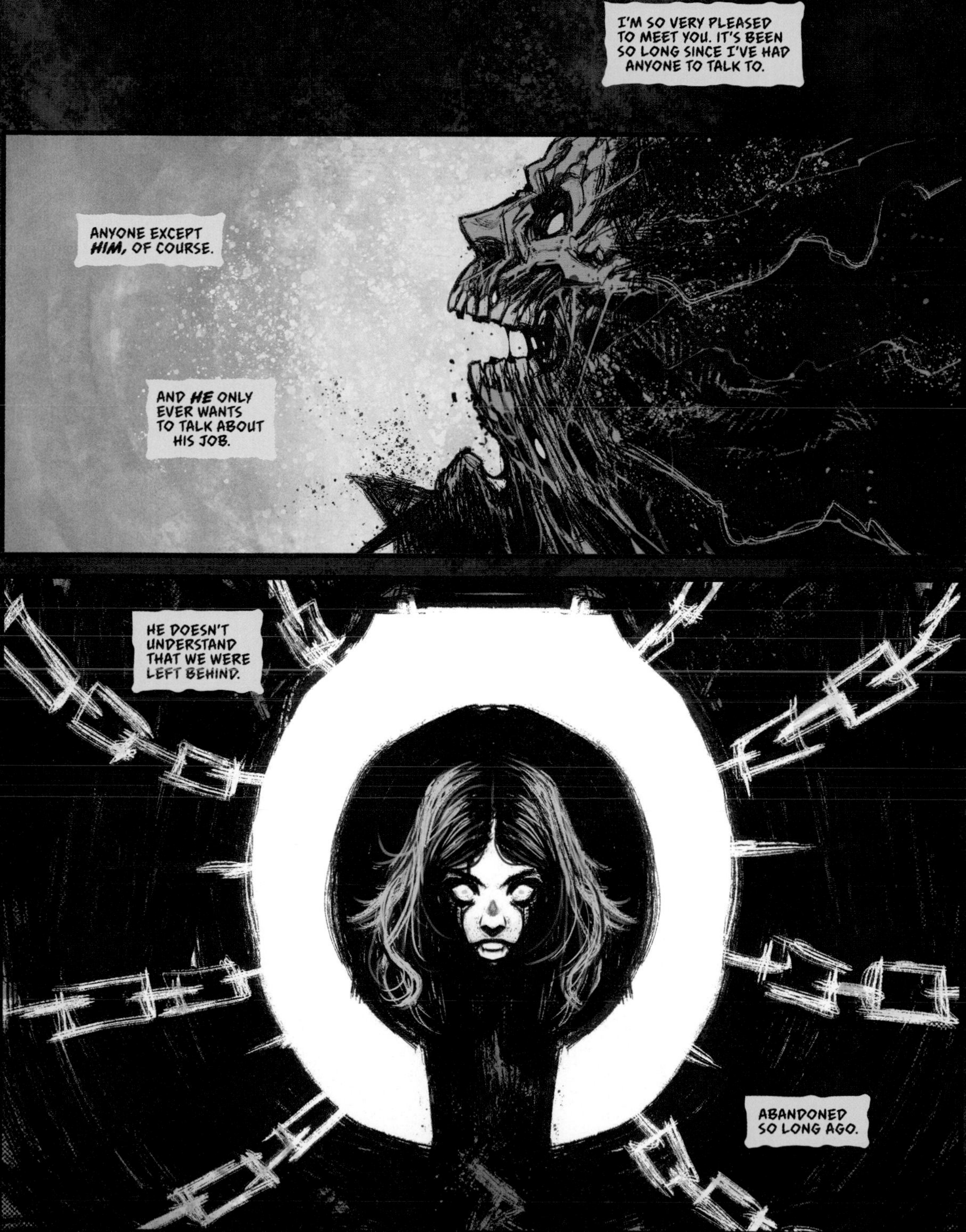
I'M SO VERY PLEASED TO MEET YOU. IT'S BEEN SO LONG SINCE I'VE HAD ANYONE TO TALK TO.
ANYONE EXCEPT *HIM,* OF COURSE.
AND *HE* ONLY EVER WANTS TO TALK ABOUT HIS JOB.
HE DOESN'T UNDERSTAND THAT WE WERE LEFT BEHIND.
ABANDONED SO LONG AGO.

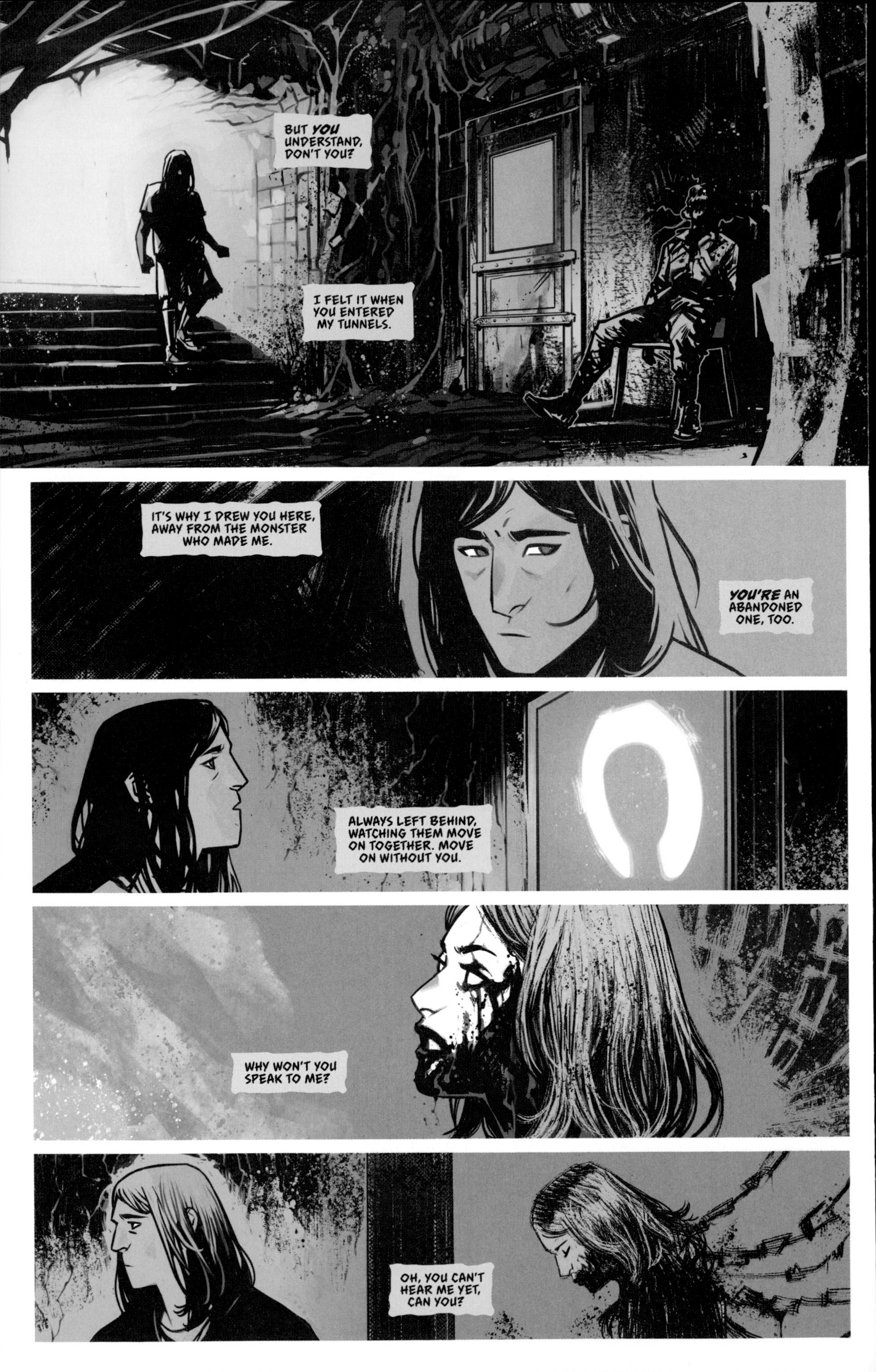
BUT YOU UNDERSTAND, DON'T YOU?
I FELT IT WHEN YOU ENTERED MY TUNNELS.
IT'S WHY I DREW YOU HERE, AWAY FROM THE MONSTER WHO MADE ME.
YOU'RE AN ABANDONED ONE, TOO.
ALWAYS LEFT BEHIND, WATCHING THEM MOVE ON TOGETHER. MOVE ON WITHOUT YOU.
WHY WON'T YOU SPEAK TO ME?
OH, YOU CAN'T HEAR ME YET, CAN YOU?

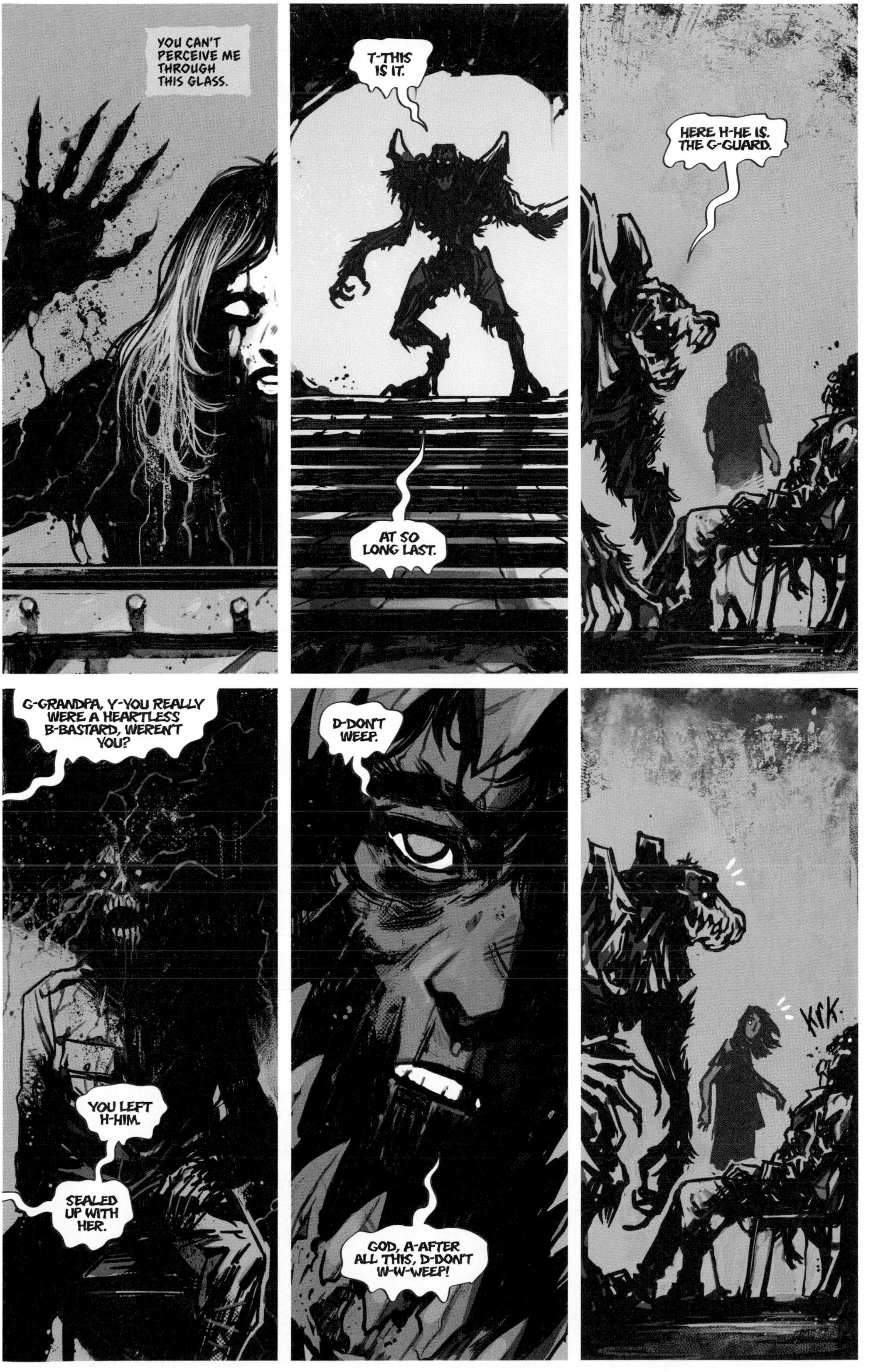
YOU CAN'T PERCEIVE ME THROUGH THIS GLASS.
T-THIS IS IT.
AT SO LONG LAST.
HERE H-HE IS. THE G-GUARD.
G-GRANDPA, Y-YOU REALLY WERE A HEARTLESS B-BASTARD, WEREN'T YOU?
YOU LEFT H-HIM.
SEALED UP WITH HER.
D-DON'T WEEP.
GOD, A-AFTER ALL THIS, D-DON'T W-W-WEEP!
KRK

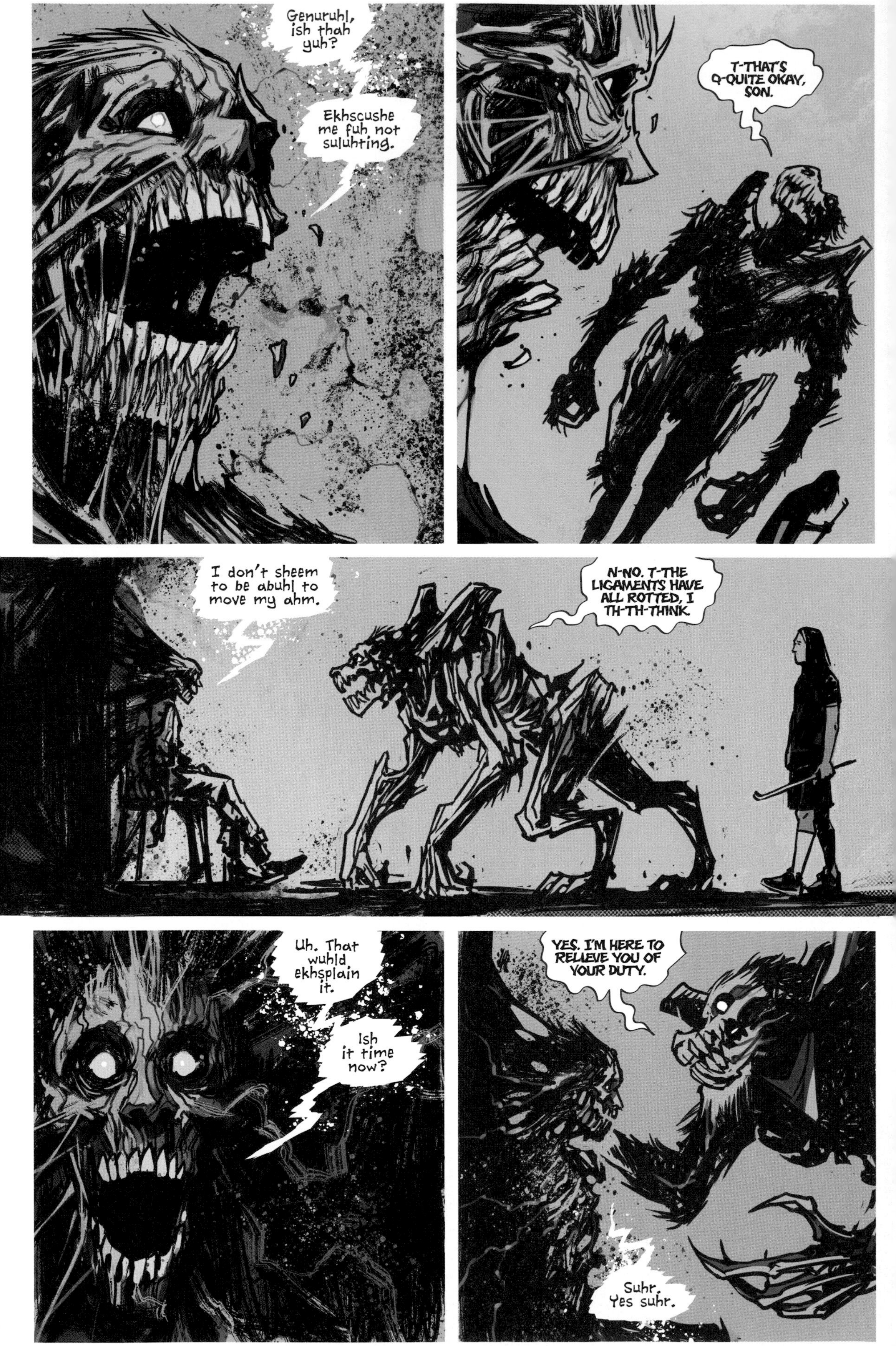
Genuruhl, ish thah yuh?
Ekhscushe me fuh not suluhting.
T-THAT'S Q-QUITE OKAY, SON.
I don't sheem to be abuhl to move my ahm.
N-NO. T-THE LIGAMENTS HAVE ALL ROTTED, I TH-TH-THINK.
Uh. That wuhld ekhsplain it.
Ish it time now?
YES. I'M HERE TO RELIEVE YOU OF YOUR DUTY.
Suhr. Yes suhr.

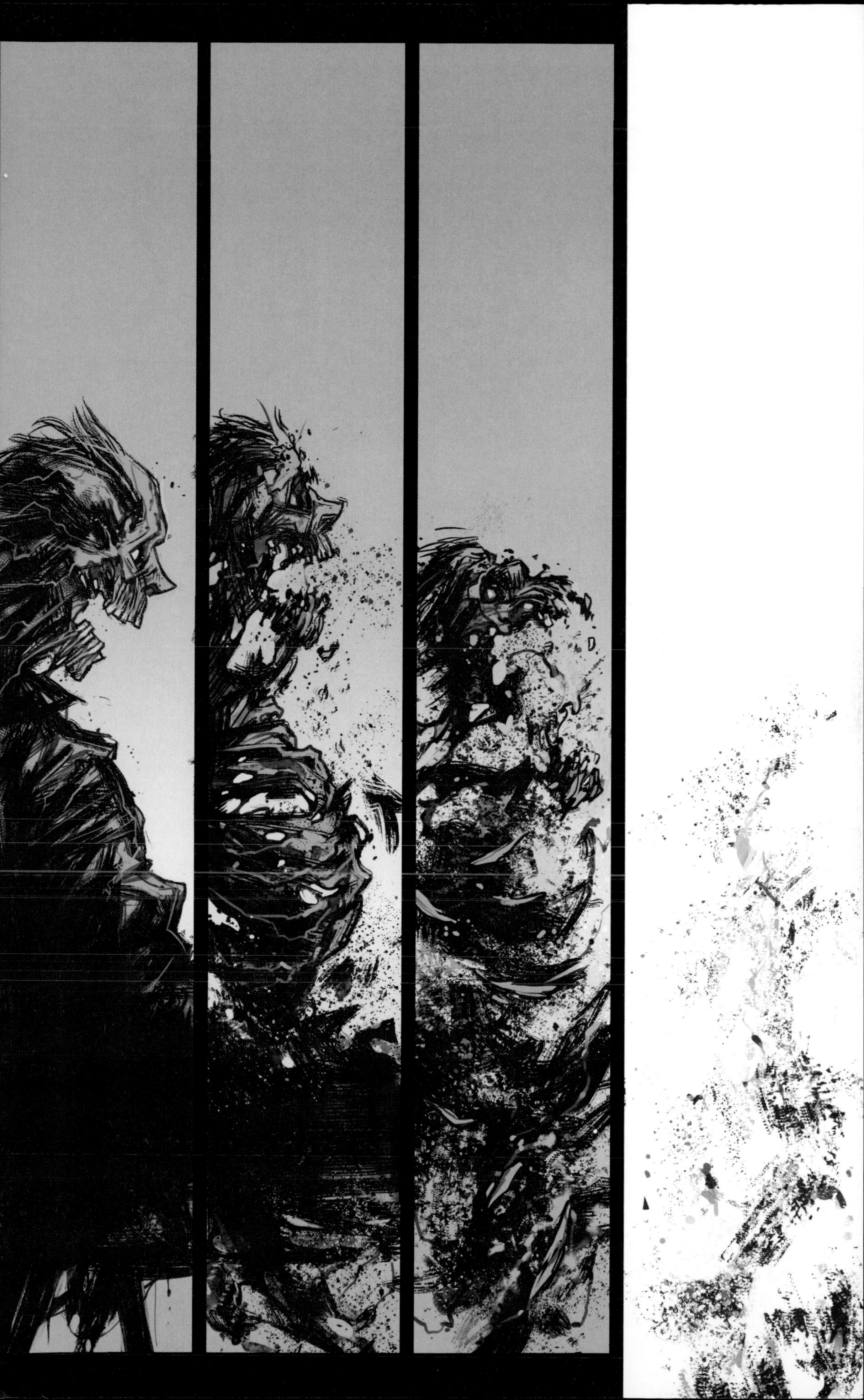

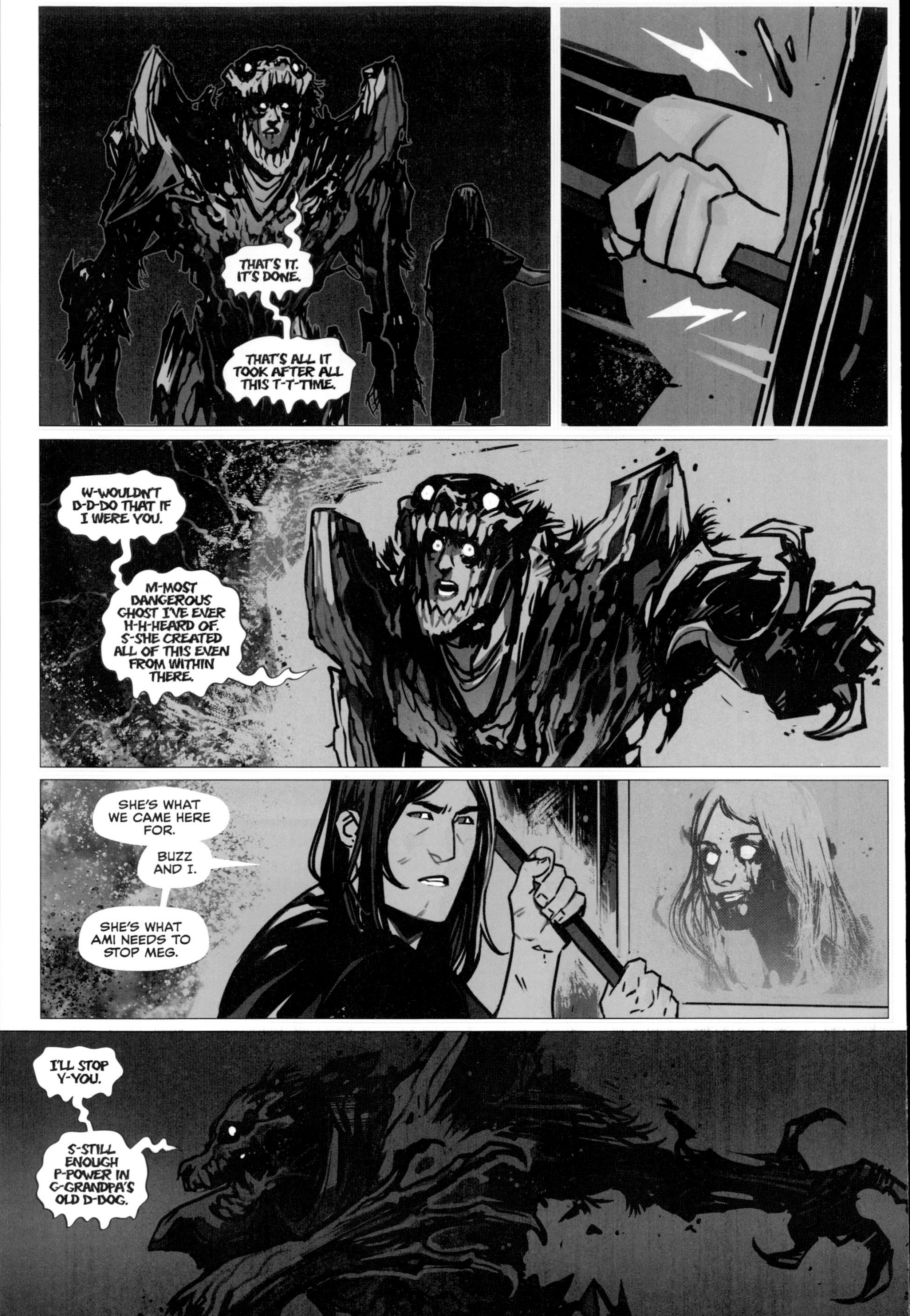
THAT'S IT. IT'S DONE.
THAT'S ALL IT TOOK AFTER ALL THIS T-T-TIME.
W-WOULDN'T D-D-DO THAT IF I WERE YOU.
M-MOST DANGEROUS GHOST I'VE EVER H-H-HEARD OF. S-SHE CREATED ALL OF THIS EVEN FROM WITHIN THERE.
SHE'S WHAT WE CAME HERE FOR.
BUZZ AND I.
SHE'S WHAT AMI NEEDS TO STOP MEG.
I'LL STOP Y-YOU.
S-STILL ENOUGH P-POWER IN G-GRANDPA'S OLD D-DOG.

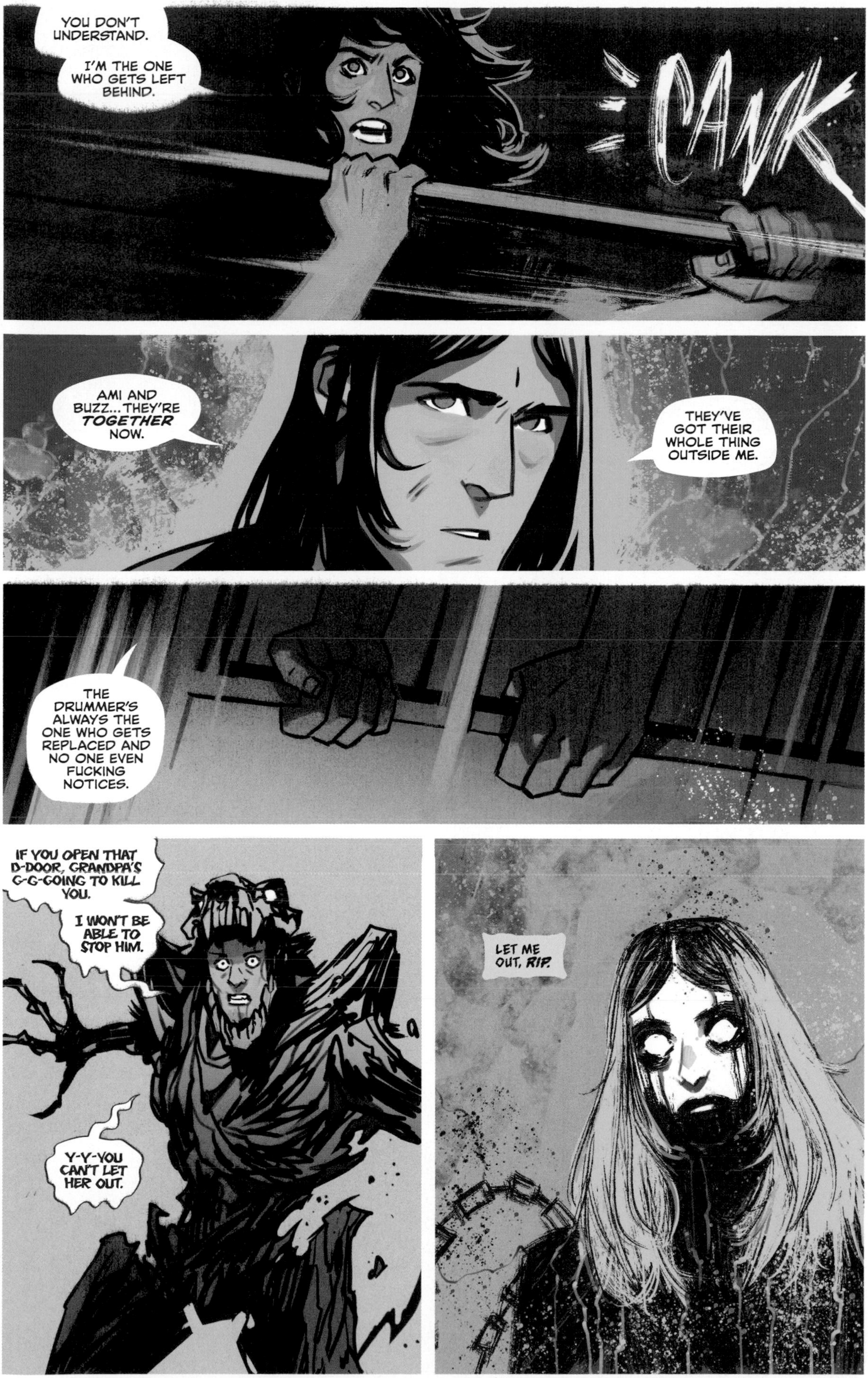
YOU DON'T UNDERSTAND.
I'M THE ONE WHO GETS LEFT BEHIND.
CANK
AMI AND BUZZ...THEY'RE TOGETHER NOW.
THEY'VE GOT THEIR WHOLE THING OUTSIDE ME.
THE DRUMMER'S ALWAYS THE ONE WHO GETS REPLACED AND NO ONE EVEN FUCKING NOTICES.
IF YOU OPEN THAT D-DOOR, GRANDPA'S G-G-GOING TO KILL YOU.
I WON'T BE ABLE TO STOP HIM.
Y-Y-YOU CAN'T LET HER OUT.
LET ME OUT, RIP.

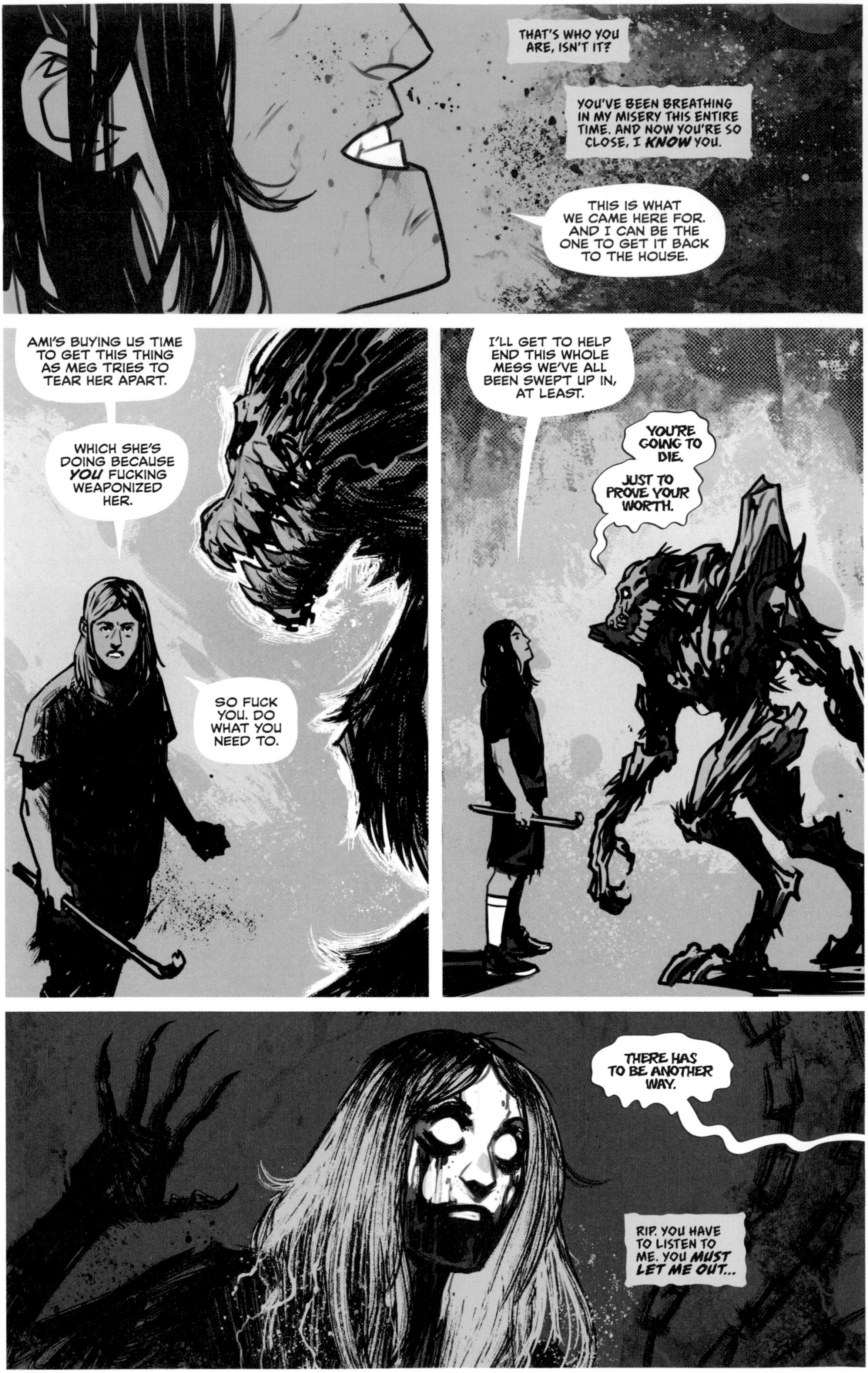
THAT'S WHO YOU ARE, ISN'T IT?
YOU'VE BEEN BREATHING IN MY MISERY THIS ENTIRE TIME. AND NOW YOU'RE SO CLOSE, I KNOW YOU.
THIS IS WHAT WE CAME HERE FOR. AND I CAN BE THE ONE TO GET IT BACK TO THE HOUSE.
AMI'S BUYING US TIME TO GET THIS THING AS MEG TRIES TO TEAR HER APART.
WHICH SHE'S DOING BECAUSE YOU FUCKING WEAPONIZED HER.
SO FUCK YOU. DO WHAT YOU NEED TO.
I'LL GET TO HELP END THIS WHOLE MESS WE'VE ALL BEEN SWEPT UP IN, AT LEAST.
YOU'RE GOING TO DIE.
JUST TO PROVE YOUR WORTH.
THERE HAS TO BE ANOTHER WAY.
RIP. YOU HAVE TO LISTEN TO ME. YOU MUST LET ME OUT...

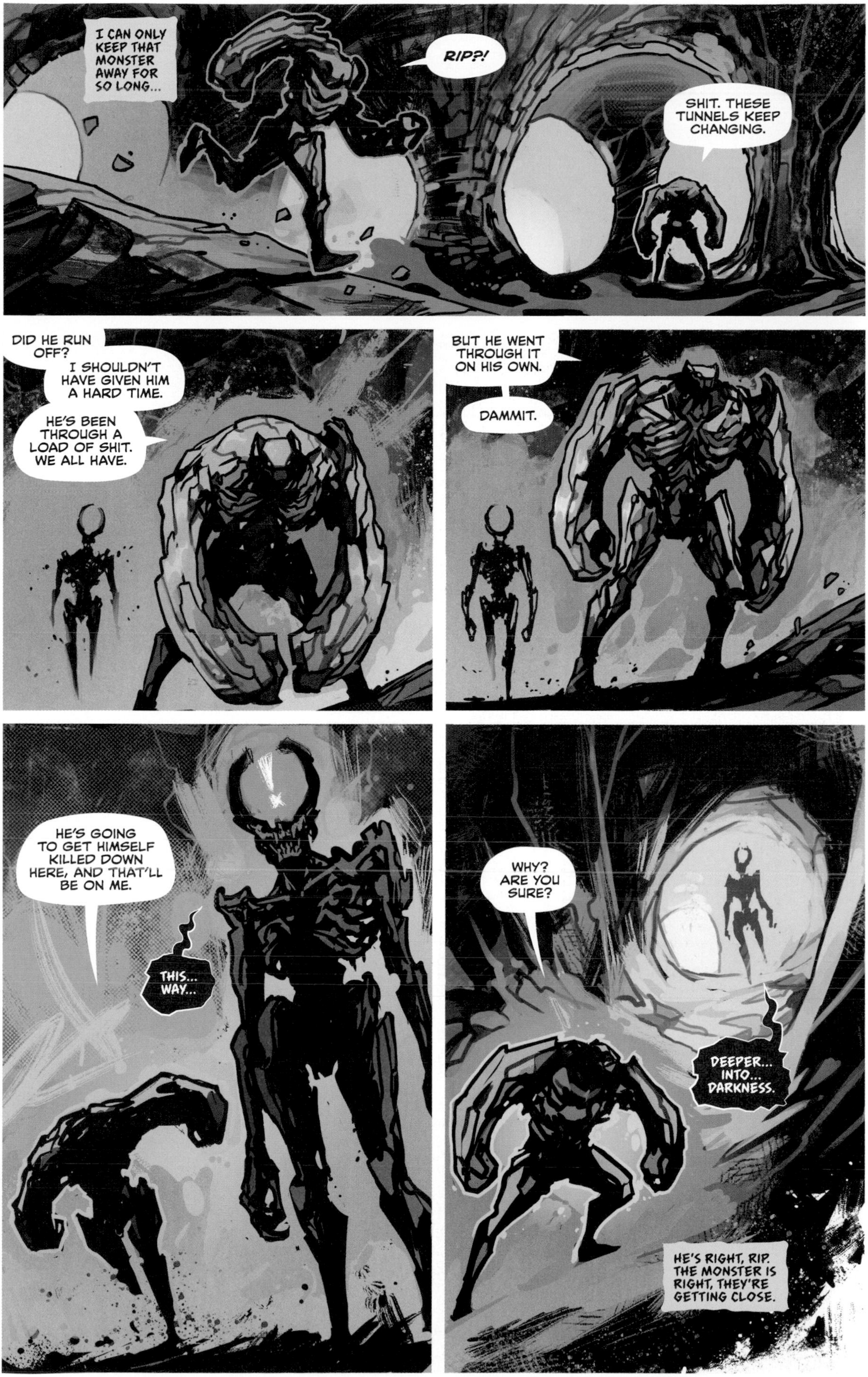
I CAN ONLY KEEP THAT MONSTER AWAY FOR SO LONG...
RIP?!
SHIT. THESE TUNNELS KEEP CHANGING.
DID HE RUN OFF?
I SHOULDN'T HAVE GIVEN HIM A HARD TIME.
HE'S BEEN THROUGH A LOAD OF SHIT. WE ALL HAVE.
BUT HE WENT THROUGH IT ON HIS OWN.
DAMMIT.
HE'S GOING TO GET HIMSELF KILLED DOWN HERE, AND THAT'LL BE ON ME.
THIS... WAY...
WHY? ARE YOU SURE?
DEEPER... INTO... DARKNESS.
HE'S RIGHT, RIP. THE MONSTER IS RIGHT, THEY'RE GETTING CLOSE.

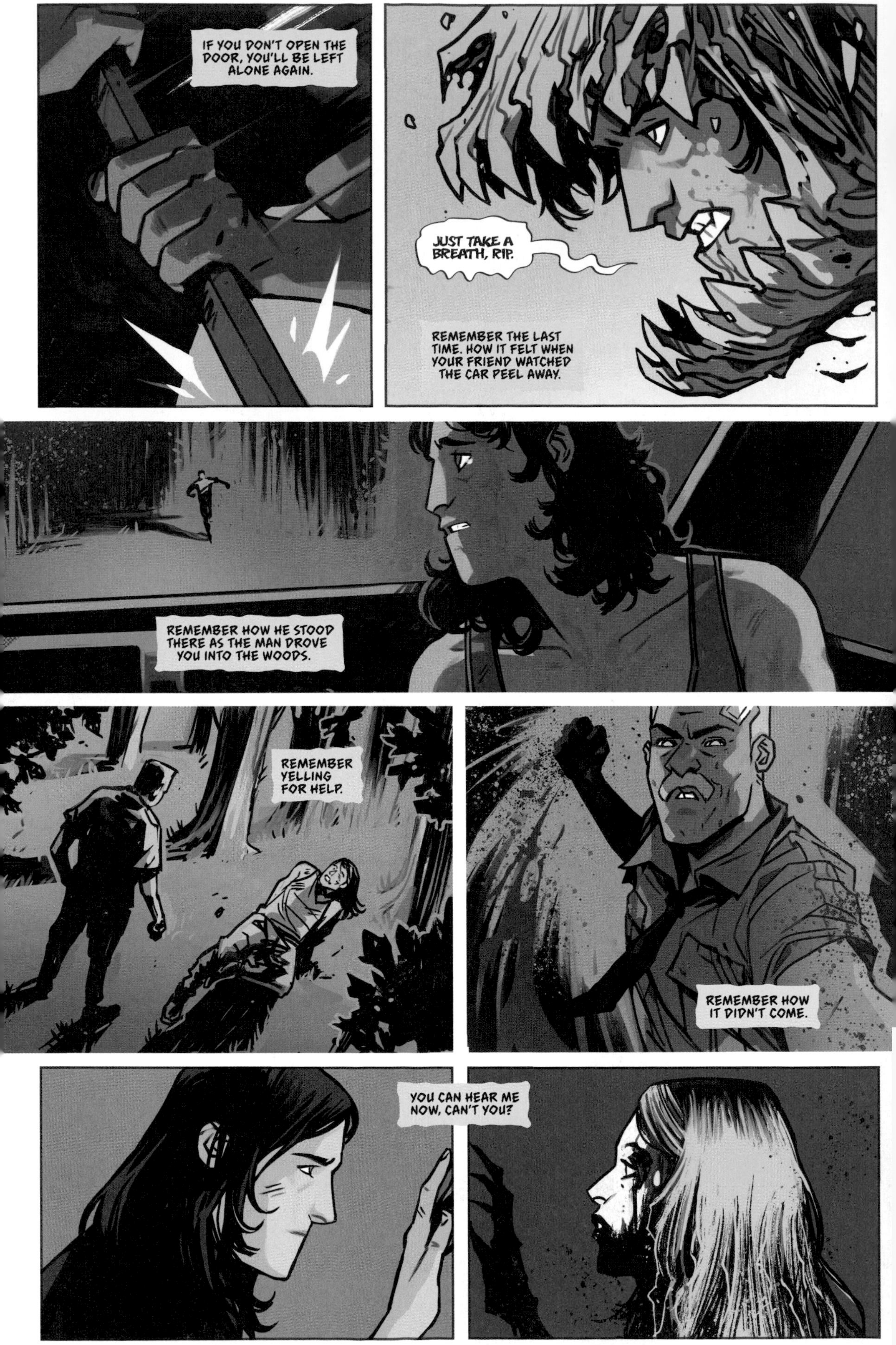
IF YOU DON'T OPEN THE DOOR, YOU'LL BE LEFT ALONE AGAIN.
JUST TAKE A BREATH, RIP.
REMEMBER THE LAST TIME. HOW IT FELT WHEN YOUR FRIEND WATCHED THE CAR PEEL AWAY.
REMEMBER HOW HE STOOD THERE AS THE MAN DROVE YOU INTO THE WOODS.
REMEMBER YELLING FOR HELP.
REMEMBER HOW IT DIDN'T COME.
YOU CAN HEAR ME NOW, CAN'T YOU?

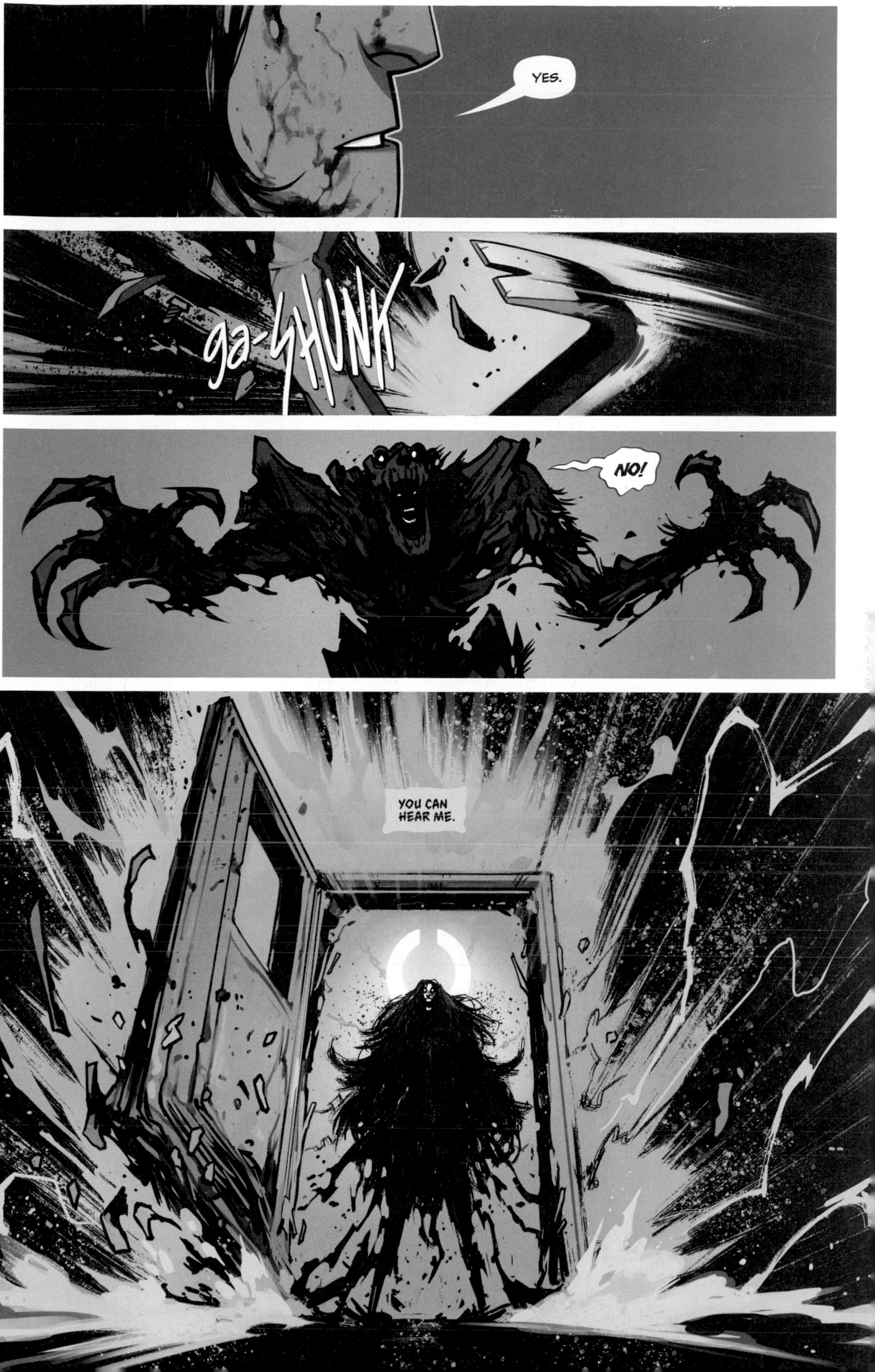
YES.
ga-SHUNK
NO!
YOU CAN HEAR ME.

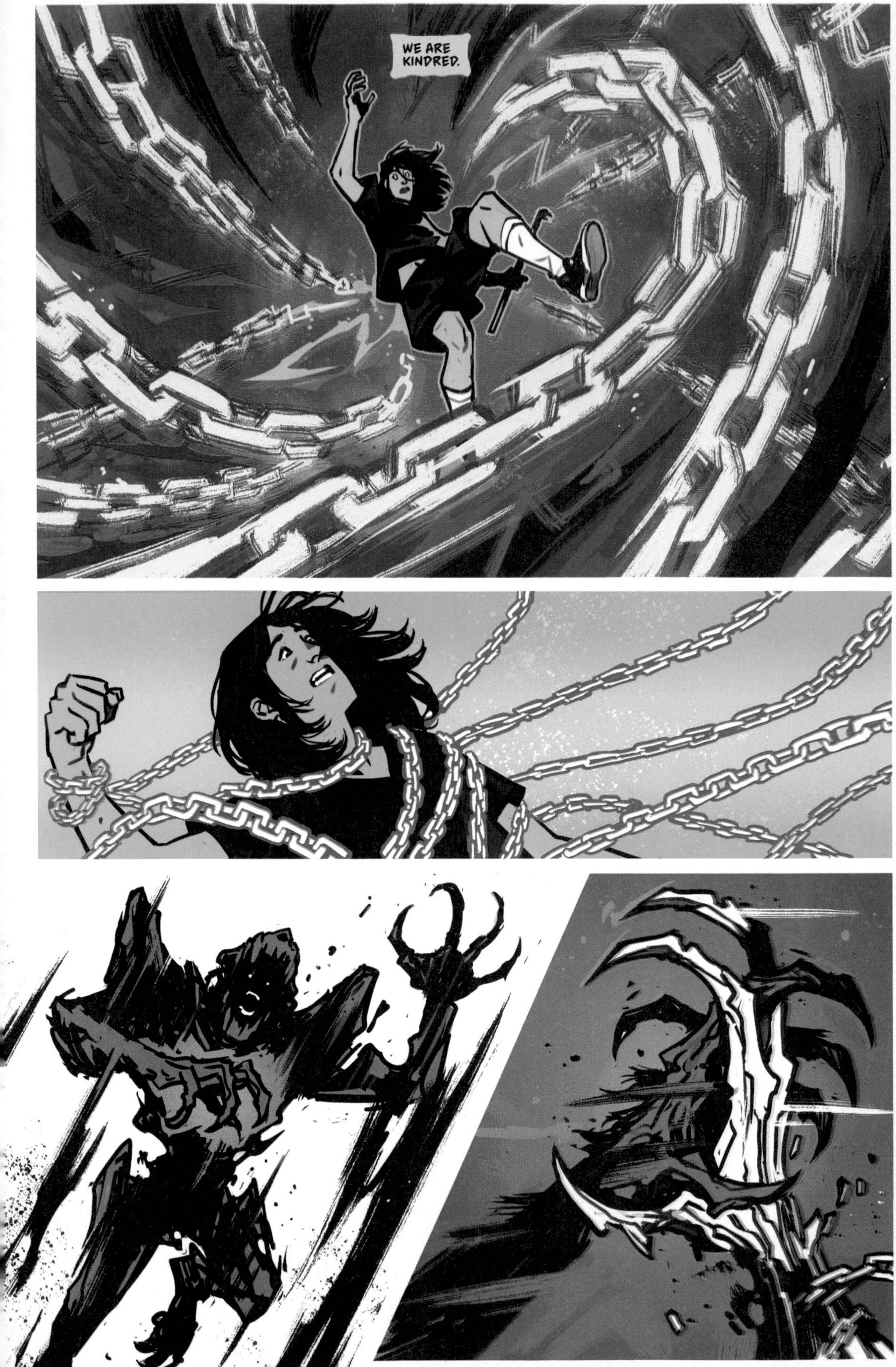
WE ARE KINDRED.

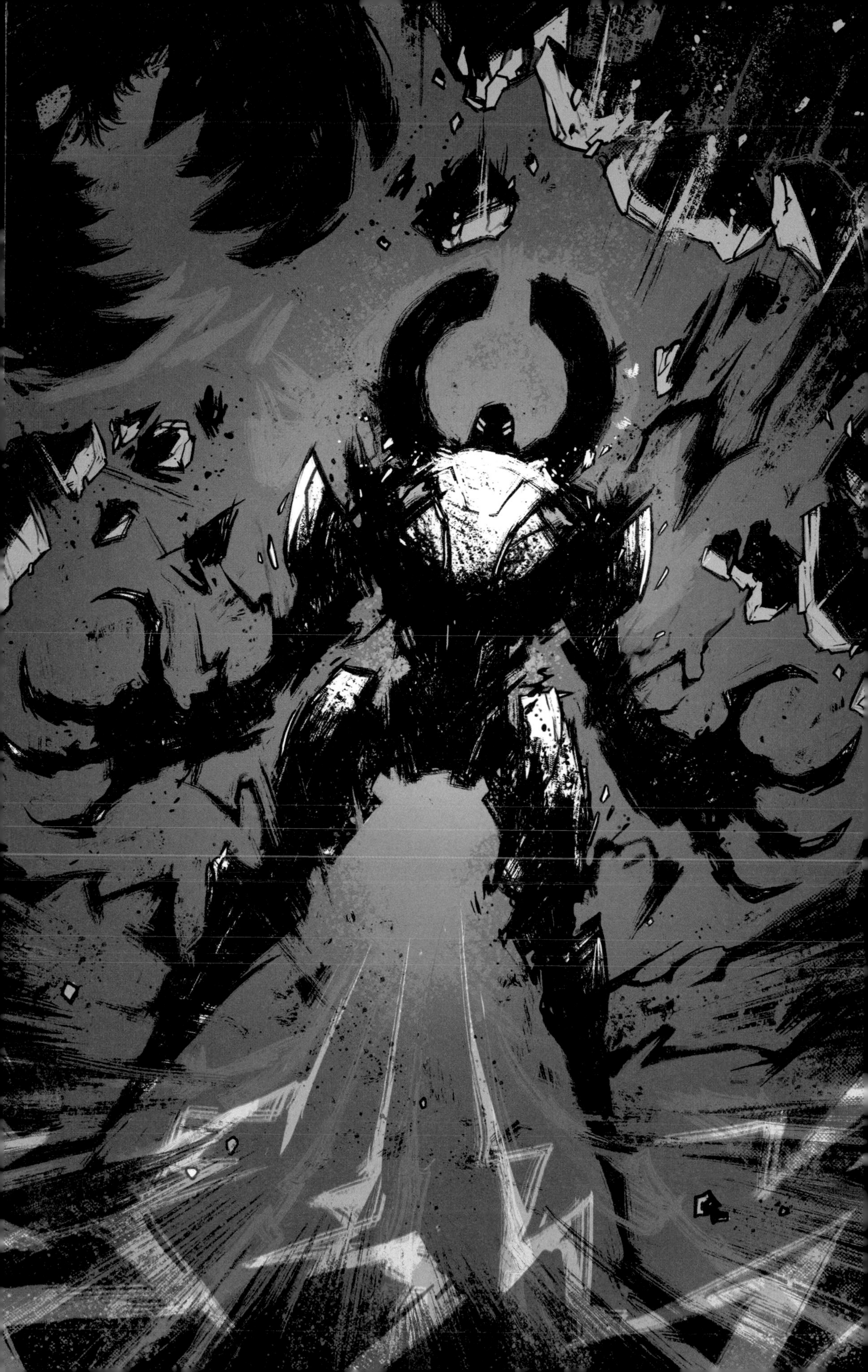

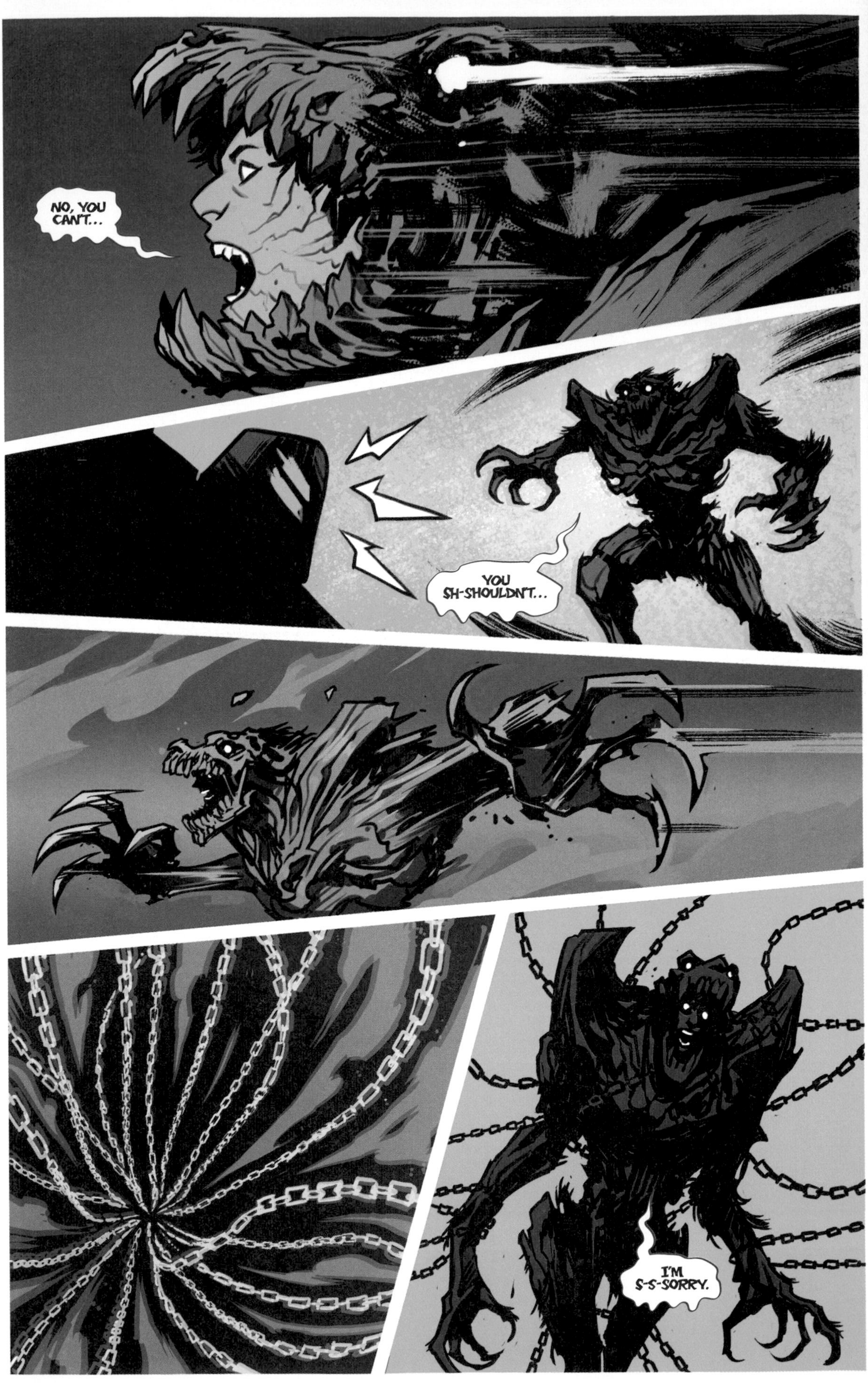
NO, YOU CAN'T...
YOU SH-SHOULDN'T...
I'M S-S-SORRY.

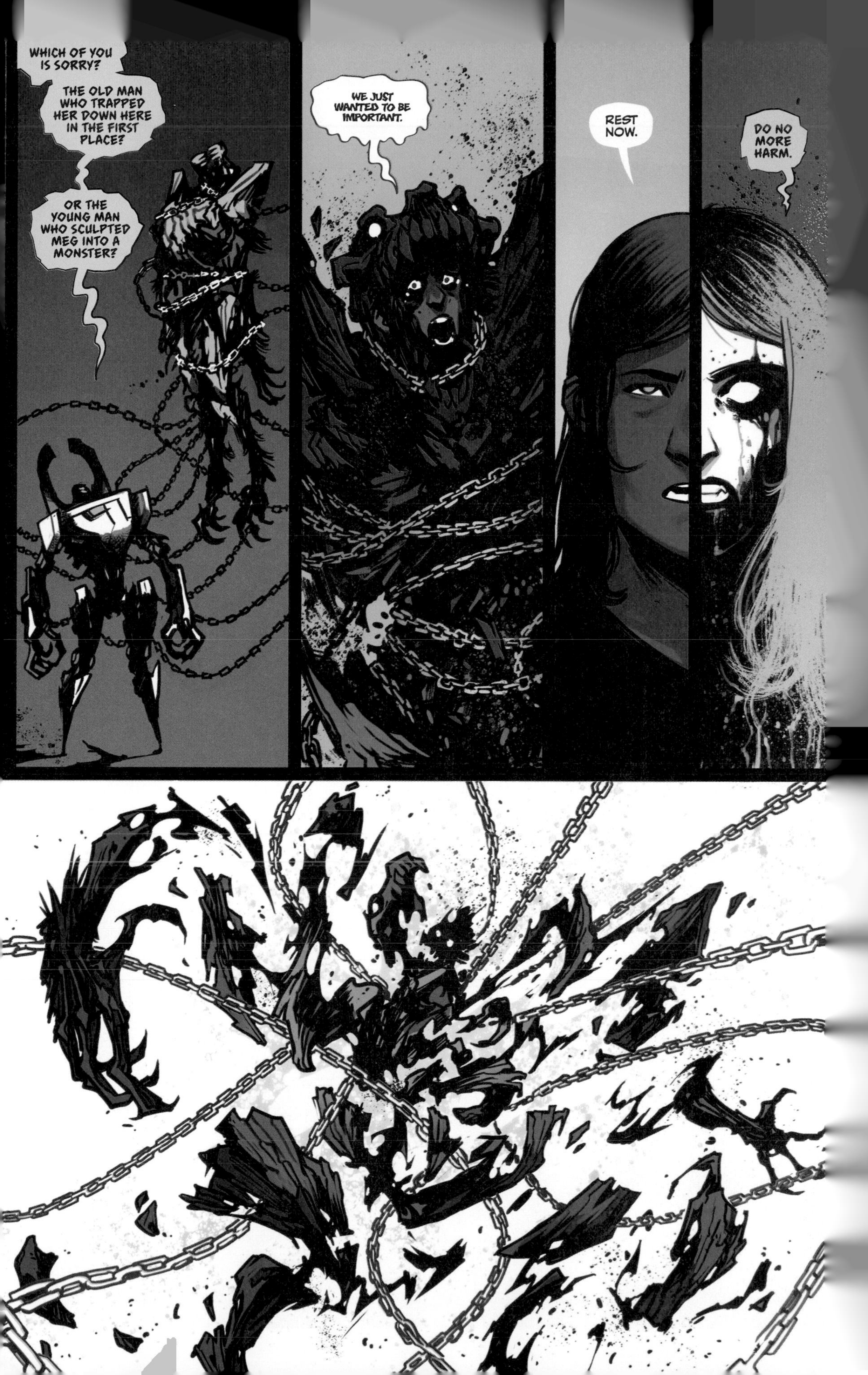
WHICH OF YOU IS SORRY?
THE OLD MAN WHO TRAPPED HER DOWN HERE IN THE FIRST PLACE?
OR THE YOUNG MAN WHO SCULPTED MEG INTO A MONSTER?
WE JUST WANTED TO BE IMPORTANT.
REST NOW.
DO NO MORE HARM.

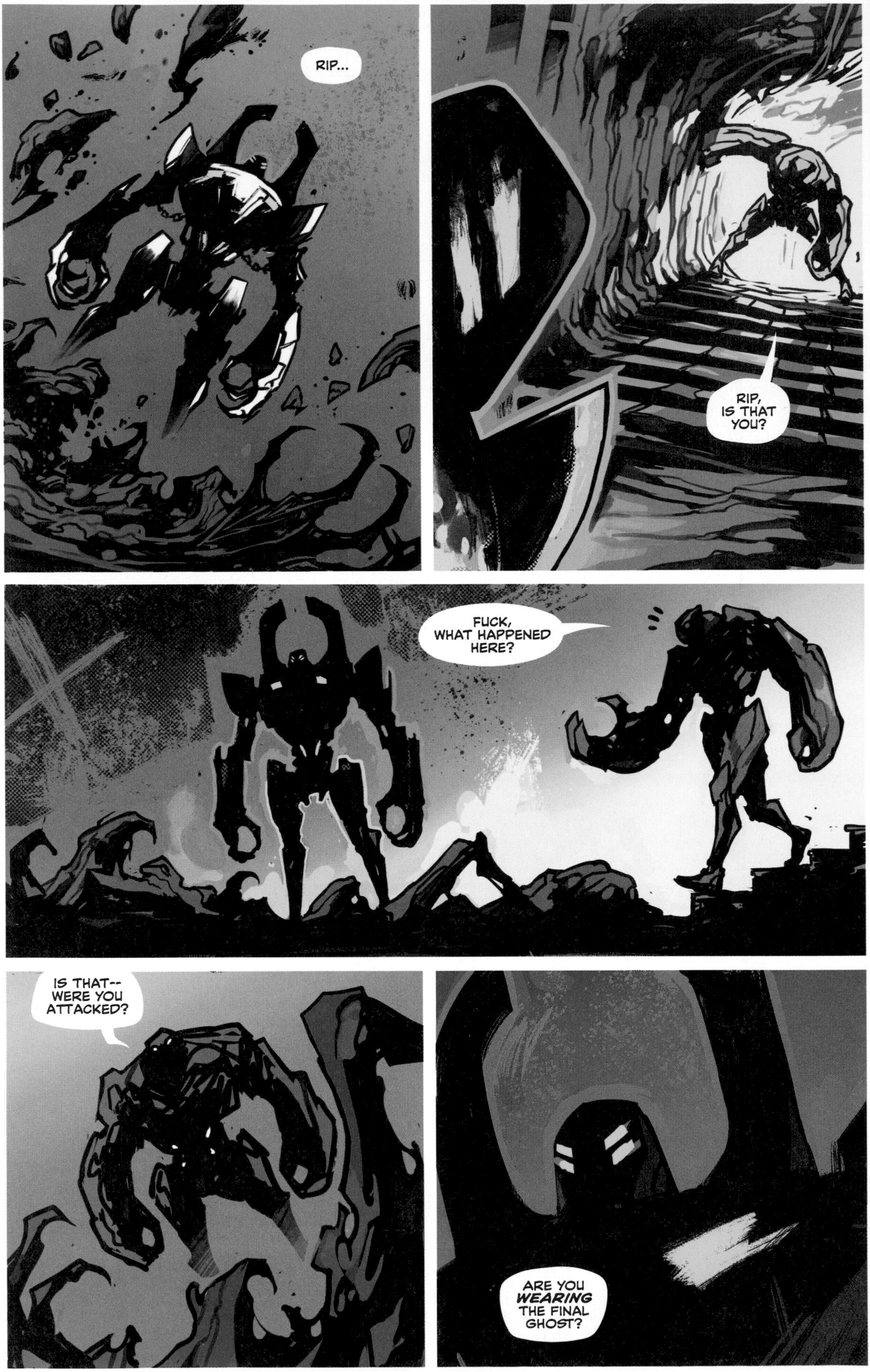
RIP...
RIP, IS THAT YOU?
FUCK, WHAT HAPPENED HERE?
IS THAT-- WERE YOU ATTACKED?
ARE YOU *WEARING* THE FINAL GHOST?

I'M GLAD YOU'RE OKAY-- AND THIS...

DON'T BLAME YOURSELF.

BRING HIM OUT.

WHAT?

MAKE HIM SHOW HIMSELF, OLD JAMES.

SHE WANTS TO SEE HIM.

I'M NOT SURE THAT'S A GOOD IDEA.

HE TOLD ME WHAT HE DID. HOW HE ABANDONED HER DOWN HERE.

HE'D BEEN TORTURED BY THIS NATION. WITH SALT AND ELECTRICITY INTO BECOMING BODY ARMOR-- INTO THIS.

WHEN HE COULD, HE RAN.

WE HAVEN'T GOT TIME FOR THEM TO FIGHT IT OUT NOW.

AMI'S IN THE OLD JAMES HOUSE RIGHT NOW, FIGHTING FOR HER LIFE AGAINST THE NUCLEAR BASTARD.

JUST TELL THE GHOST WE'RE GOING BACK TO THE HOUSE. THAT'S WHAT THEY WANT. THEY WANT TO GO BACK.

NO.

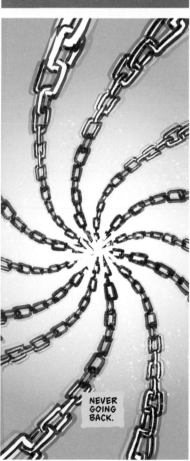

NEVER GOING BACK.

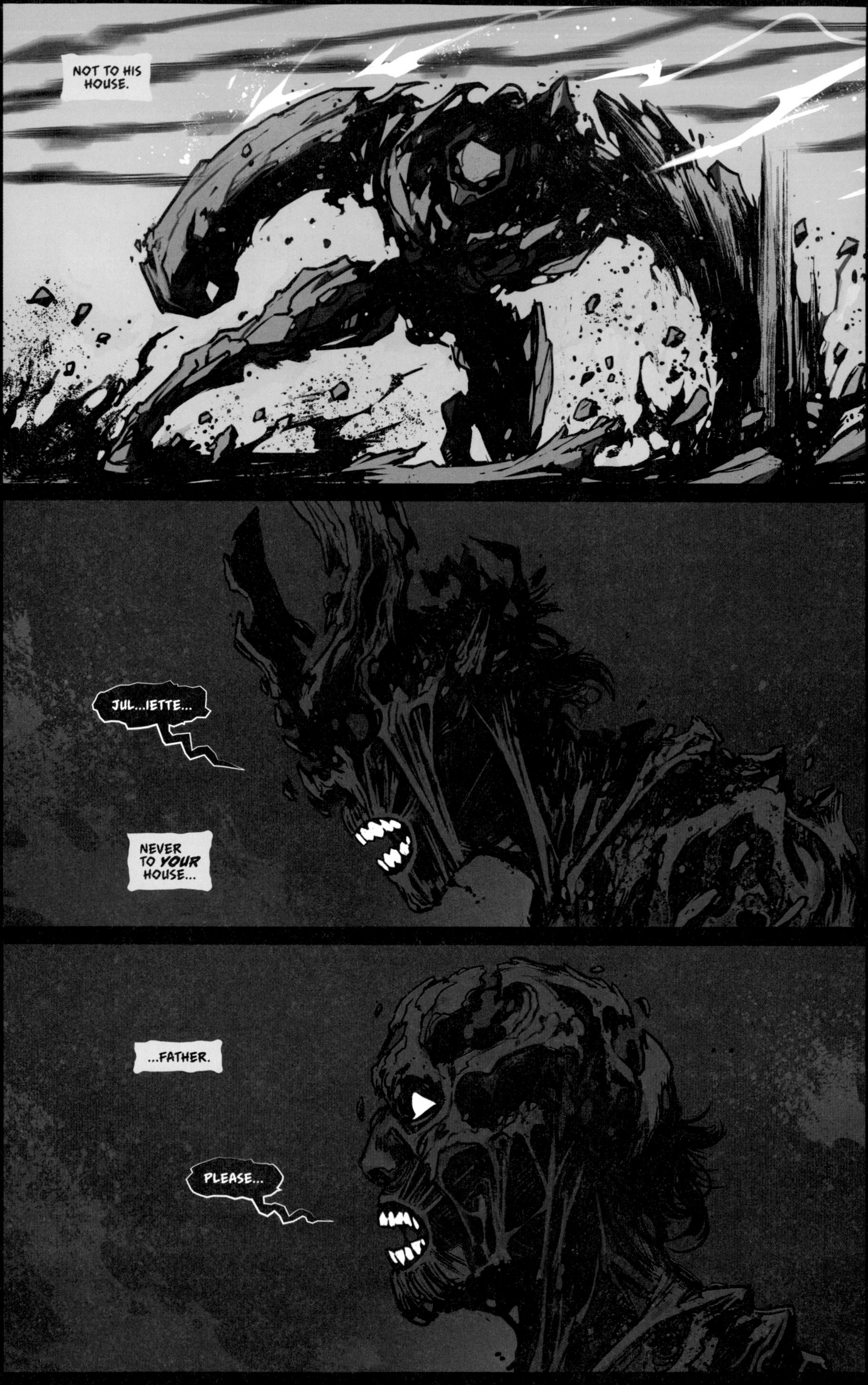
NOT TO HIS HOUSE.
JUL...IETTE...
NEVER TO YOUR HOUSE...
...FATHER.
PLEASE...

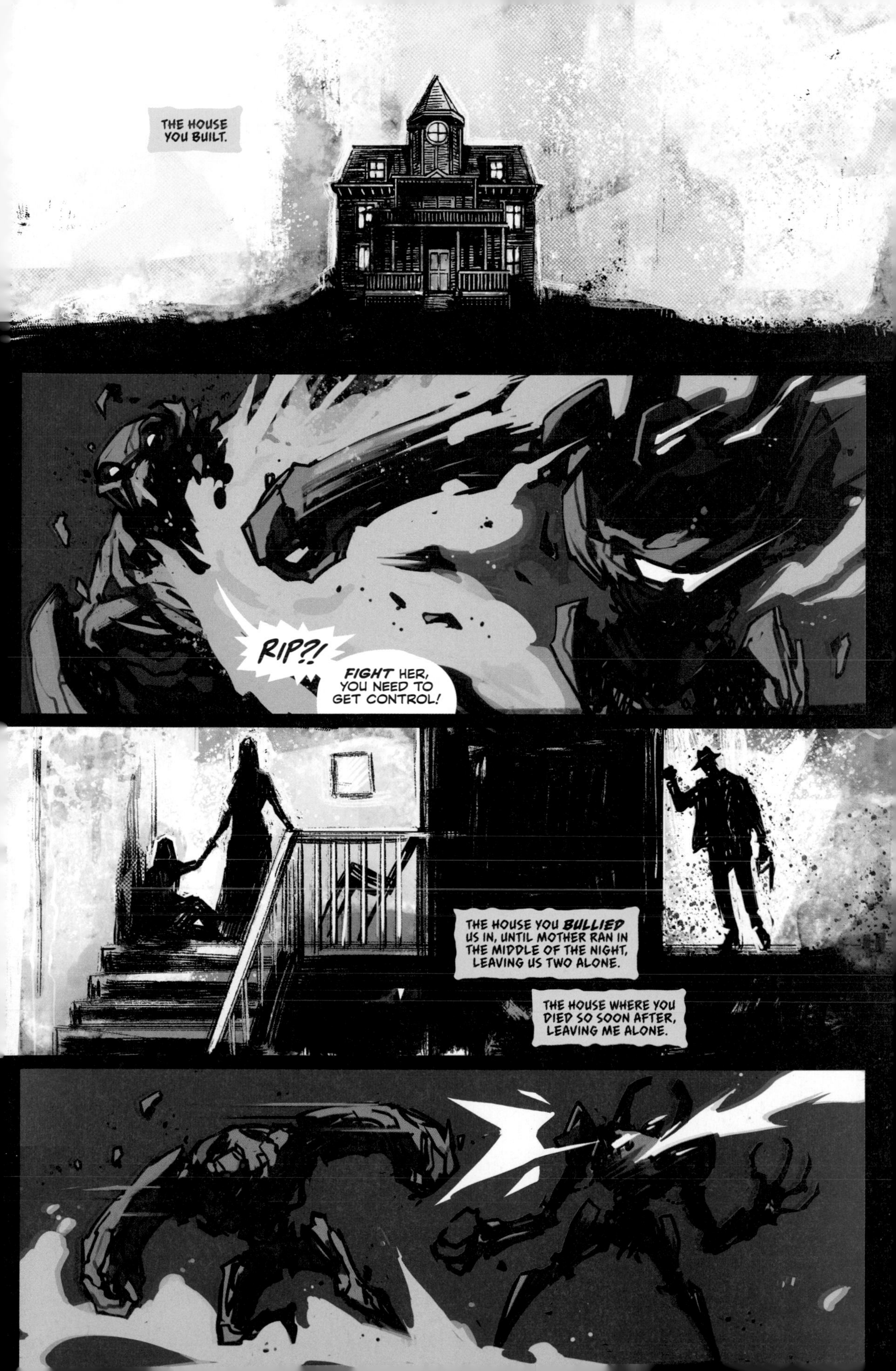
THE HOUSE YOU BUILT.
RIP?!
FIGHT HER, YOU NEED TO GET CONTROL!
THE HOUSE YOU BULLIED US IN, UNTIL MOTHER RAN IN THE MIDDLE OF THE NIGHT, LEAVING US TWO ALONE.
THE HOUSE WHERE YOU DIED SO SOON AFTER, LEAVING ME ALONE.

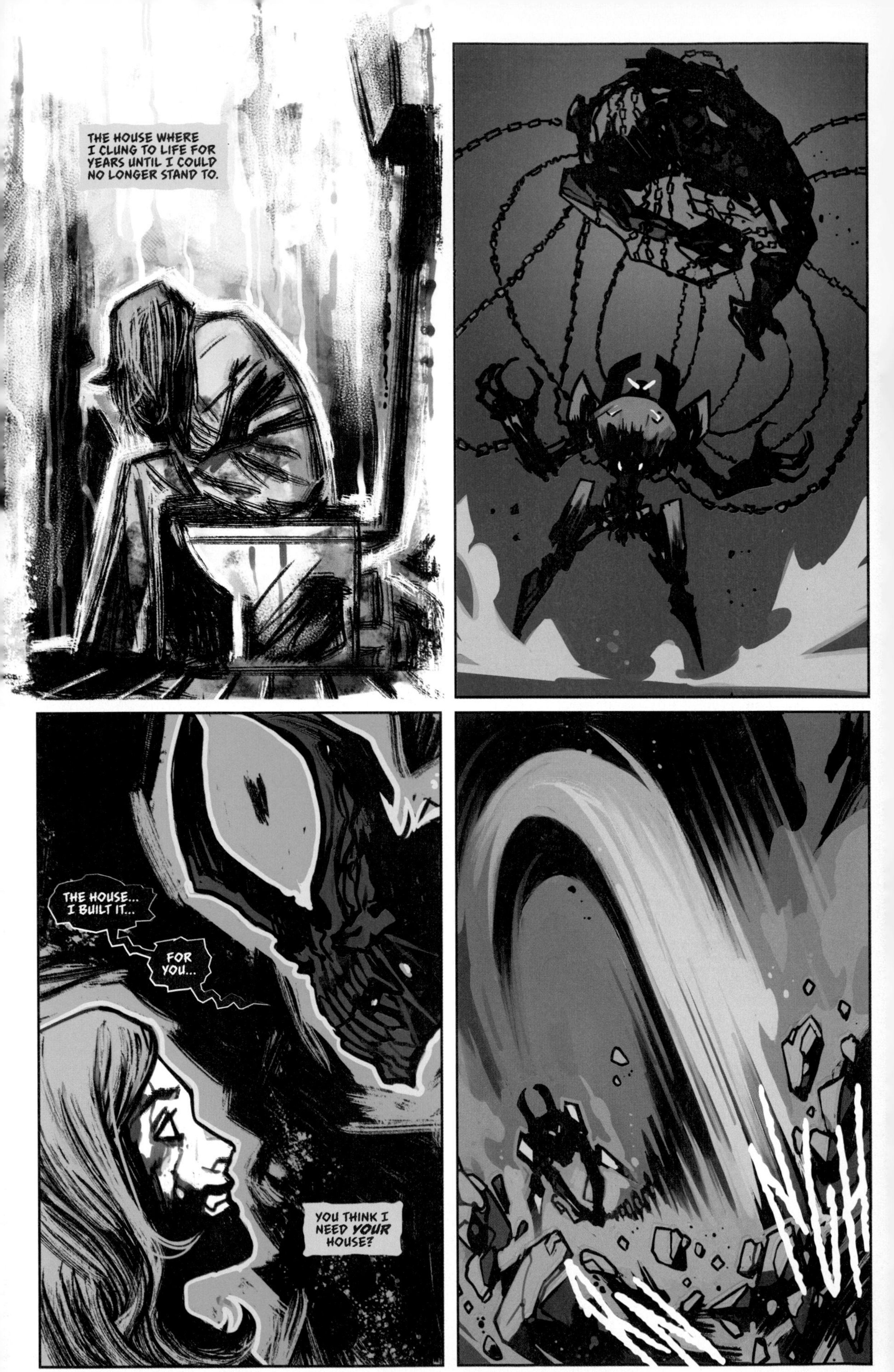
THE HOUSE WHERE I CLUNG TO LIFE FOR YEARS UNTIL I COULD NO LONGER STAND TO.
THE HOUSE... I BUILT IT...
FOR YOU...
YOU THINK I NEED *YOUR* HOUSE?
NGH

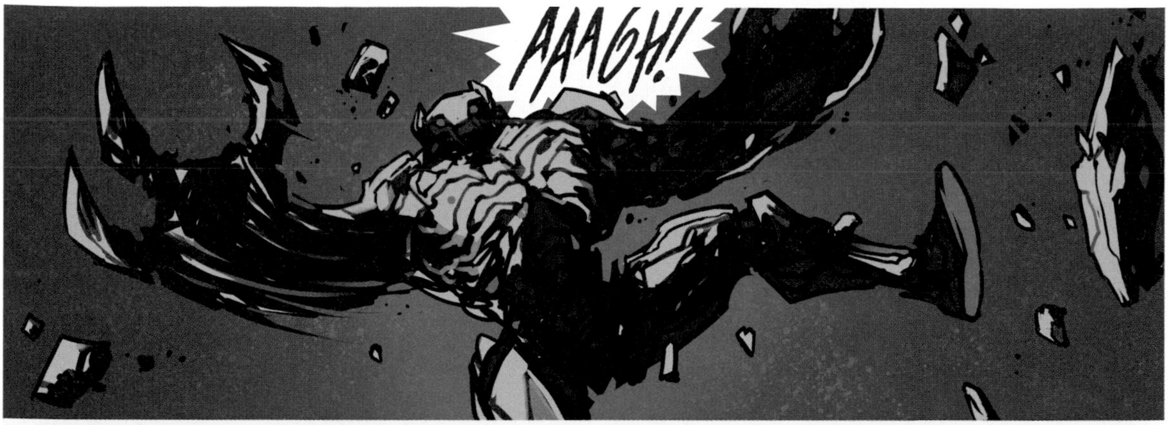
AAAGH!

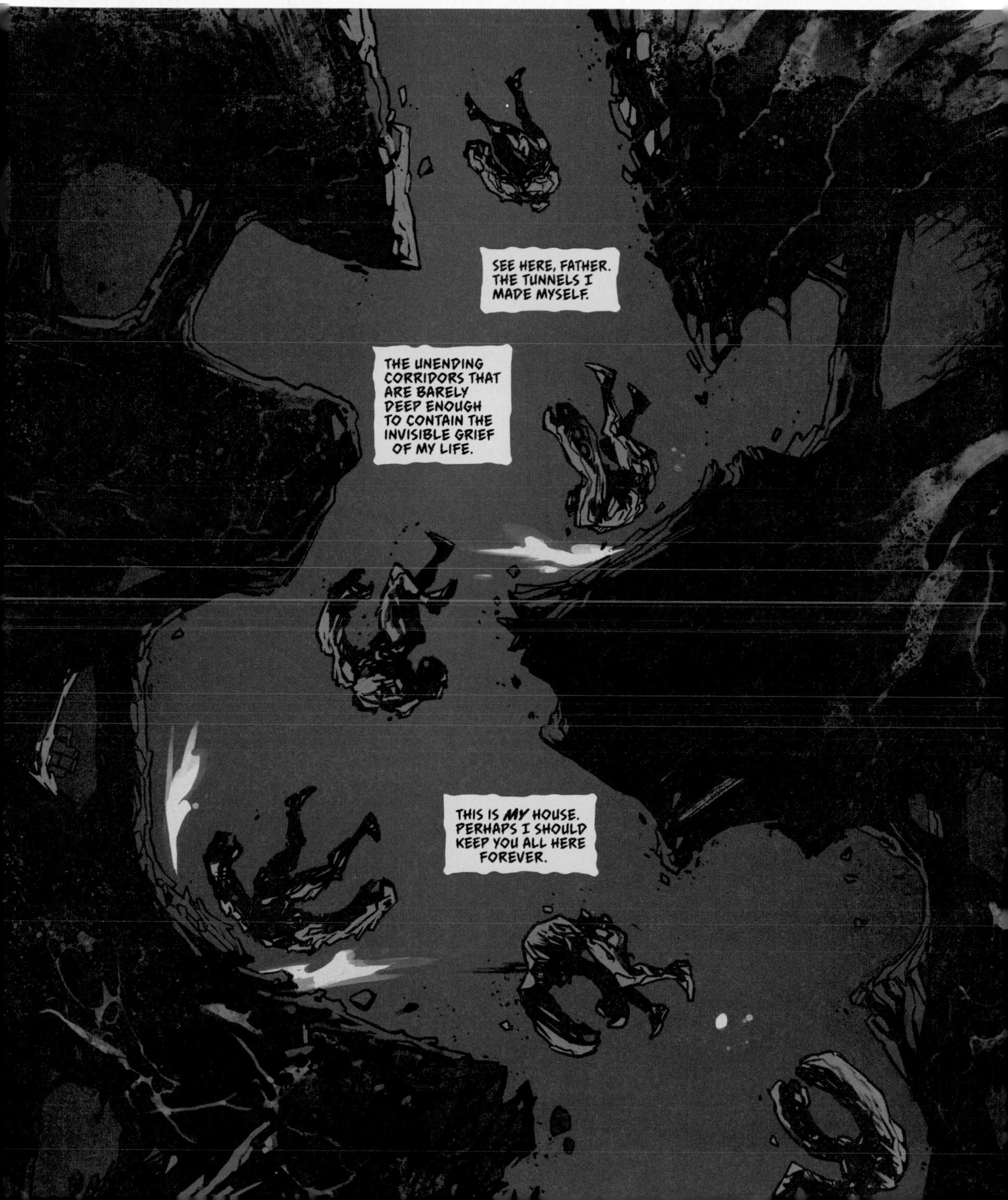
SEE HERE, FATHER. THE TUNNELS I MADE MYSELF.
THE UNENDING CORRIDORS THAT ARE BARELY DEEP ENOUGH TO CONTAIN THE INVISIBLE GRIEF OF MY LIFE.
THIS IS MY HOUSE. PERHAPS I SHOULD KEEP YOU ALL HERE FOREVER.

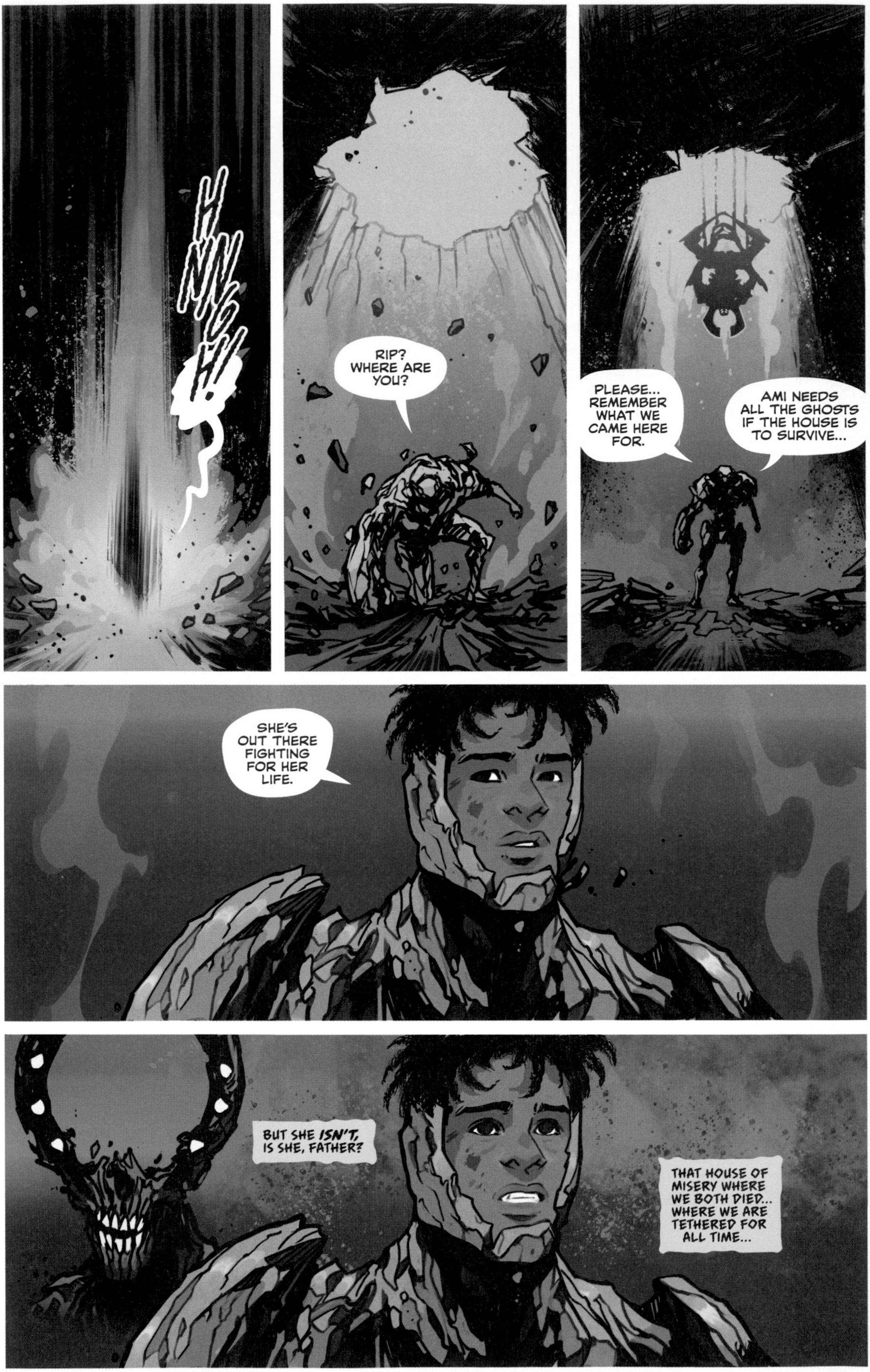
HNNGGH!
RIP? WHERE ARE YOU?
PLEASE... REMEMBER WHAT WE CAME HERE FOR.
AMI NEEDS ALL THE GHOSTS IF THE HOUSE IS TO SURVIVE...
SHE'S OUT THERE FIGHTING FOR HER LIFE.
BUT SHE *ISN'T*, IS SHE, FATHER?
THAT HOUSE OF MISERY WHERE WE BOTH DIED... WHERE WE ARE TETHERED FOR ALL TIME...

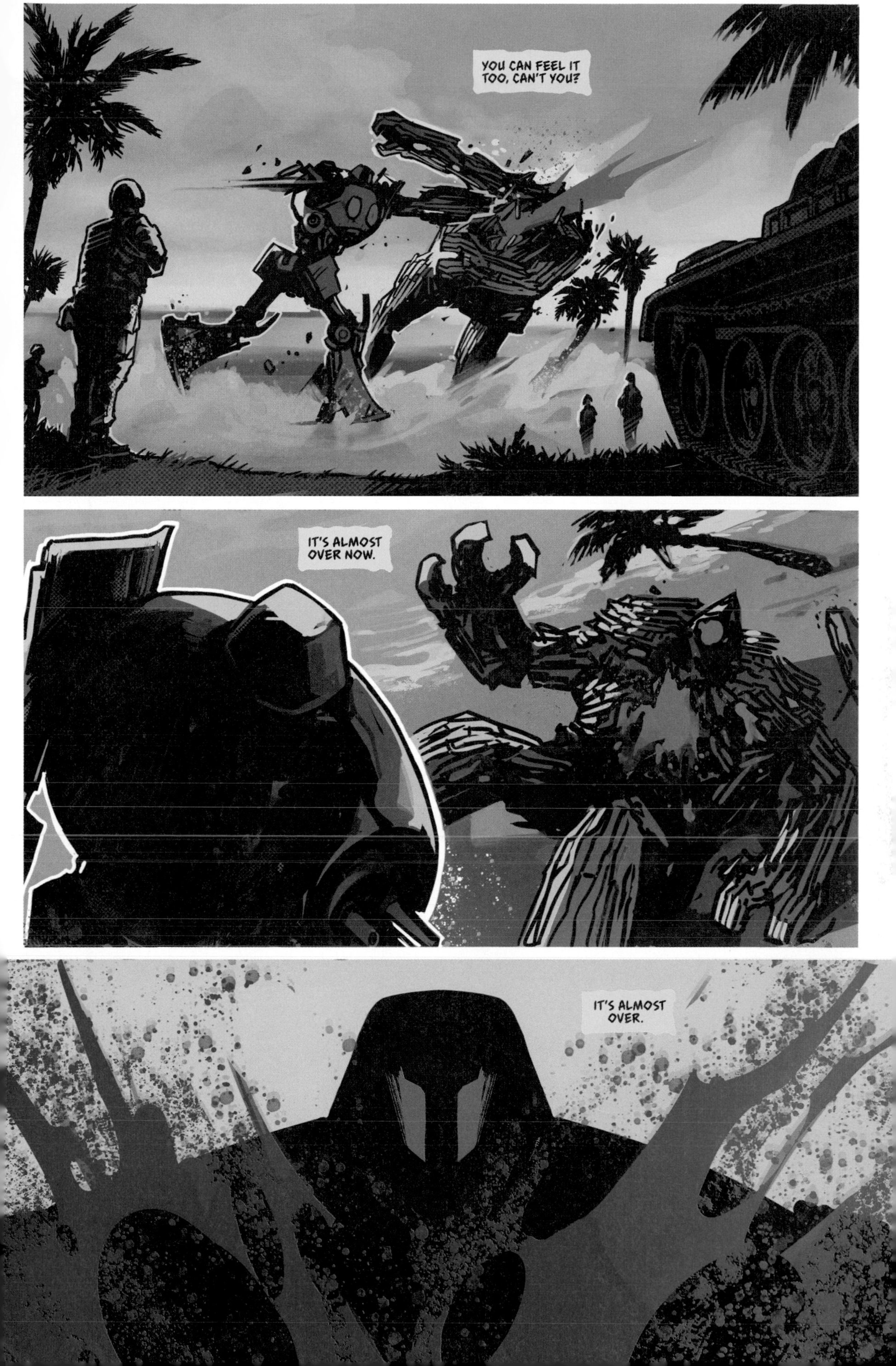
YOU CAN FEEL IT TOO, CAN'T YOU?
IT'S ALMOST OVER NOW.
IT'S ALMOST OVER.

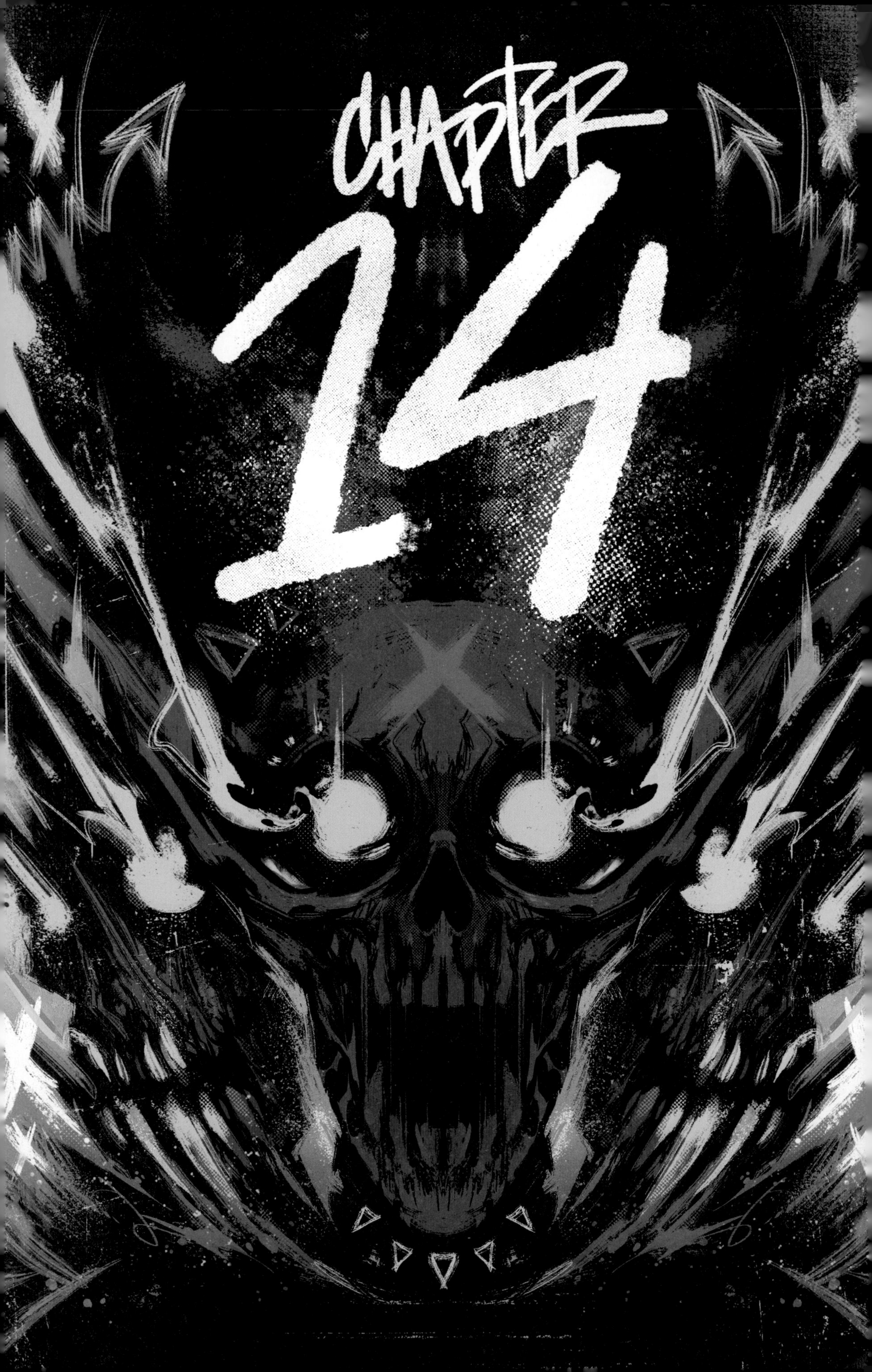
CHAPTER
24

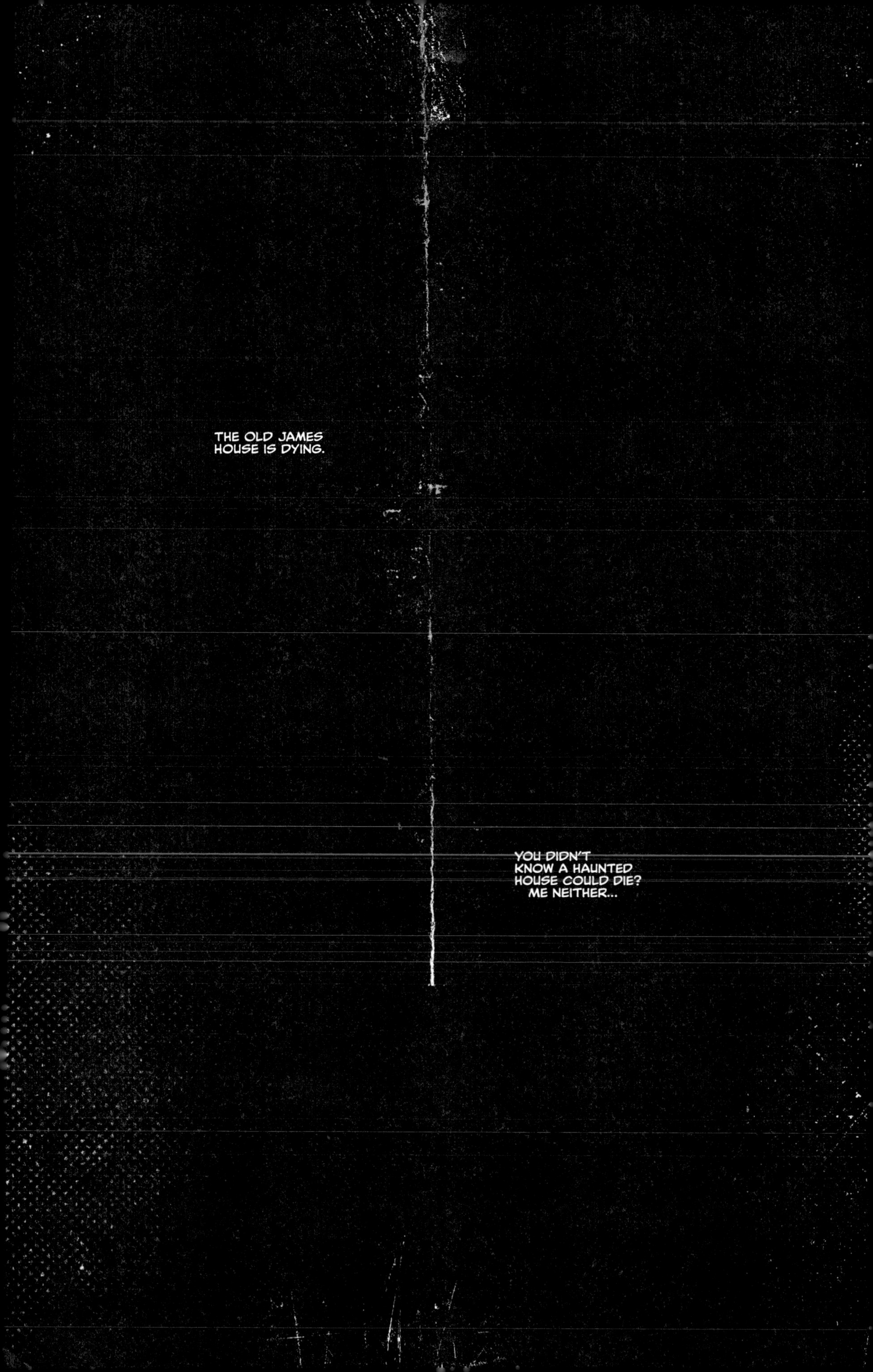
THE OLD JAMES HOUSE IS DYING.
YOU DIDN'T KNOW A HAUNTED HOUSE COULD DIE? ME NEITHER...

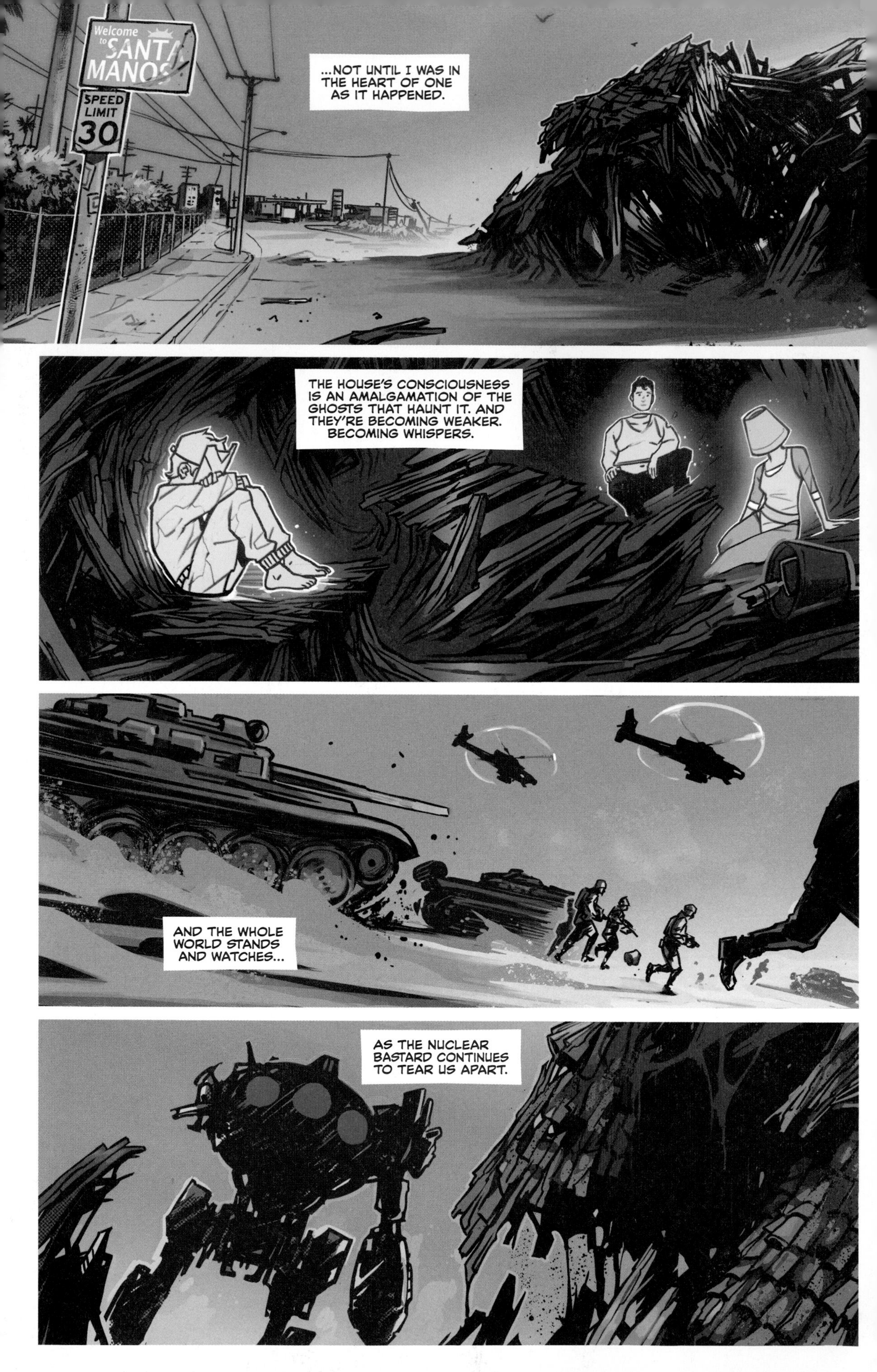
Welcome to SANTA MANOS
SPEED LIMIT 30
...NOT UNTIL I WAS IN THE HEART OF ONE AS IT HAPPENED.
THE HOUSE'S CONSCIOUSNESS IS AN AMALGAMATION OF THE GHOSTS THAT HAUNT IT. AND THEY'RE BECOMING WEAKER. BECOMING WHISPERS.
AND THE WHOLE WORLD STANDS AND WATCHES...
AS THE NUCLEAR BASTARD CONTINUES TO TEAR US APART.

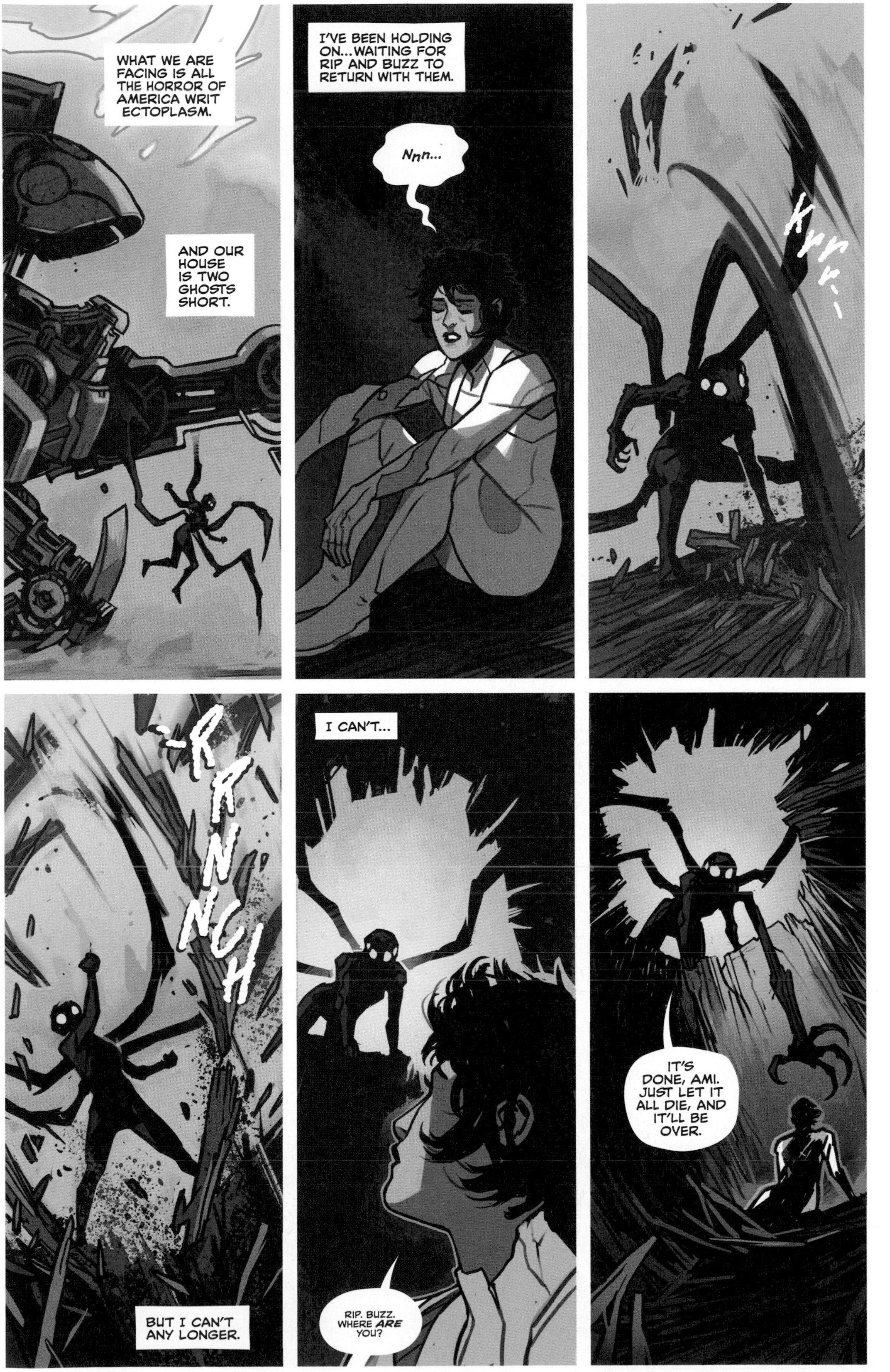
WHAT WE ARE FACING IS ALL THE HORROR OF AMERICA WRIT ECTOPLASM.
AND OUR HOUSE IS TWO GHOSTS SHORT.
I'VE BEEN HOLDING ON...WAITING FOR RIP AND BUZZ TO RETURN WITH THEM.
Nnn...
Kyrr-
-RRNNCH
BUT I CAN'T ANY LONGER.
I CAN'T...
RIP. BUZZ. WHERE *ARE* YOU?
IT'S DONE, AMI. JUST LET IT ALL DIE, AND IT'LL BE OVER.

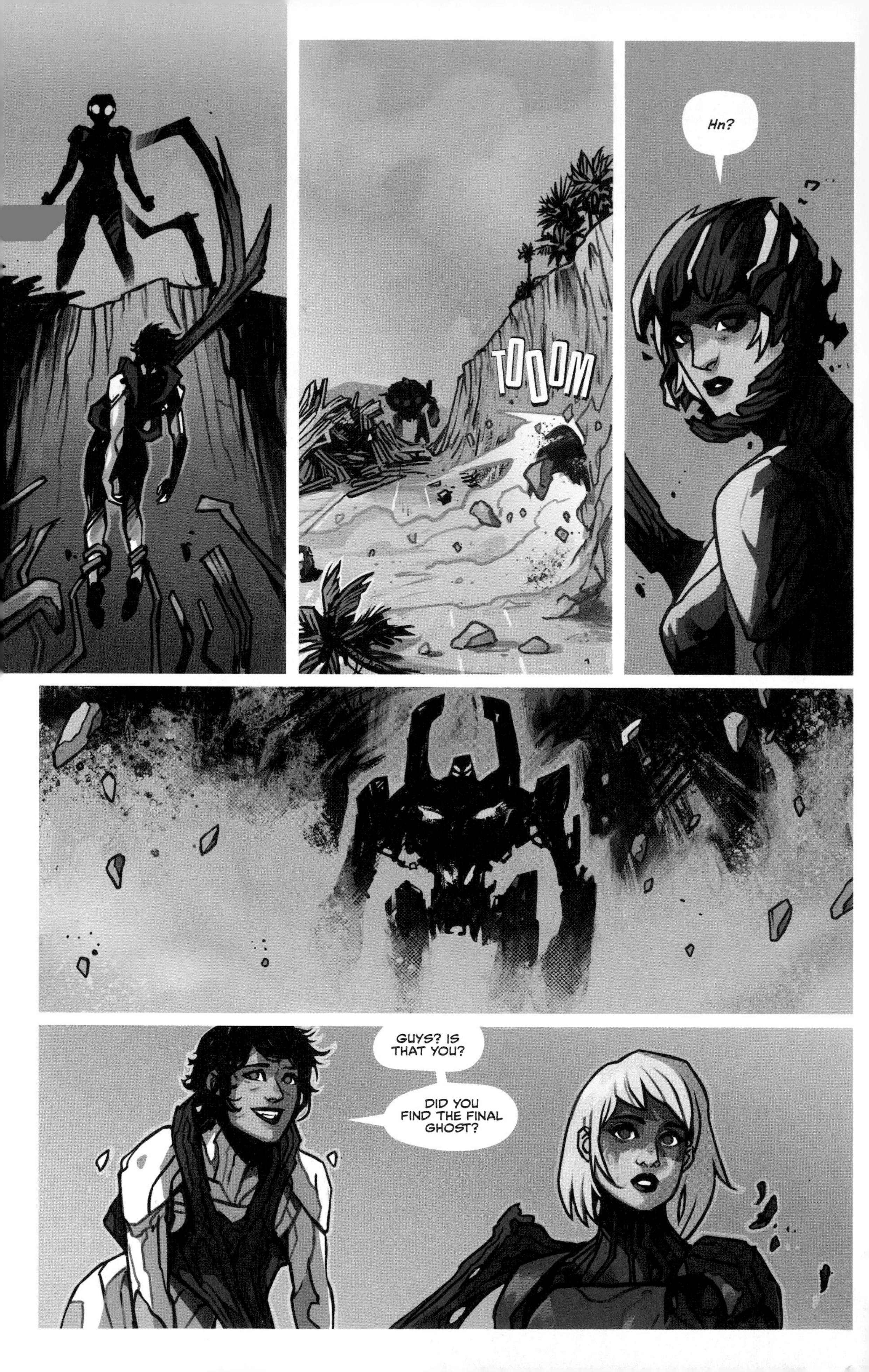
TOOOM
Hn?
GUYS? IS THAT YOU?
DID YOU FIND THE FINAL GHOST?

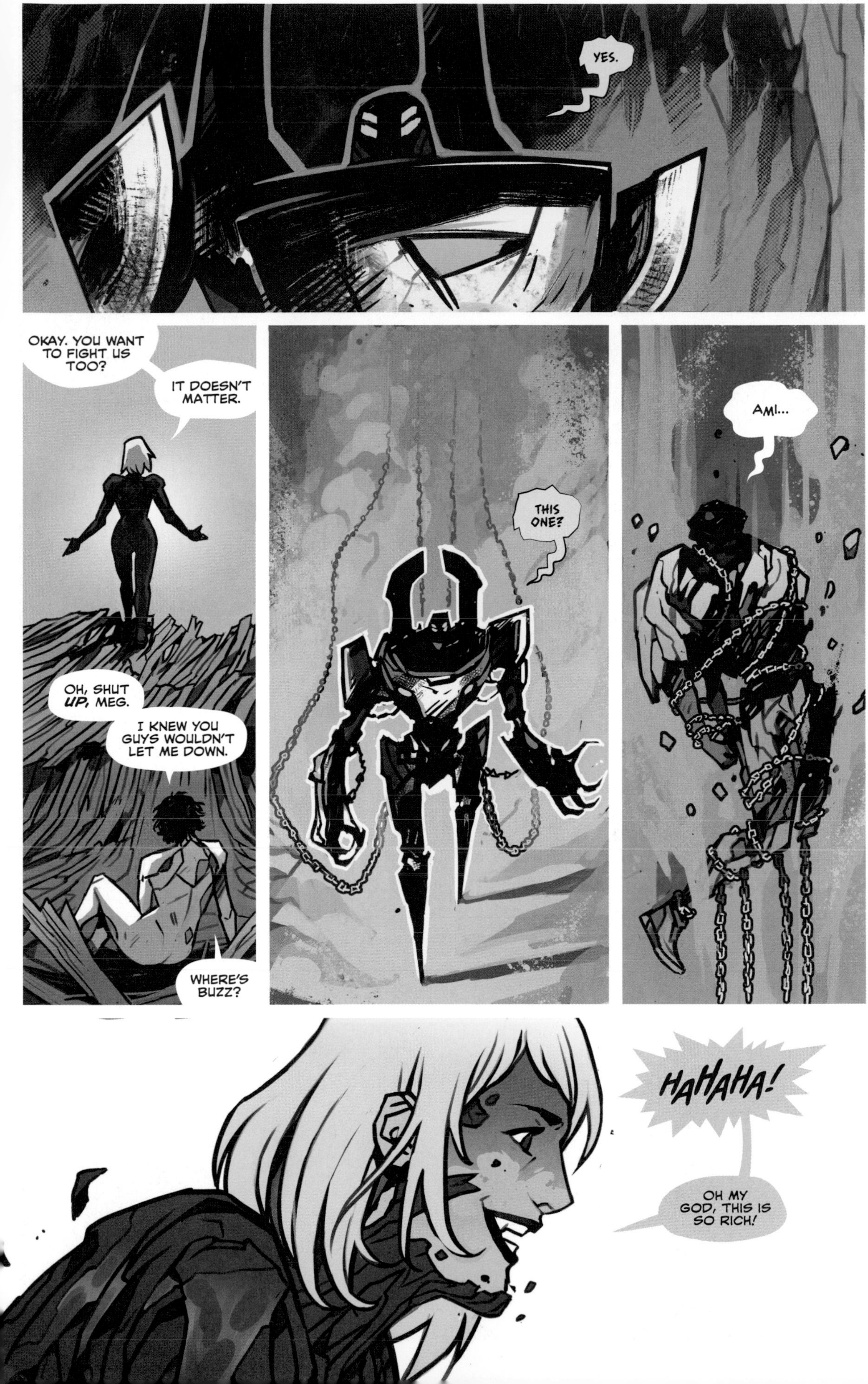
YES.
OKAY. YOU WANT TO FIGHT US TOO?
IT DOESN'T MATTER.
OH, SHUT *UP*, MEG.
I KNEW YOU GUYS WOULDN'T LET ME DOWN.
WHERE'S BUZZ?
THIS ONE?
AMI...
HAHAHA!
OH MY GOD, THIS IS SO RICH!

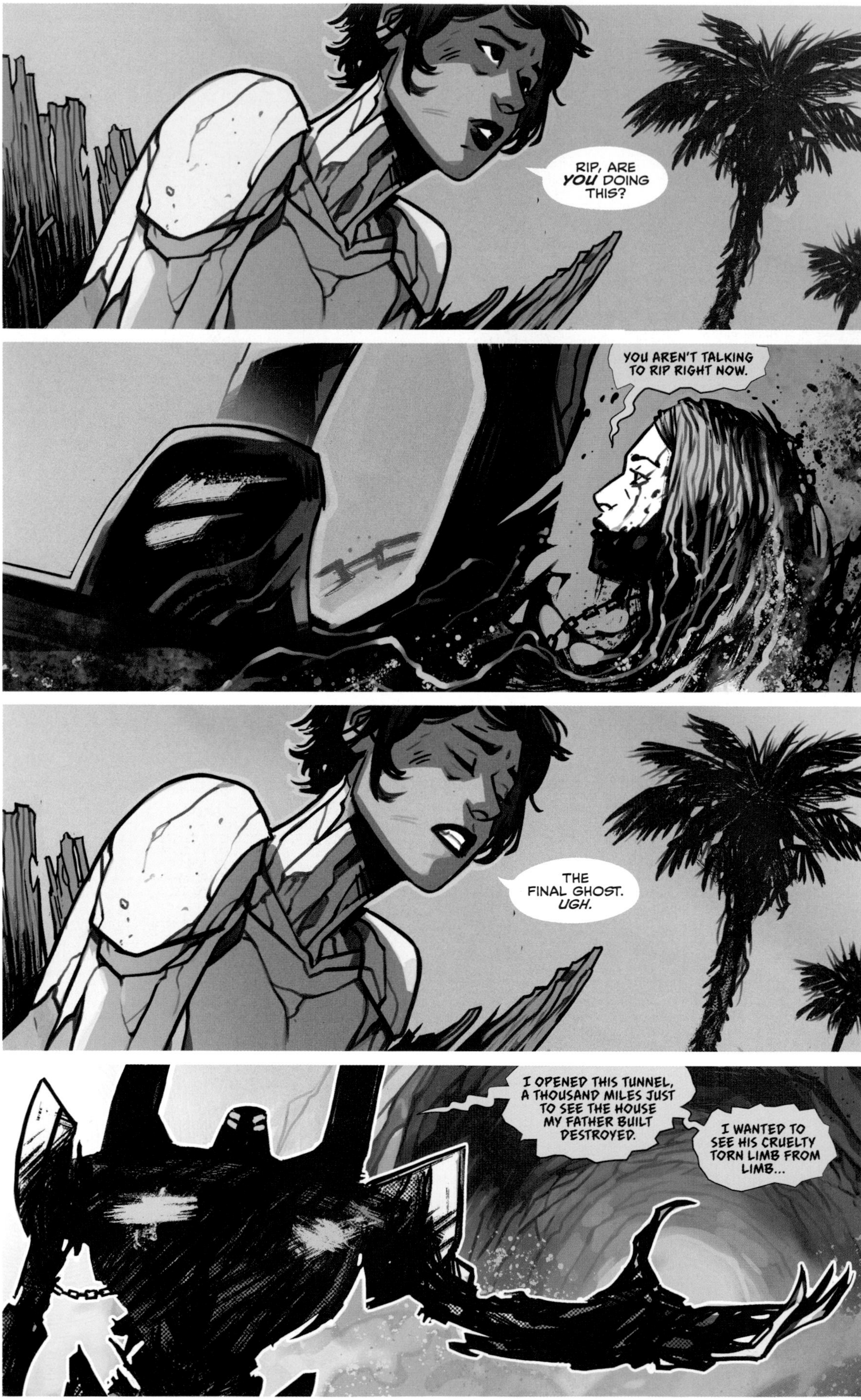
RIP, ARE *YOU* DOING THIS?
YOU AREN'T TALKING TO RIP RIGHT NOW.
THE FINAL GHOST. *UGH.*
I OPENED THIS TUNNEL, A THOUSAND MILES JUST TO SEE THE HOUSE MY FATHER BUILT DESTROYED.
I WANTED TO SEE HIS CRUELTY TORN LIMB FROM LIMB...

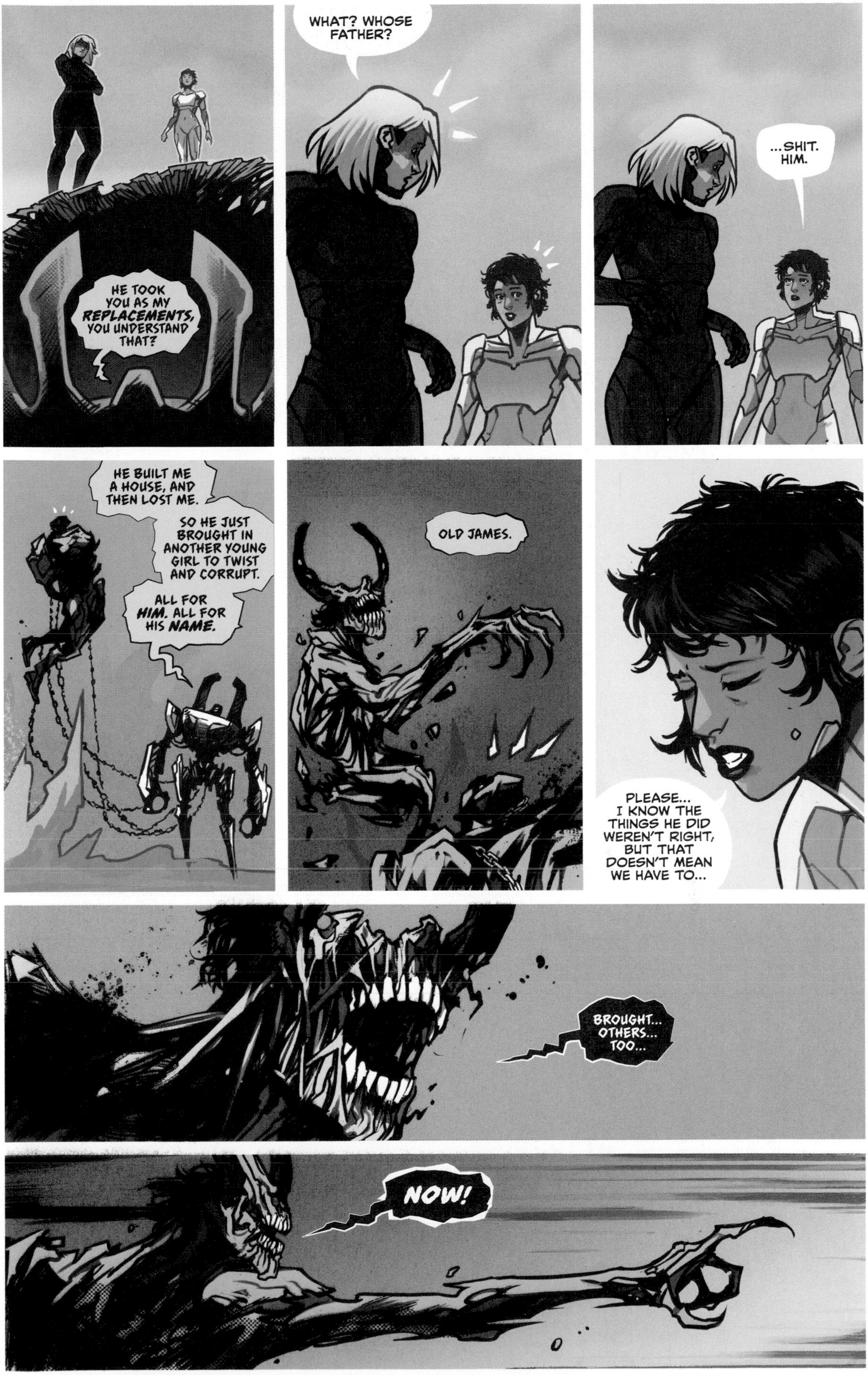
HE TOOK YOU AS MY REPLACEMENTS, YOU UNDERSTAND THAT?
WHAT? WHOSE FATHER?
...SHIT. HIM.
HE BUILT ME A HOUSE, AND THEN LOST ME.
SO HE JUST BROUGHT IN ANOTHER YOUNG GIRL TO TWIST AND CORRUPT.
ALL FOR HIM. ALL FOR HIS NAME.
OLD JAMES.
PLEASE... I KNOW THE THINGS HE DID WEREN'T RIGHT, BUT THAT DOESN'T MEAN WE HAVE TO...
BROUGHT... OTHERS... TOO...
NOW!

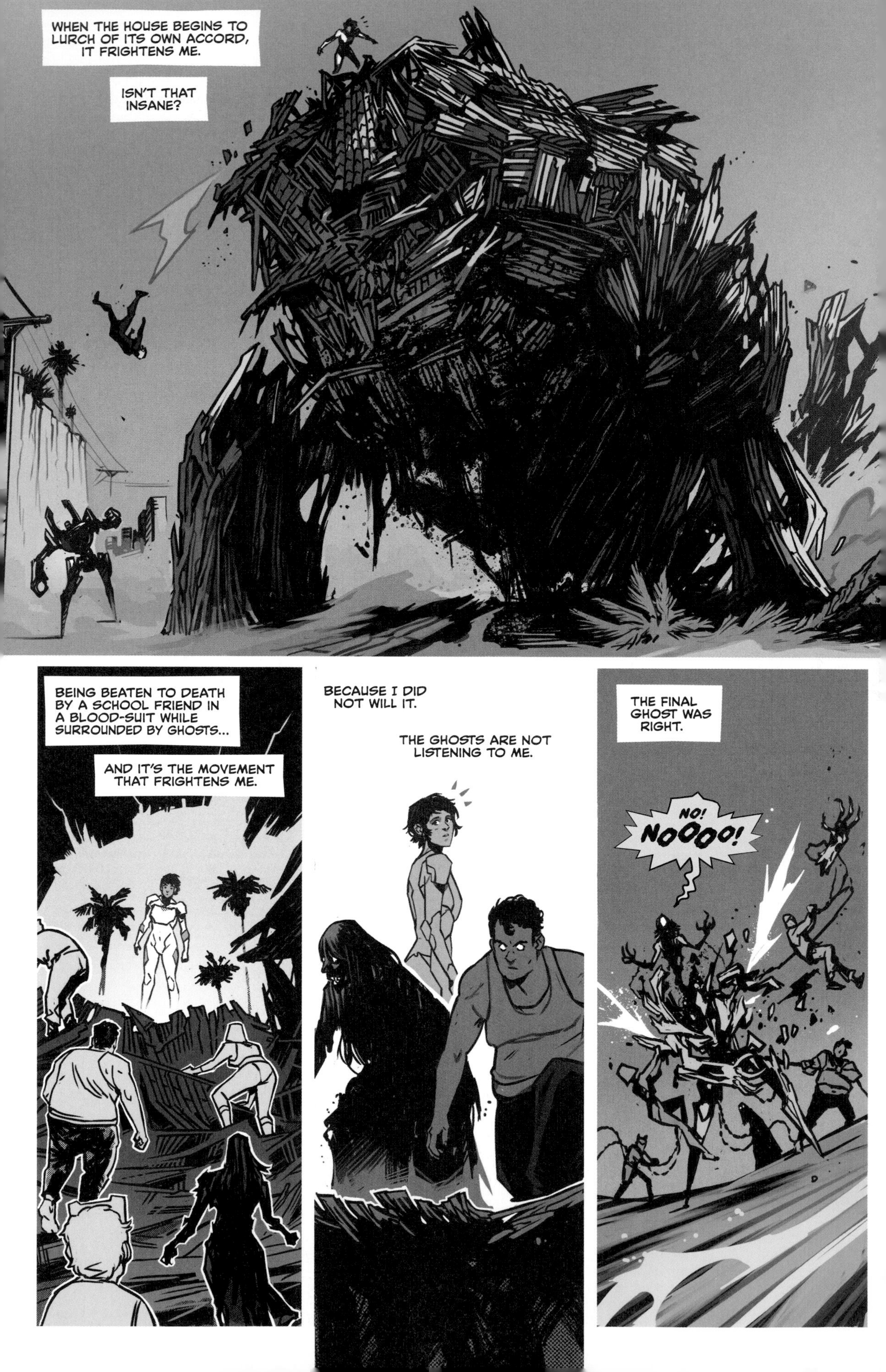

WHEN THE HOUSE BEGINS TO LURCH OF ITS OWN ACCORD, IT FRIGHTENS ME.
ISN'T THAT INSANE?
BEING BEATEN TO DEATH BY A SCHOOL FRIEND IN A BLOOD-SUIT WHILE SURROUNDED BY GHOSTS...
AND IT'S THE MOVEMENT THAT FRIGHTENS ME.
BECAUSE I DID NOT WILL IT.
THE GHOSTS ARE NOT LISTENING TO ME.
THE FINAL GHOST WAS RIGHT.
NO! NOOOO!

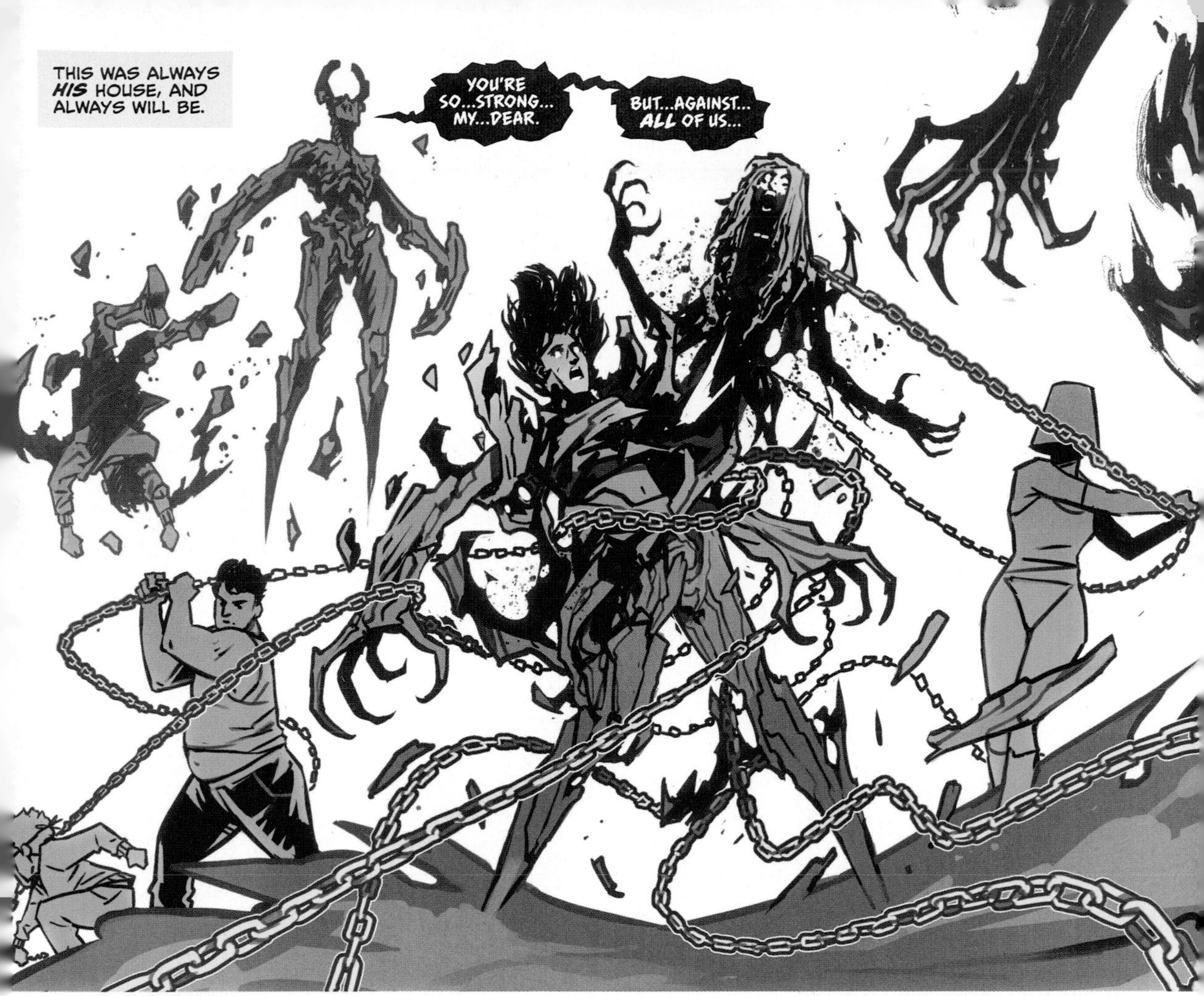
THIS WAS ALWAYS *HIS* HOUSE, AND ALWAYS WILL BE.
YOU'RE SO...STRONG... MY...DEAR.
BUT...AGAINST... *ALL* OF US...

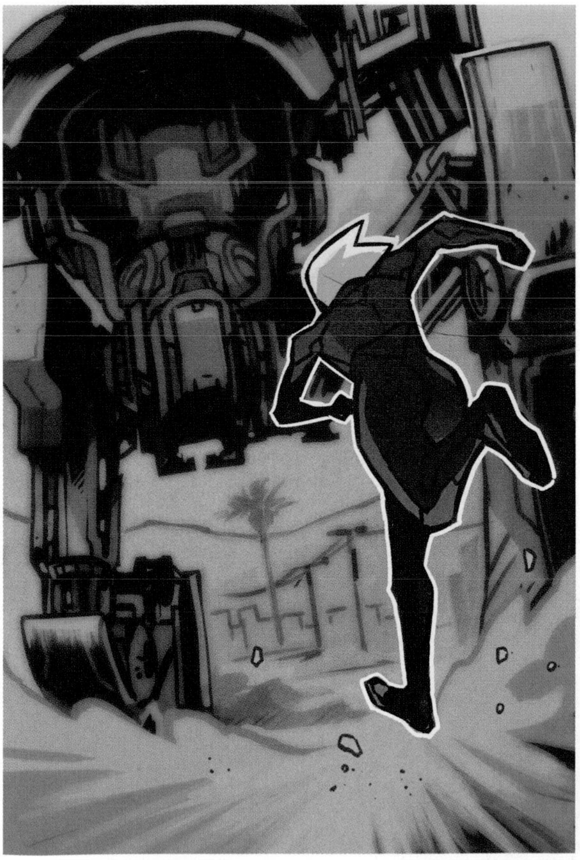

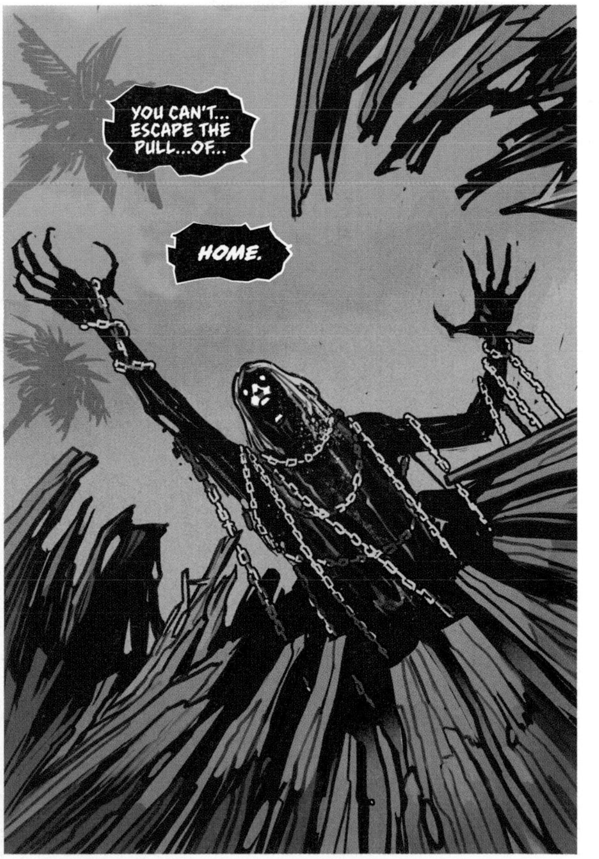
YOU CAN'T... ESCAPE THE PULL...OF...
HOME.

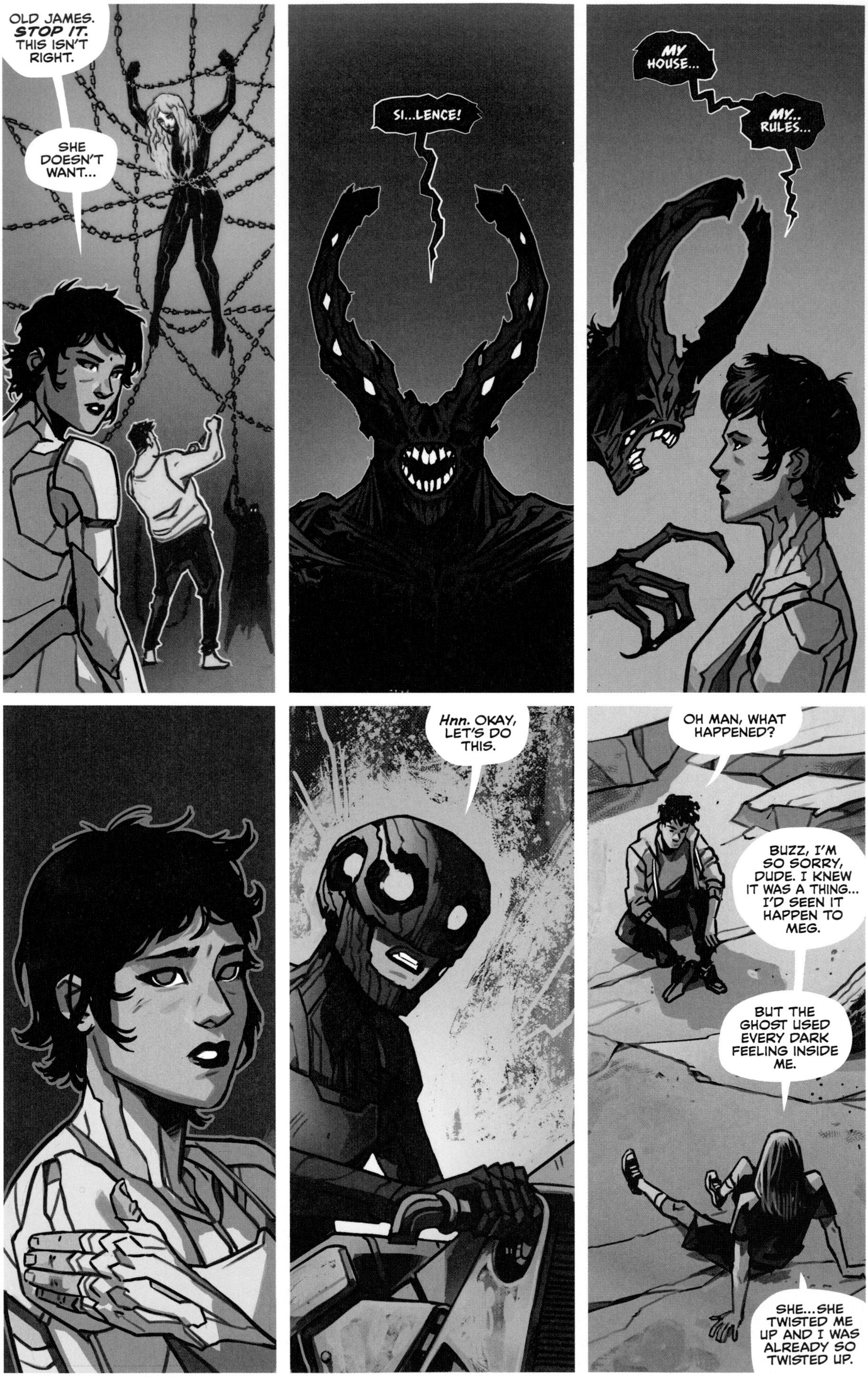

OLD JAMES. **STOP IT.** THIS ISN'T RIGHT.
SHE DOESN'T WANT...
SI...LENCE!
MY HOUSE...
MY... RULES...
Hnn. OKAY, LET'S DO THIS.
OH MAN, WHAT HAPPENED?
BUZZ, I'M SO SORRY, DUDE. I KNEW IT WAS A THING... I'D SEEN IT HAPPEN TO MEG.
BUT THE GHOST USED EVERY DARK FEELING INSIDE ME.
SHE...SHE TWISTED ME UP AND I WAS ALREADY SO TWISTED UP.

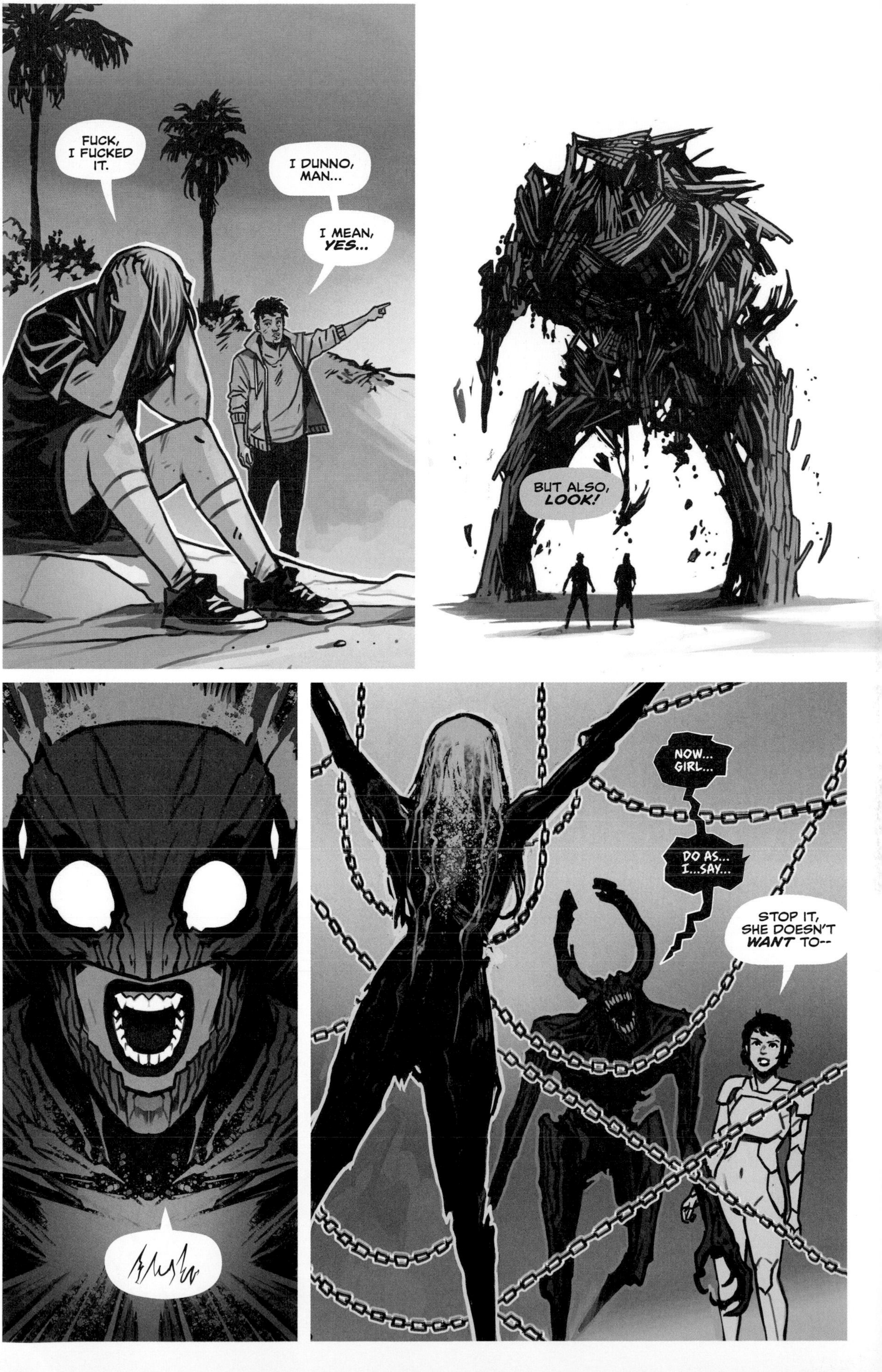
FUCK, I FUCKED IT.
I DUNNO, MAN...
I MEAN, YES...
BUT ALSO, LOOK!
NOW... GIRL...
DO AS... I...SAY...
STOP IT, SHE DOESN'T WANT TO--

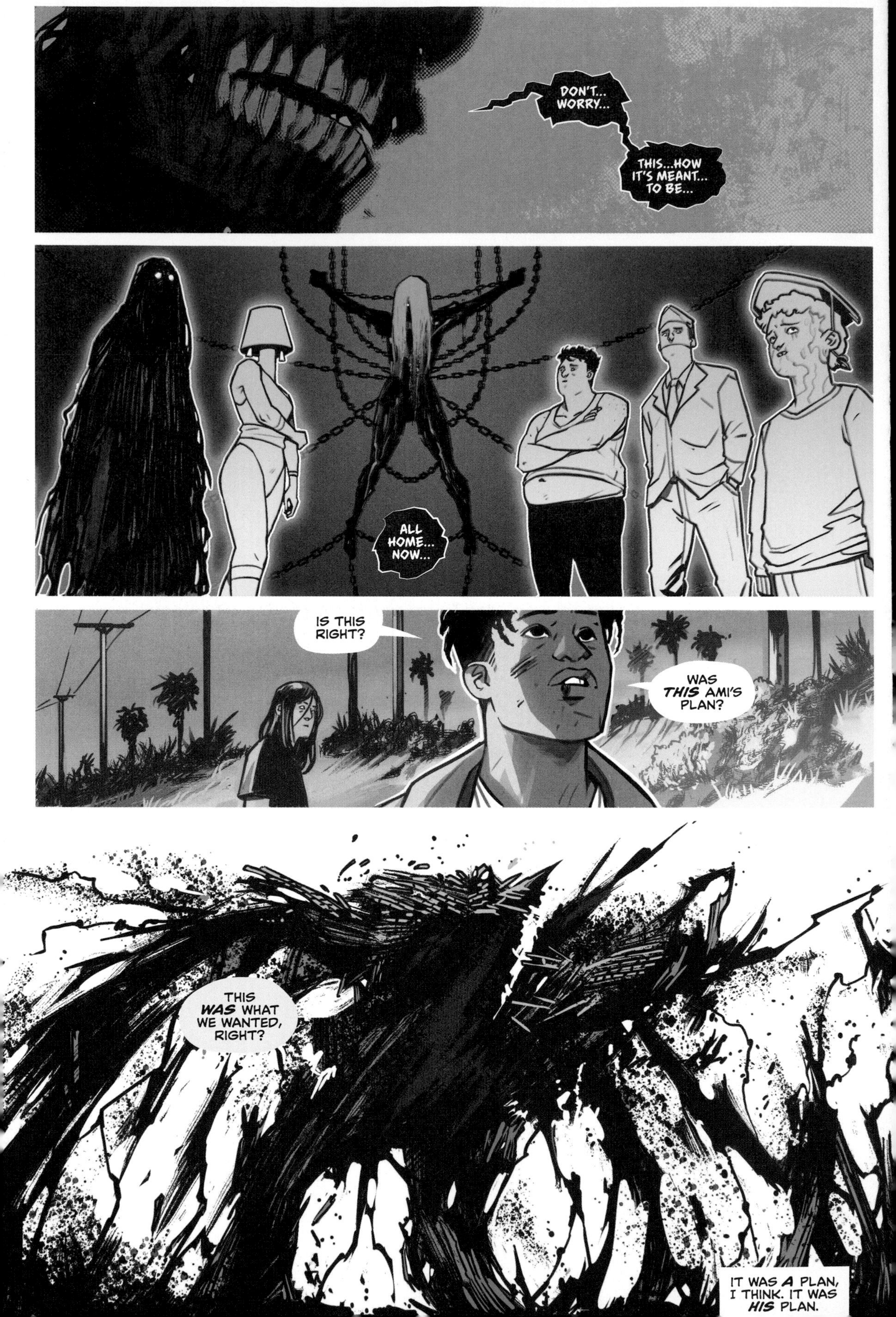
DON'T... WORRY...
THIS...HOW IT'S MEANT... TO BE...
ALL HOME... NOW...
IS THIS RIGHT?
WAS *THIS* AMI'S PLAN?
THIS *WAS* WHAT WE WANTED, RIGHT?
IT WAS *A* PLAN, I THINK. IT WAS *HIS* PLAN.

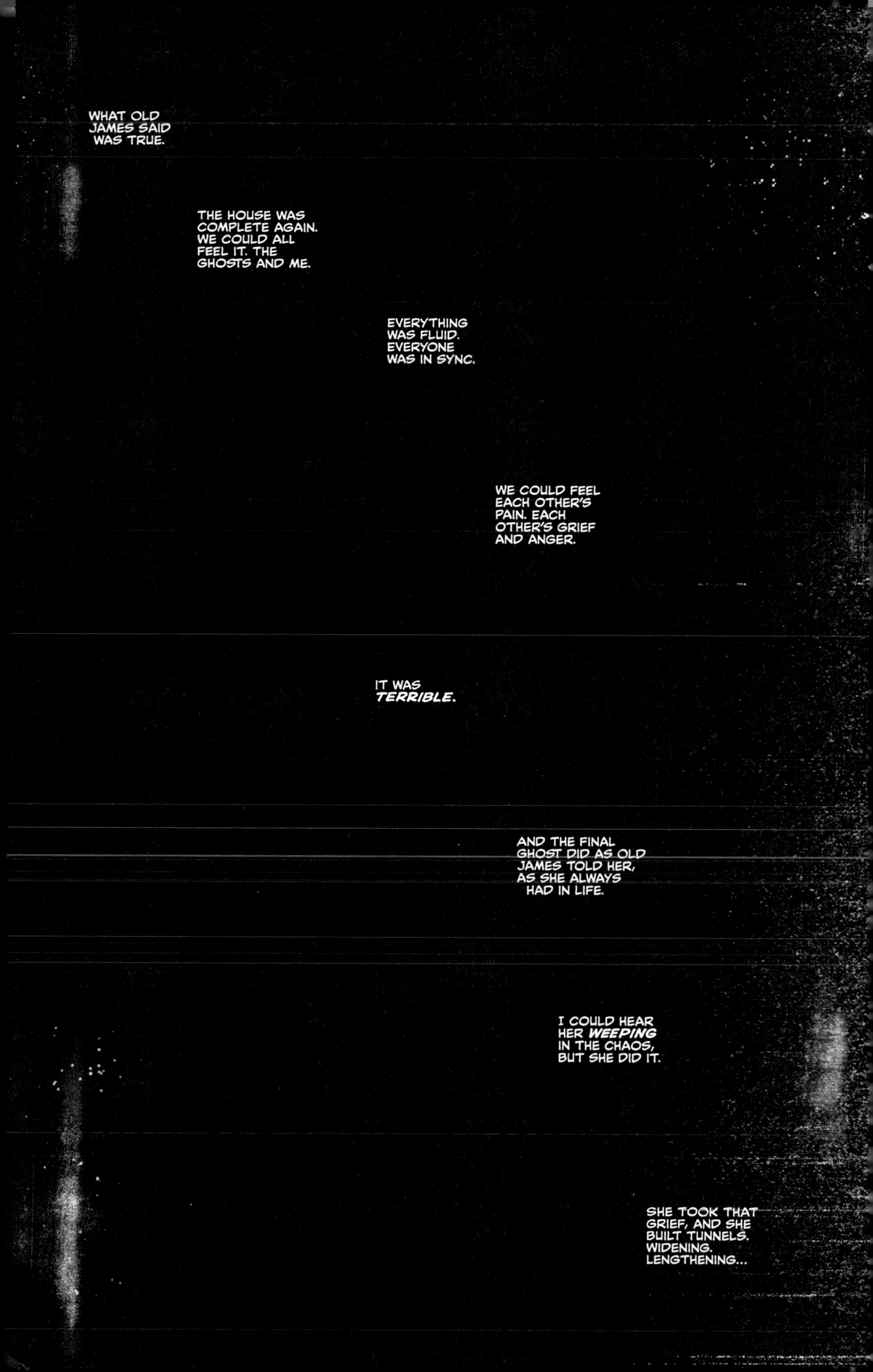
WHAT OLD JAMES SAID WAS TRUE.
THE HOUSE WAS COMPLETE AGAIN. WE COULD ALL FEEL IT. THE GHOSTS AND ME.
EVERYTHING WAS FLUID. EVERYONE WAS IN SYNC.
WE COULD FEEL EACH OTHER'S PAIN. EACH OTHER'S GRIEF AND ANGER.
IT WAS ***TERRIBLE***.
AND THE FINAL GHOST DID AS OLD JAMES TOLD HER, AS SHE ALWAYS HAD IN LIFE.
I COULD HEAR HER ***WEEPING*** IN THE CHAOS, BUT SHE DID IT.
SHE TOOK THAT GRIEF, AND SHE BUILT TUNNELS. WIDENING. LENGTHENING...

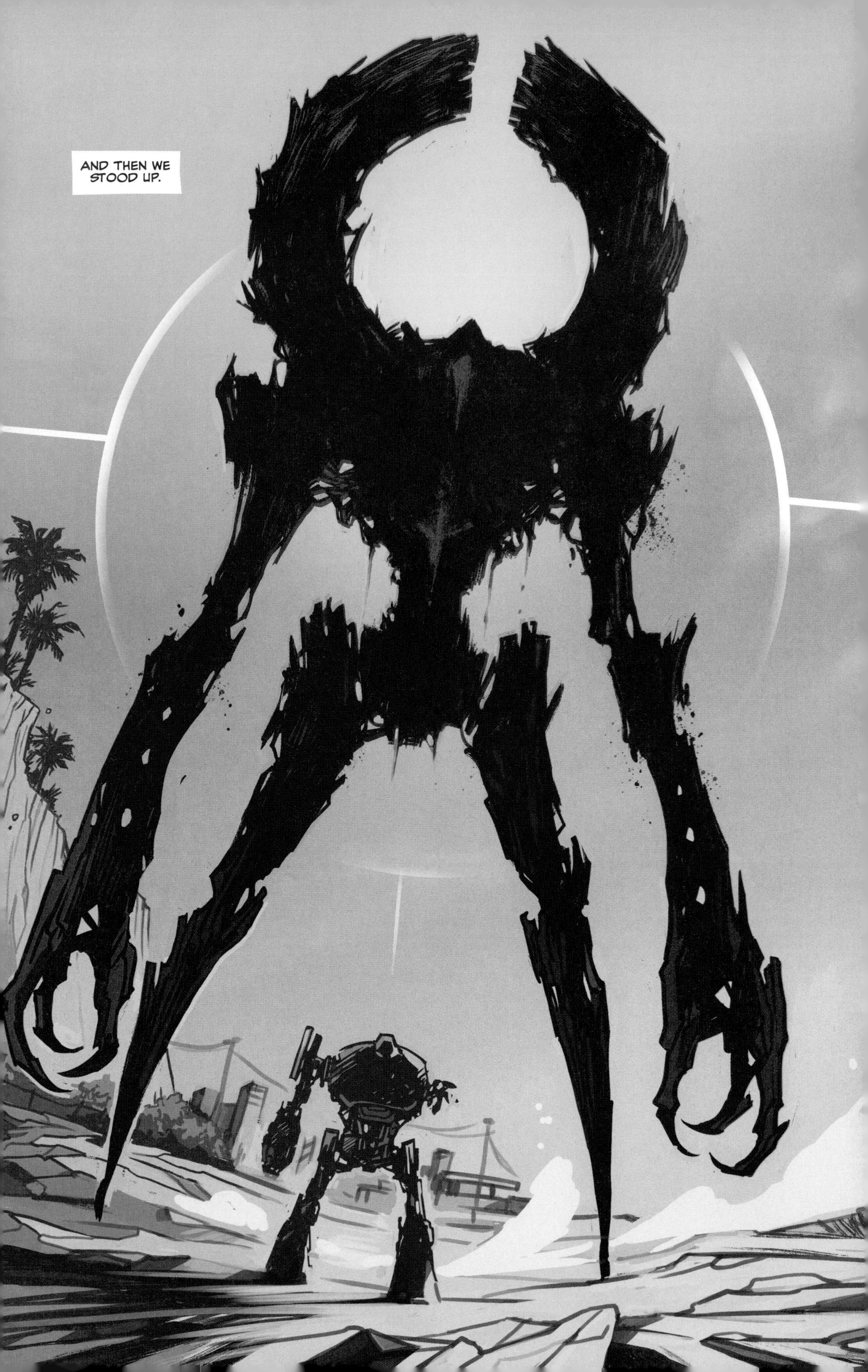
AND THEN WE STOOD UP.

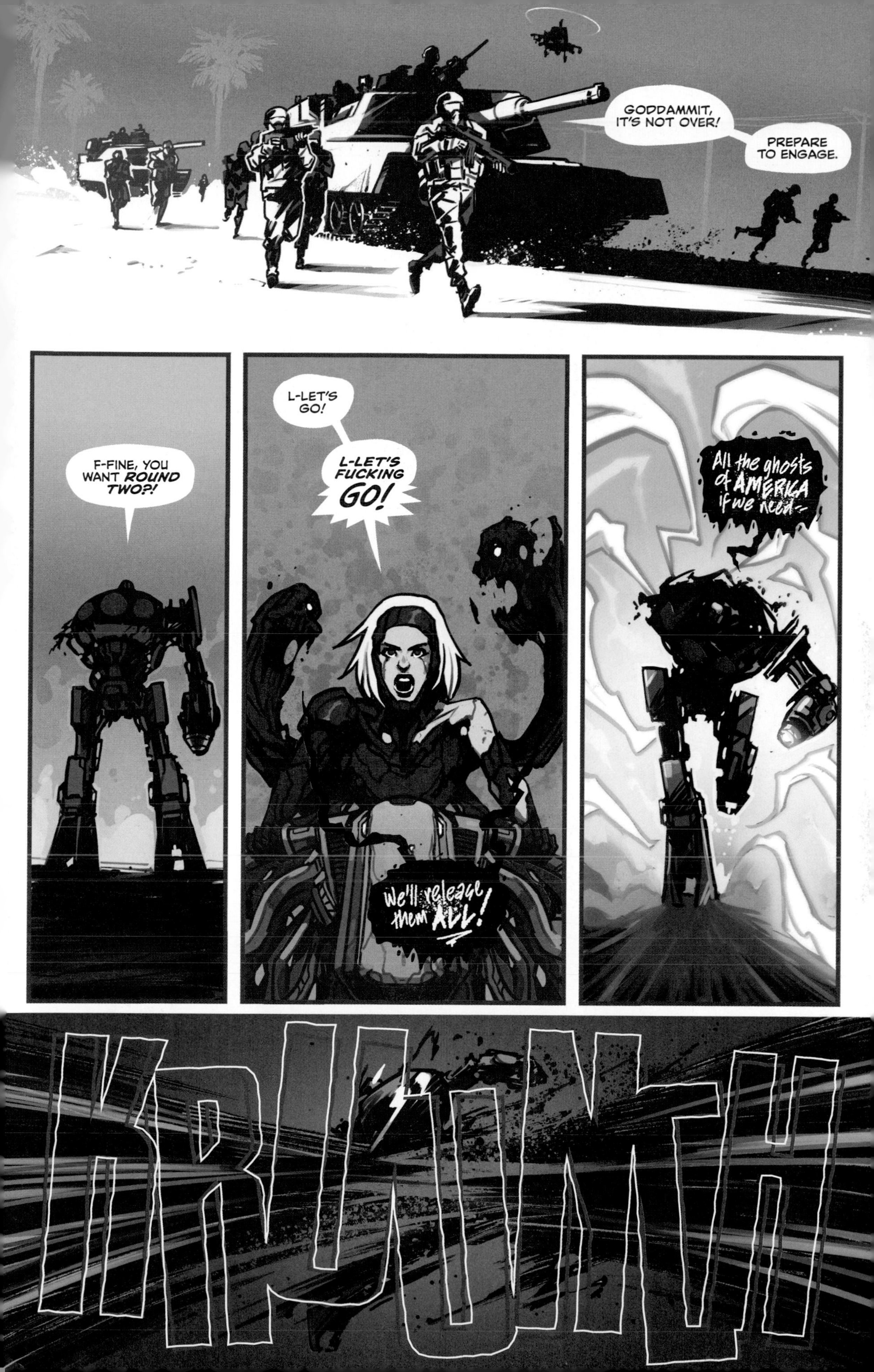
GODDAMMIT, IT'S NOT OVER!
PREPARE TO ENGAGE.
F-FINE, YOU WANT ROUND TWO?!
L-LET'S GO!
L-LET'S FUCKING GO!
We'll release them ALL!
All the ghosts of AMERICA if we need--
KRUNCH

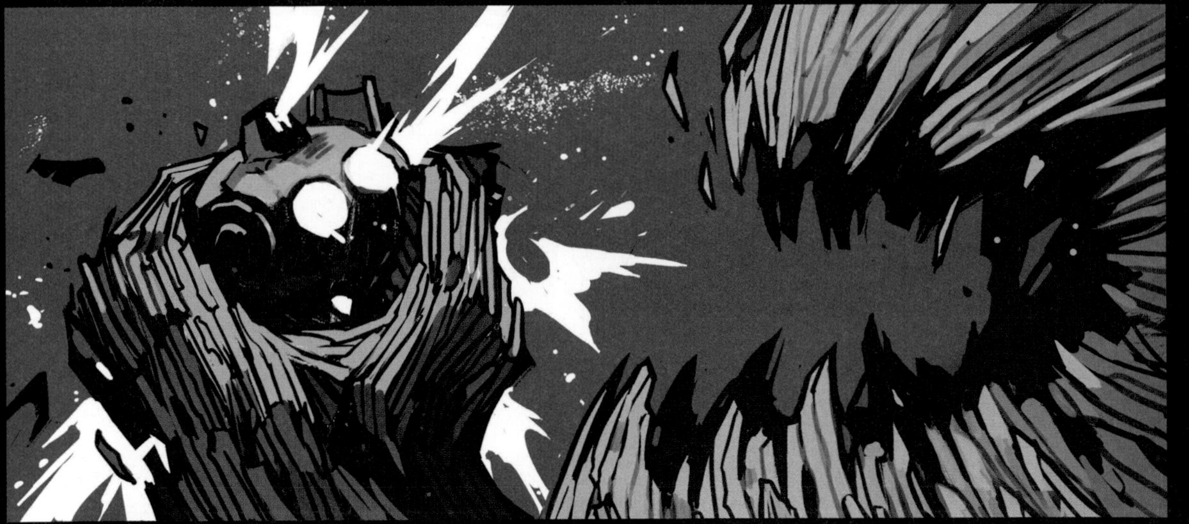
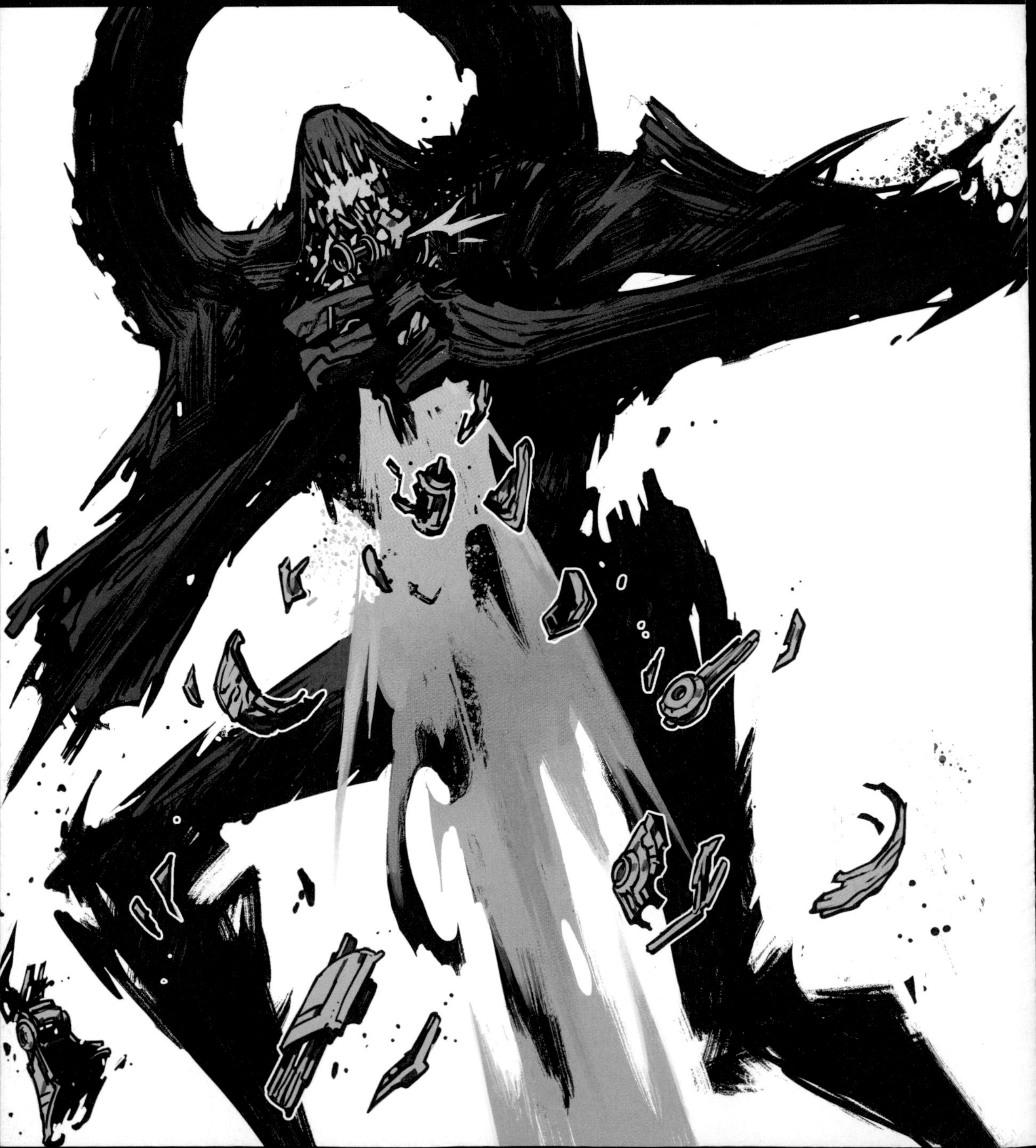

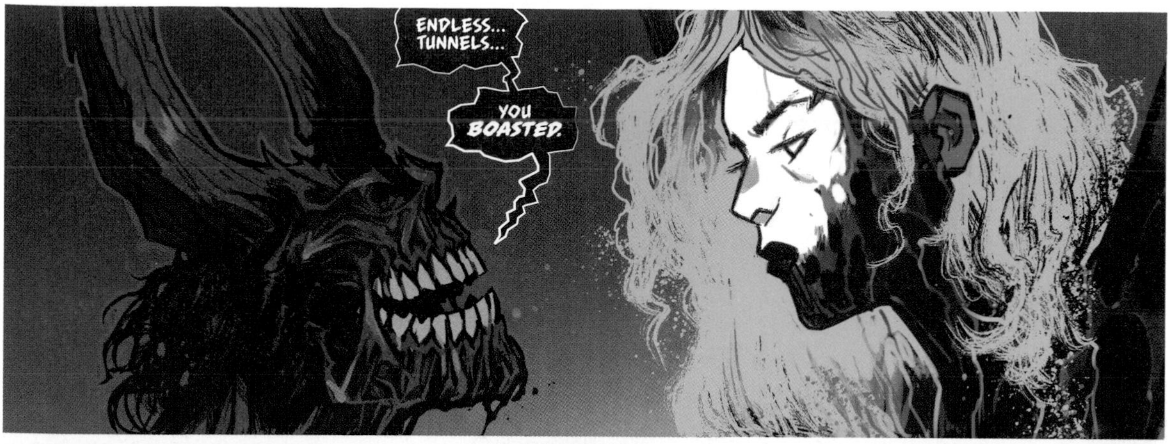
ENDLESS... TUNNELS...
YOU BOASTED.

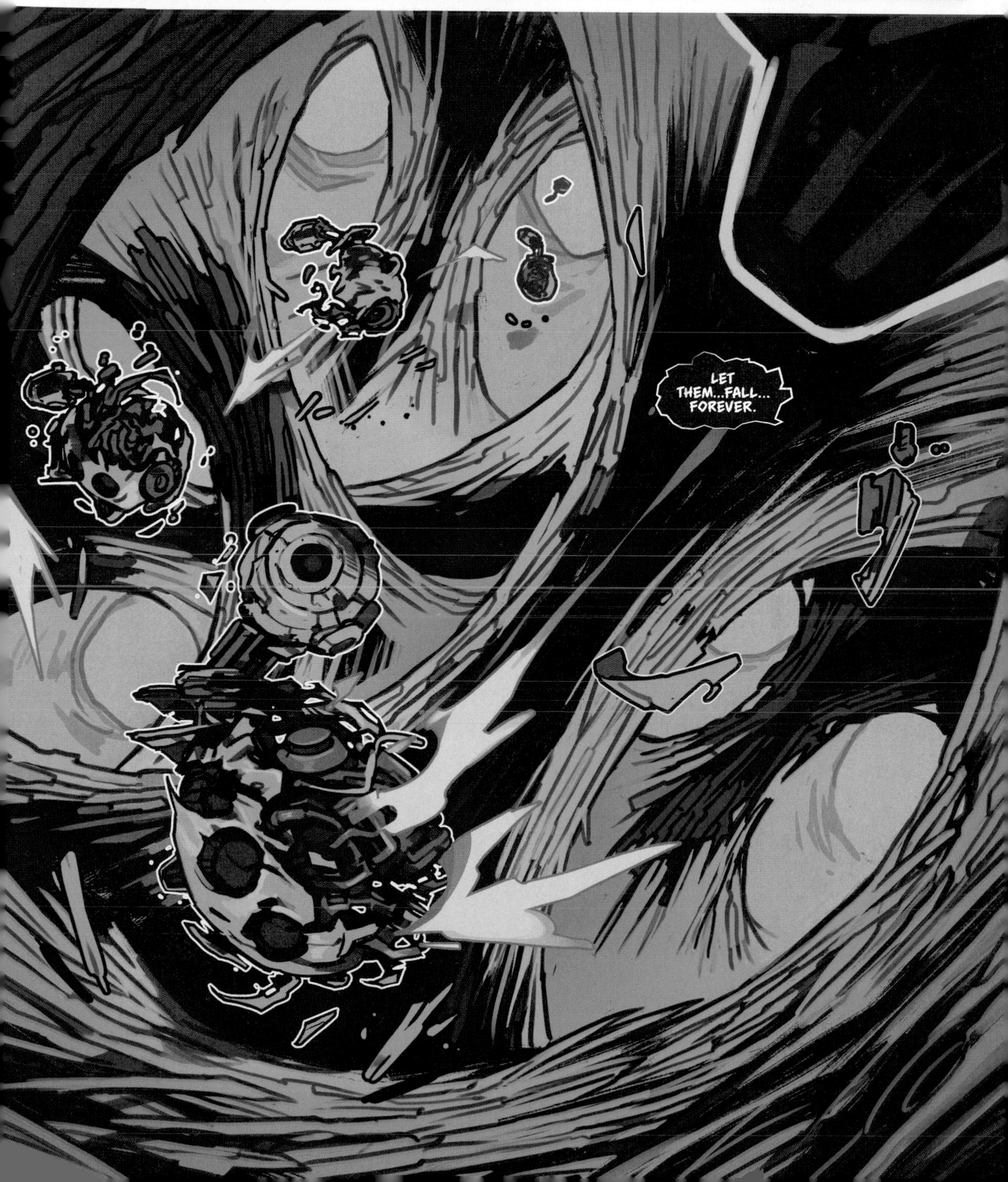
LET THEM...FALL... FOREVER.

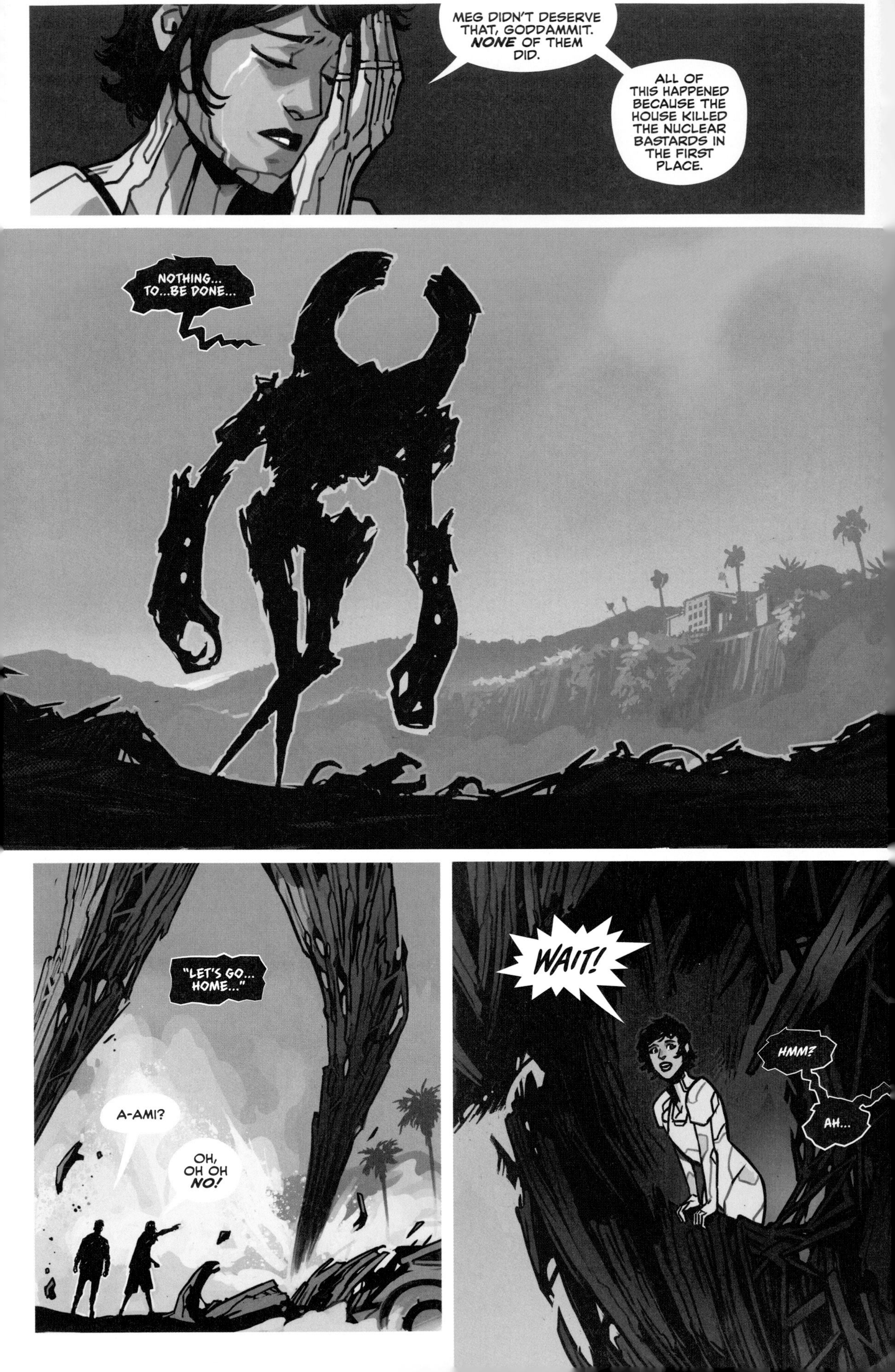
MEG DIDN'T DESERVE THAT, GODDAMMIT. NONE OF THEM DID.
ALL OF THIS HAPPENED BECAUSE THE HOUSE KILLED THE NUCLEAR BASTARDS IN THE FIRST PLACE.
NOTHING... TO...BE DONE...
"LET'S GO... HOME..."
A-AMI?
OH, OH OH NO!
WAIT!
HMM?
AH...

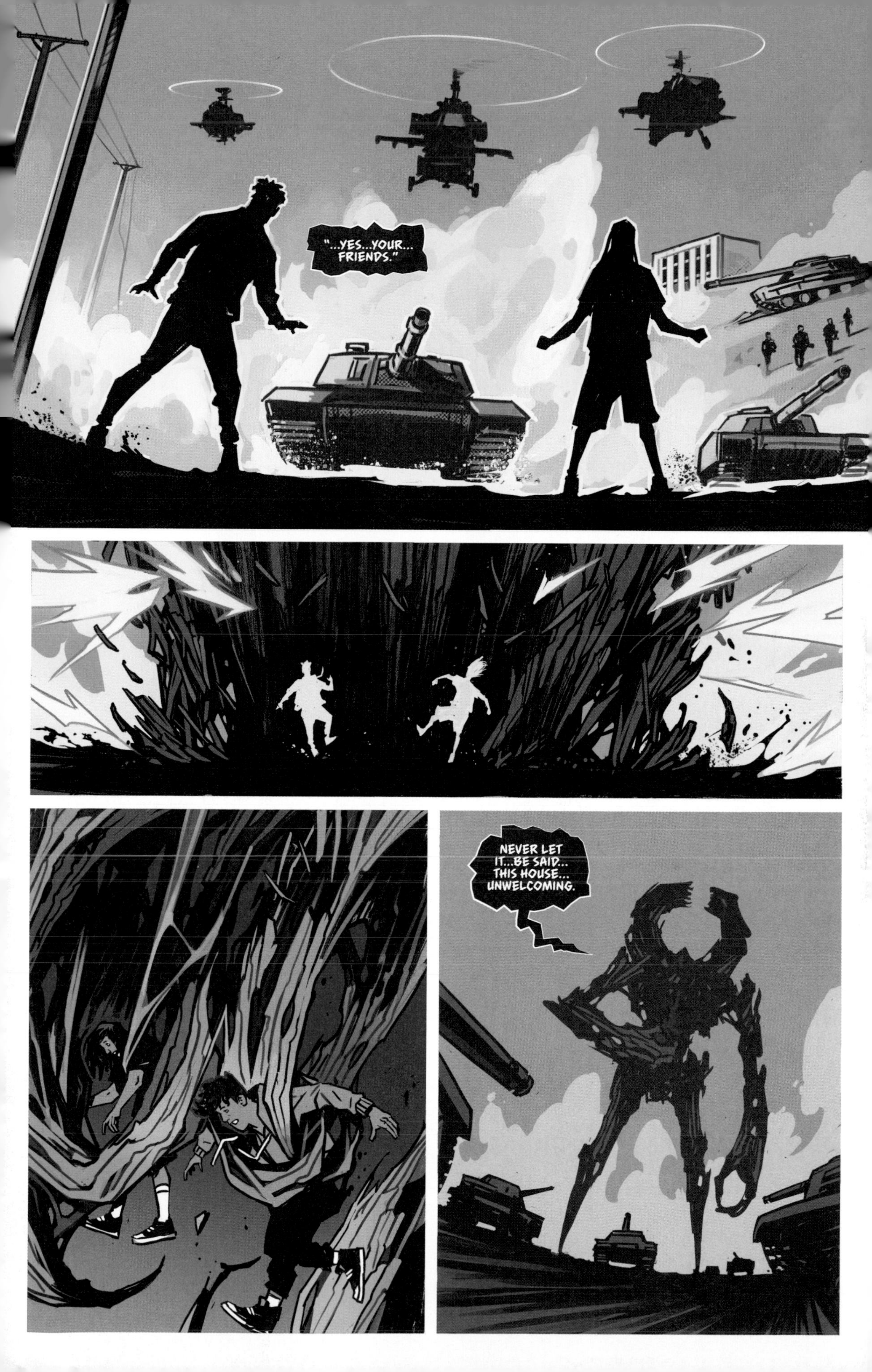
"...YES...YOUR... FRIENDS."
NEVER LET IT...BE SAID... THIS HOUSE... UNWELCOMING.

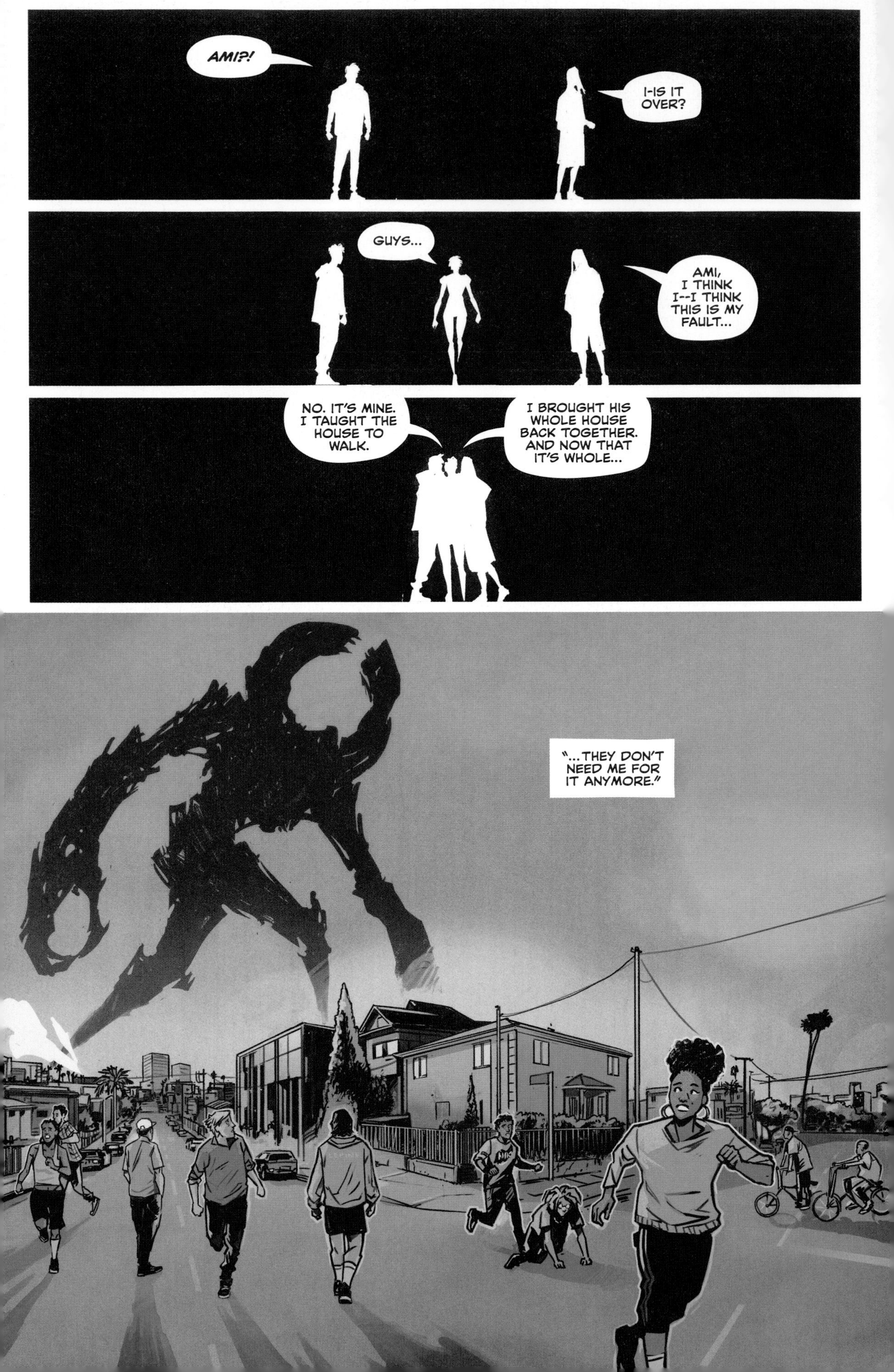
AMI?!
I-IS IT OVER?
GUYS...
AMI, I THINK I--I THINK THIS IS MY FAULT...
NO. IT'S MINE. I TAUGHT THE HOUSE TO WALK.
I BROUGHT HIS WHOLE HOUSE BACK TOGETHER. AND NOW THAT IT'S WHOLE...
"...THEY DON'T NEED ME FOR IT ANYMORE."

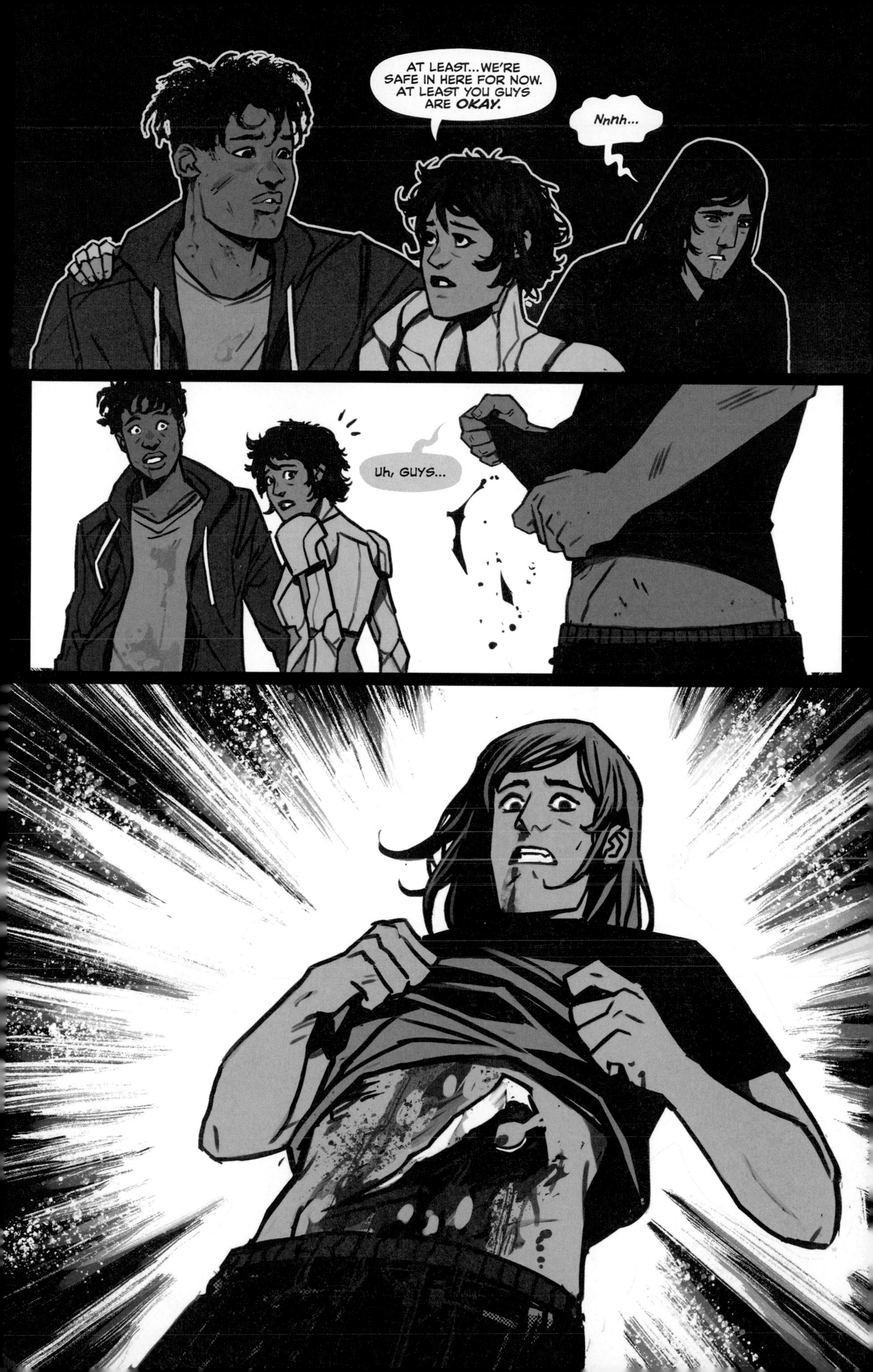
AT LEAST...WE'RE SAFE IN HERE FOR NOW. AT LEAST YOU GUYS ARE OKAY.
Nnnh...
Uh, GUYS...

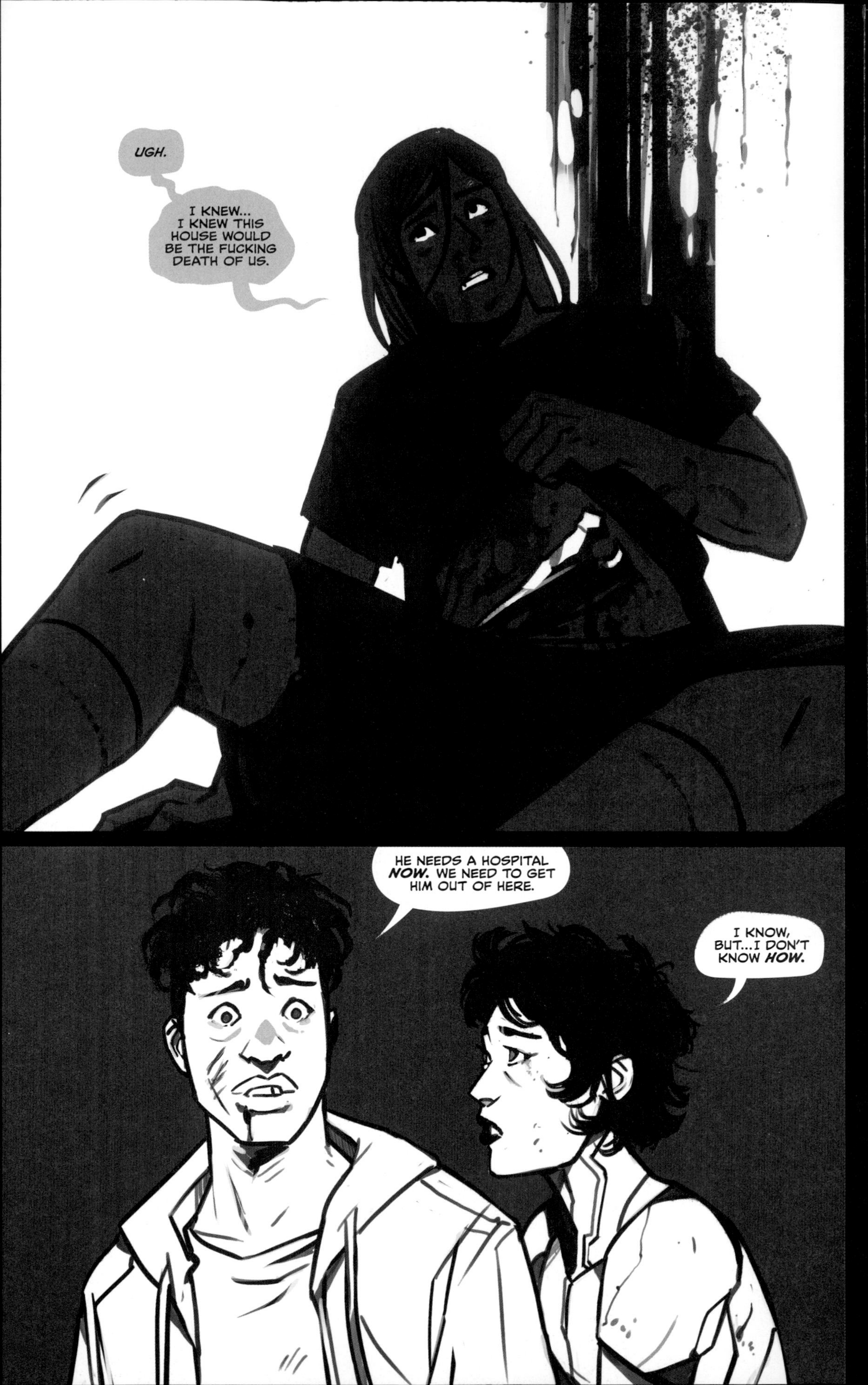
UGH.
I KNEW... I KNEW THIS HOUSE WOULD BE THE FUCKING DEATH OF US.
HE NEEDS A HOSPITAL *NOW.* WE NEED TO GET HIM OUT OF HERE.
I KNOW, BUT...I DON'T KNOW *HOW.*

DON'T FALL ASLEEP, RIP. DON'T PASS OUT.

YOU HAVE TO HOLD ON. WE MIGHT HAVE TO WAIT A MINUTE TO GET YOU OUT...

"...OLD JAMES THINKS IT'S ALL OVER. HE'S TRYING TO TAKE US ALL *HOME.*"

"LIKE...THE AFTERLIFE OR SOMETHING?"

"NO...

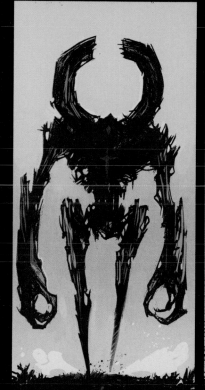

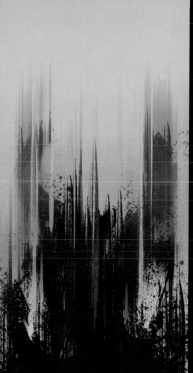

"...LITERALLY.

"HE JUST WANTS TO TAKE THE HOUSE BACK...

"BACK TO WHERE HE BUILT IT.

"SO EVERY- THING CAN BE NORMAL AGAIN."

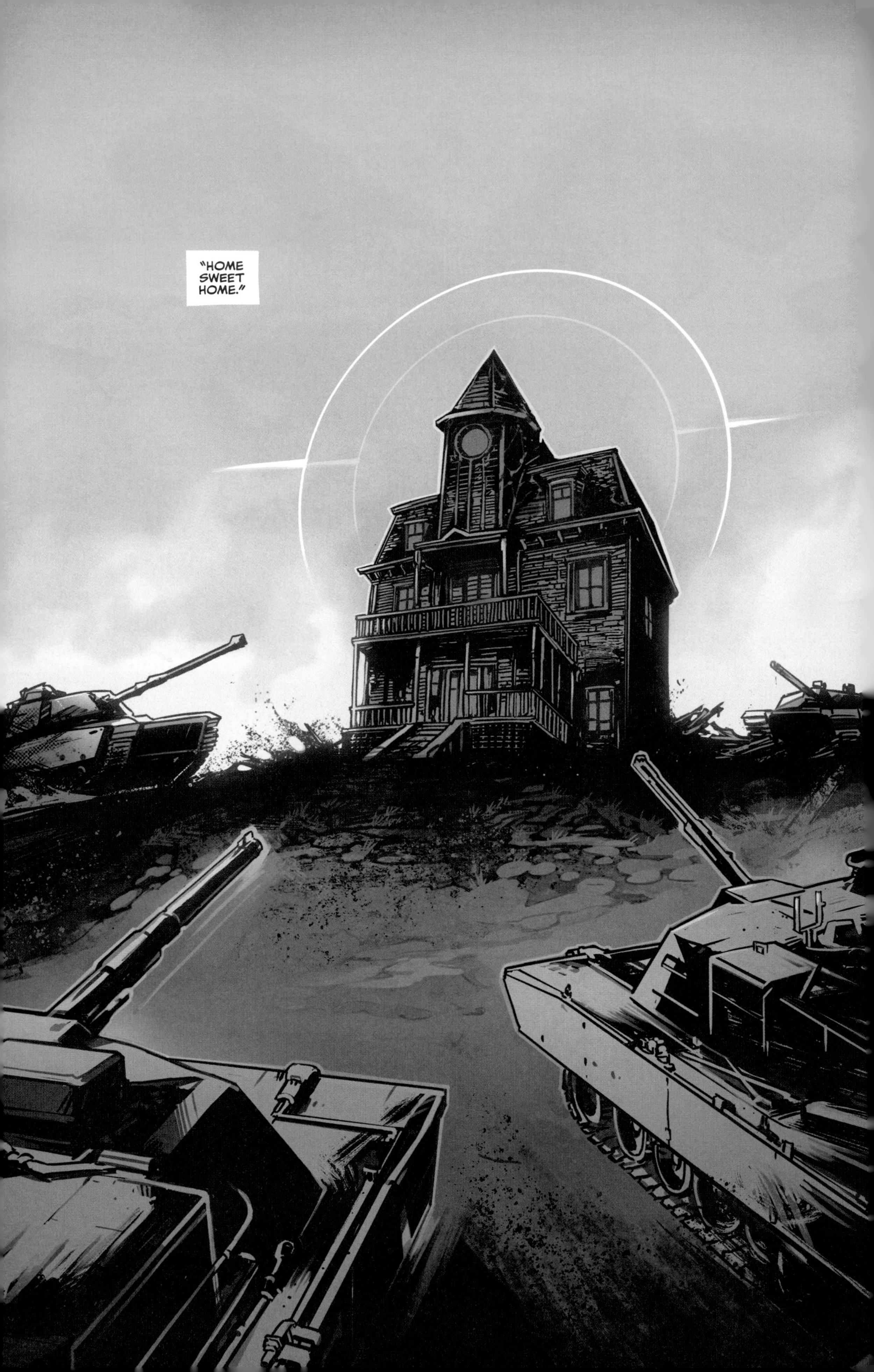
"HOME SWEET HOME."

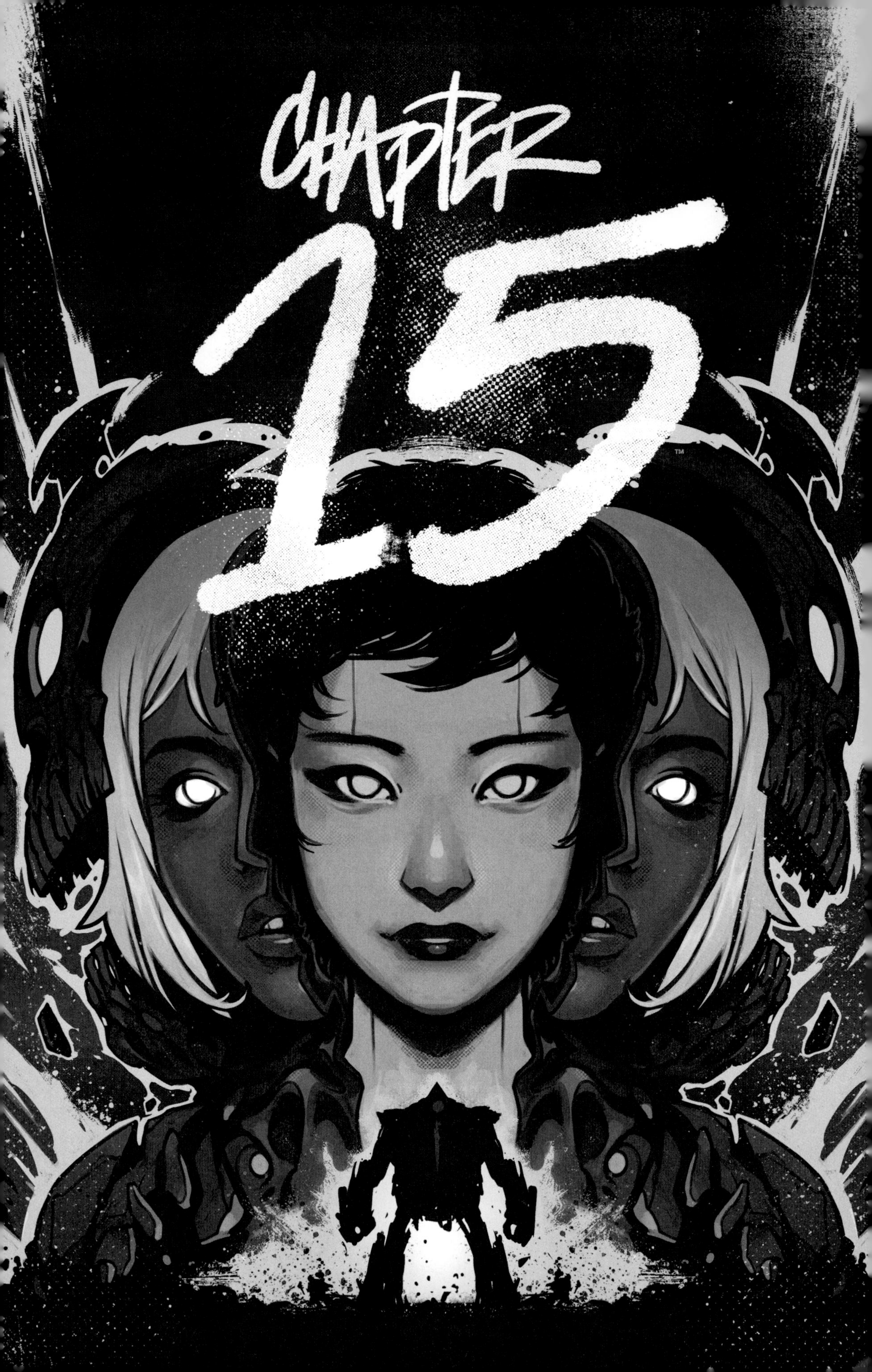
CHAPTER
15™

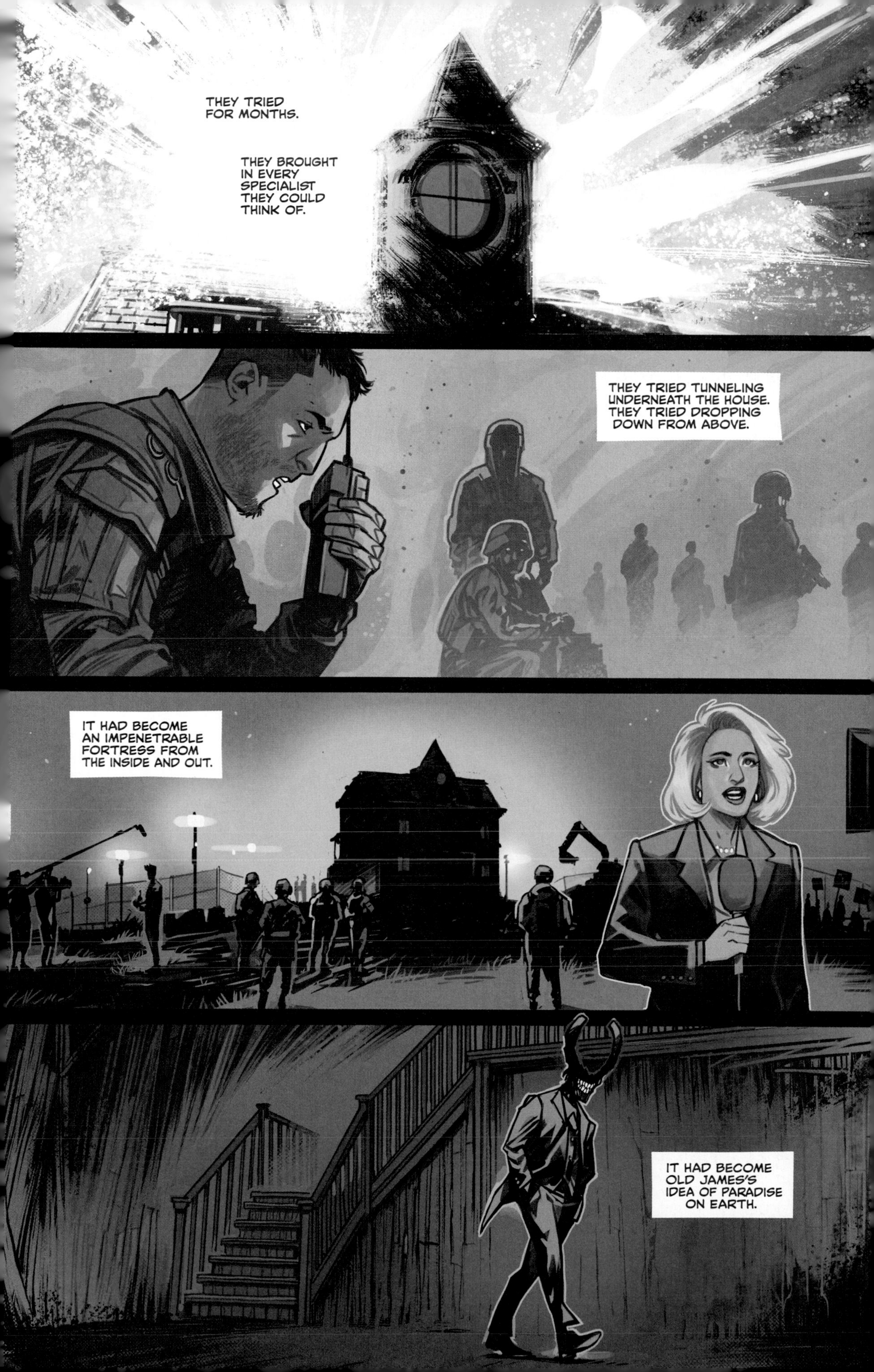
THEY TRIED FOR MONTHS.
THEY BROUGHT IN EVERY SPECIALIST THEY COULD THINK OF.
THEY TRIED TUNNELING UNDERNEATH THE HOUSE. THEY TRIED DROPPING DOWN FROM ABOVE.
IT HAD BECOME AN IMPENETRABLE FORTRESS FROM THE INSIDE AND OUT.
IT HAD BECOME OLD JAMES'S IDEA OF PARADISE ON EARTH.

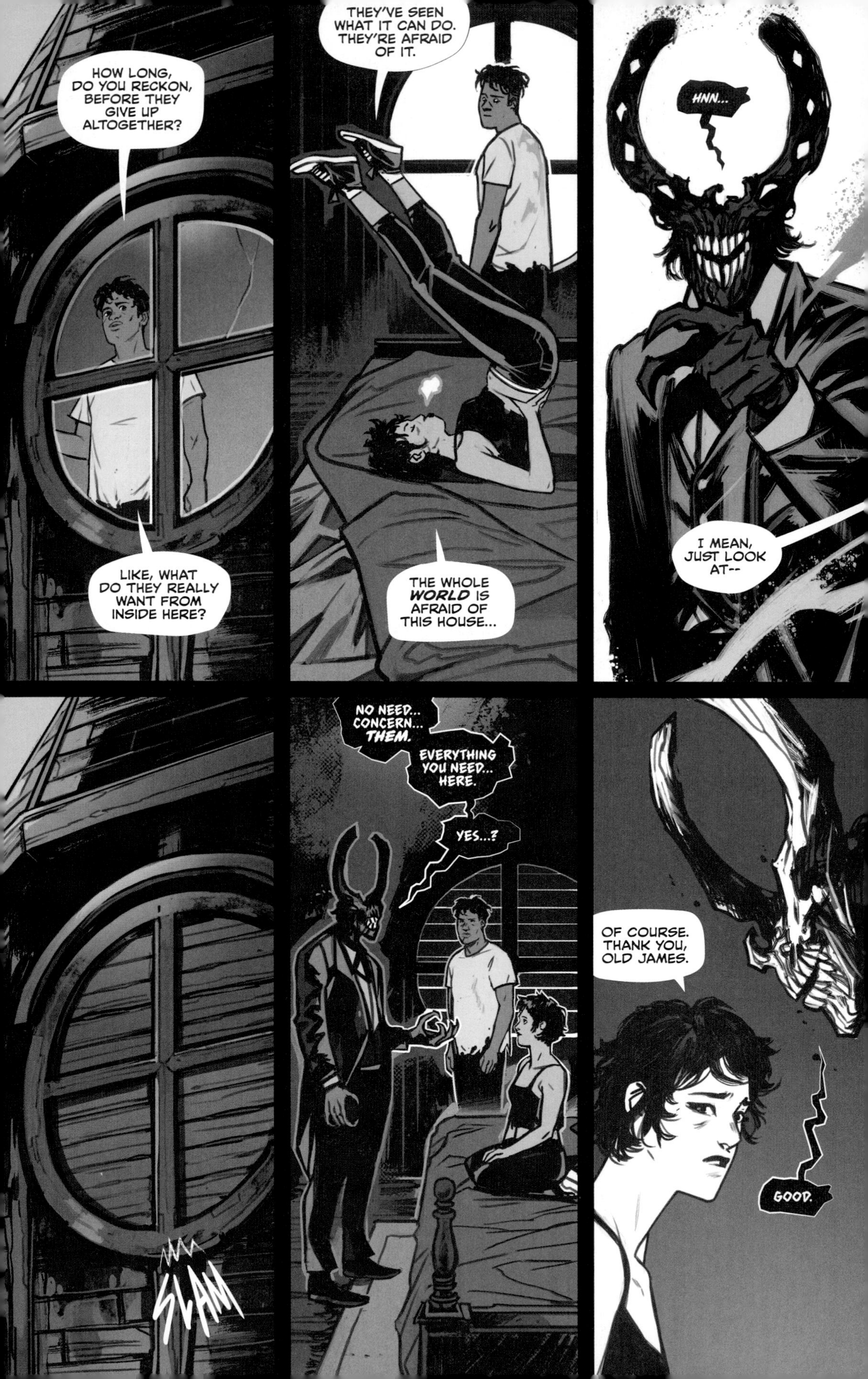
HOW LONG, DO YOU RECKON, BEFORE THEY GIVE UP ALTOGETHER?
LIKE, WHAT DO THEY REALLY WANT FROM INSIDE HERE?
THEY'VE SEEN WHAT IT CAN DO. THEY'RE AFRAID OF IT.
THE WHOLE *WORLD* IS AFRAID OF THIS HOUSE...
HNN...
I MEAN, JUST LOOK AT--
SLAM
NO NEED... CONCERN... *THEM.*
EVERYTHING YOU NEED... HERE.
YES...?
OF COURSE. THANK YOU, OLD JAMES.
GOOD.

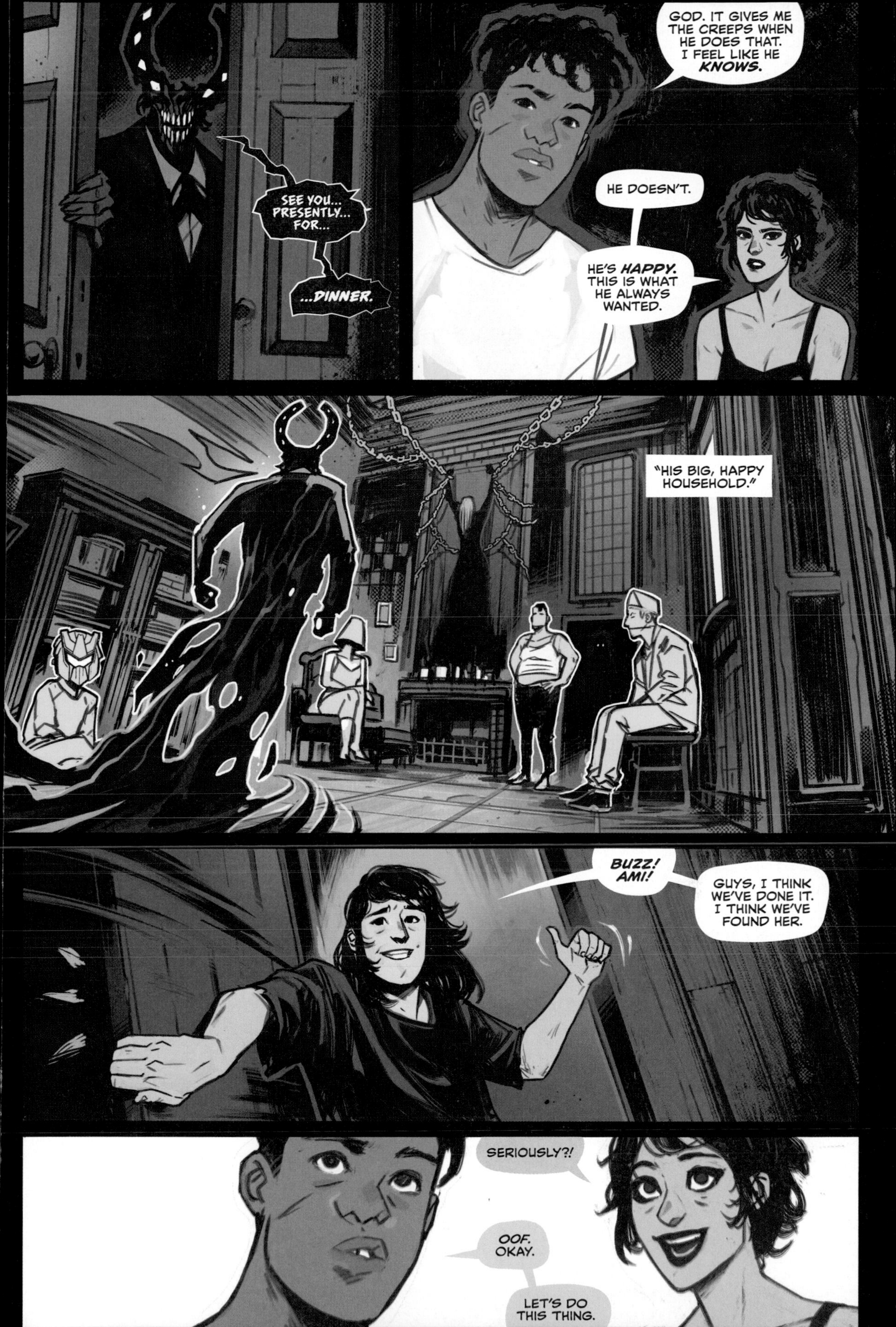
SEE YOU... PRESENTLY... FOR...
...DINNER.
GOD. IT GIVES ME THE CREEPS WHEN HE DOES THAT. I FEEL LIKE HE KNOWS.
HE DOESN'T.
HE'S HAPPY. THIS IS WHAT HE ALWAYS WANTED.
"HIS BIG, HAPPY HOUSEHOLD."
BUZZ! AMI!
GUYS, I THINK WE'VE DONE IT. I THINK WE'VE FOUND HER.
SERIOUSLY?!
OOF. OKAY.
LET'S DO THIS THING.

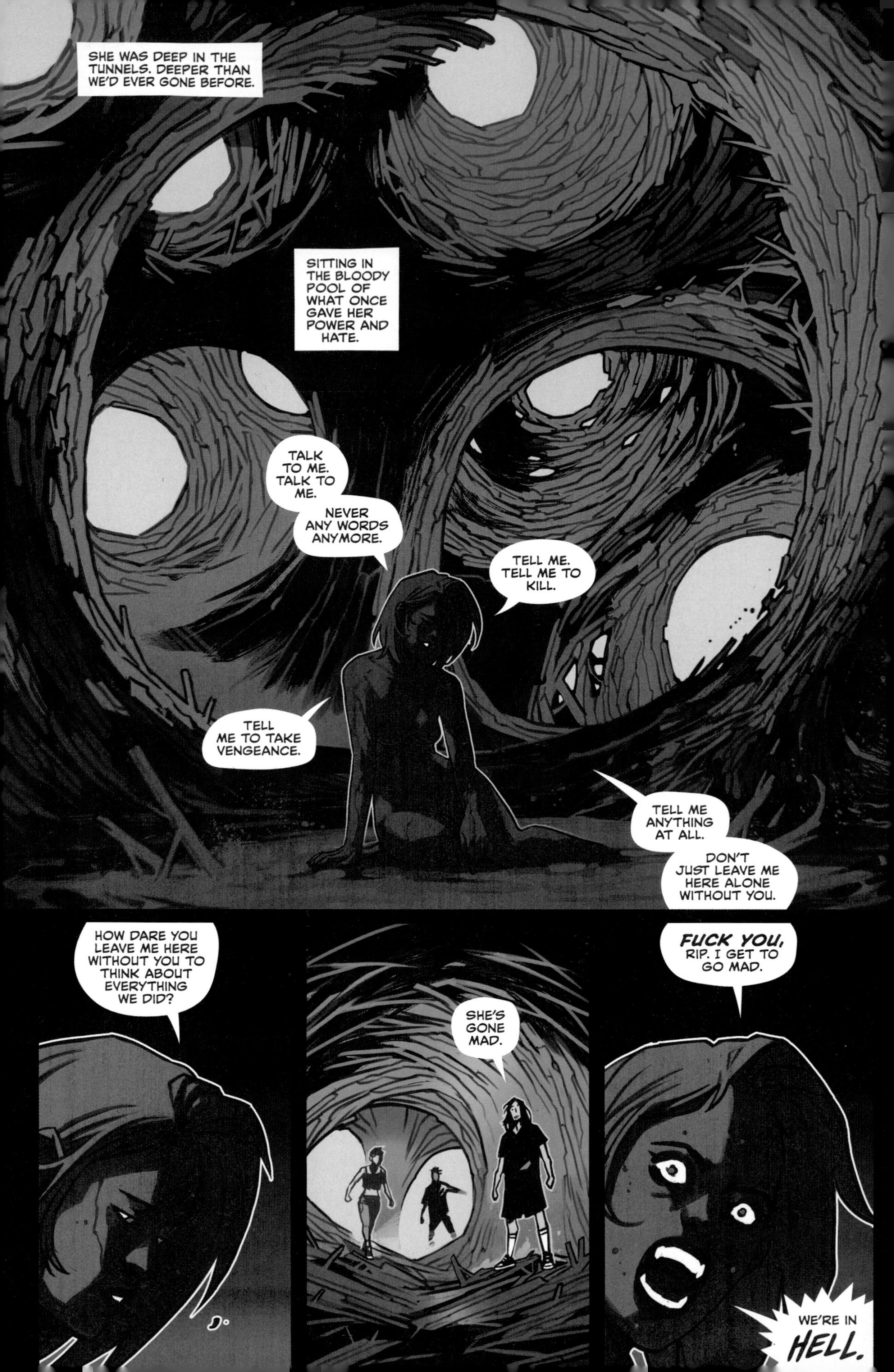
SHE WAS DEEP IN THE TUNNELS. DEEPER THAN WE'D EVER GONE BEFORE.
SITTING IN THE BLOODY POOL OF WHAT ONCE GAVE HER POWER AND HATE.
TALK TO ME. TALK TO ME.
NEVER ANY WORDS ANYMORE.
TELL ME. TELL ME TO KILL.
TELL ME TO TAKE VENGEANCE.
TELL ME ANYTHING AT ALL.
DON'T JUST LEAVE ME HERE ALONE WITHOUT YOU.
HOW DARE YOU LEAVE ME HERE WITHOUT YOU TO THINK ABOUT EVERYTHING WE DID?
SHE'S GONE MAD.
FUCK YOU, RIP. I GET TO GO MAD.
WE'RE IN HELL.

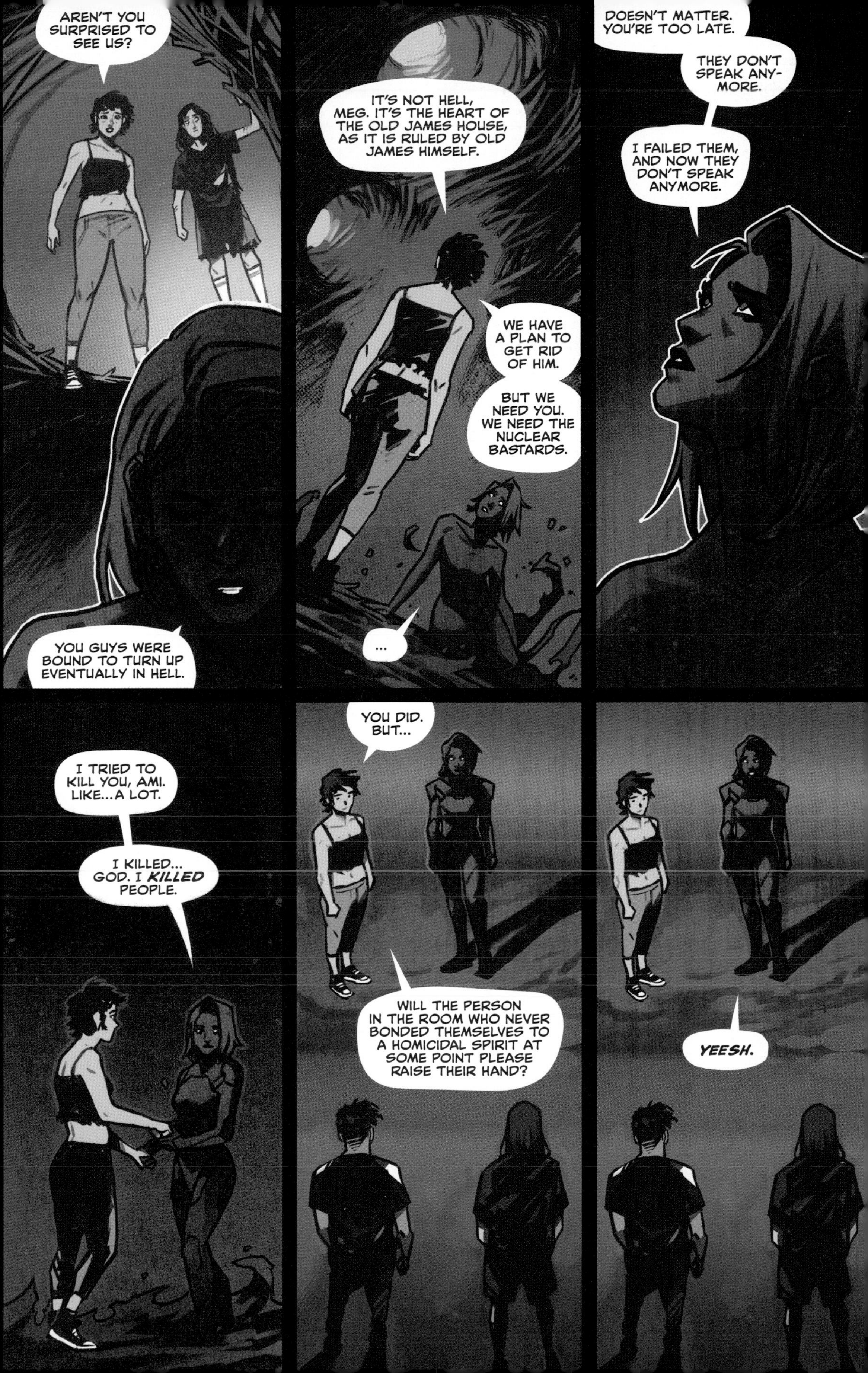
AREN'T YOU SURPRISED TO SEE US?
YOU GUYS WERE BOUND TO TURN UP EVENTUALLY IN HELL.
IT'S NOT HELL, MEG. IT'S THE HEART OF THE OLD JAMES HOUSE, AS IT IS RULED BY OLD JAMES HIMSELF.
WE HAVE A PLAN TO GET RID OF HIM.
BUT WE NEED YOU. WE NEED THE NUCLEAR BASTARDS.
...
DOESN'T MATTER. YOU'RE TOO LATE.
THEY DON'T SPEAK ANY-MORE.
I FAILED THEM, AND NOW THEY DON'T SPEAK ANYMORE.
I TRIED TO KILL YOU, AMI. LIKE...A LOT.
I KILLED... GOD. I *KILLED* PEOPLE.
YOU DID. BUT...
WILL THE PERSON IN THE ROOM WHO NEVER BONDED THEMSELVES TO A HOMICIDAL SPIRIT AT SOME POINT PLEASE RAISE THEIR HAND?
YEESH.

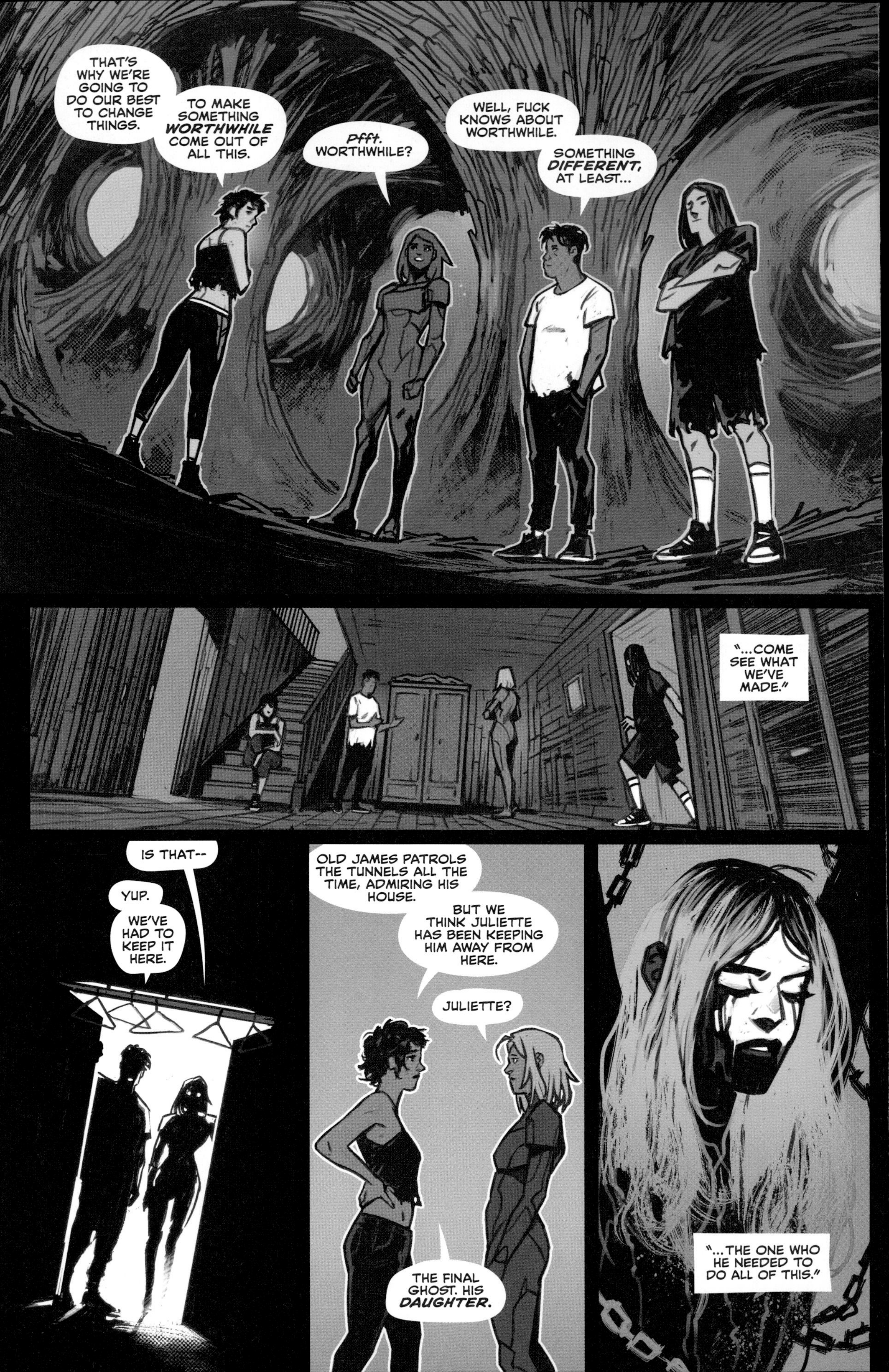
THAT'S WHY WE'RE GOING TO DO OUR BEST TO CHANGE THINGS.
TO MAKE SOMETHING WORTHWHILE COME OUT OF ALL THIS.
Pfft. WORTHWHILE?
WELL, FUCK KNOWS ABOUT WORTHWHILE.
SOMETHING DIFFERENT, AT LEAST...
"...COME SEE WHAT WE'VE MADE."
IS THAT--
YUP.
WE'VE HAD TO KEEP IT HERE.
OLD JAMES PATROLS THE TUNNELS ALL THE TIME, ADMIRING HIS HOUSE.
BUT WE THINK JULIETTE HAS BEEN KEEPING HIM AWAY FROM HERE.
JULIETTE?
THE FINAL GHOST. HIS DAUGHTER.
"...THE ONE WHO HE NEEDED TO DO ALL OF THIS."

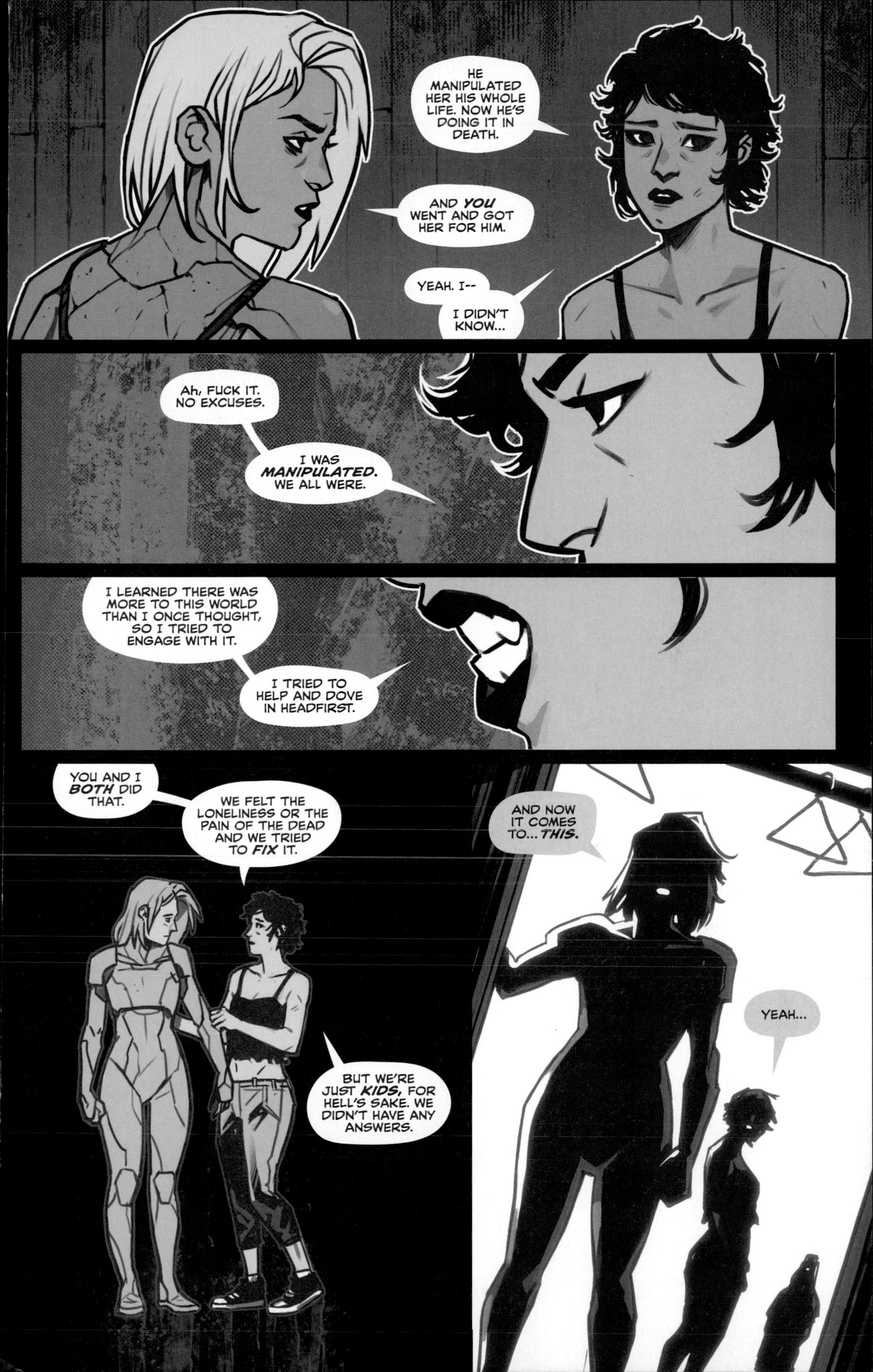
HE MANIPULATED HER HIS WHOLE LIFE. NOW HE'S DOING IT IN DEATH.
AND YOU WENT AND GOT HER FOR HIM.
YEAH. I--
I DIDN'T KNOW...
Ah, FUCK IT. NO EXCUSES.
I WAS MANIPULATED. WE ALL WERE.
I LEARNED THERE WAS MORE TO THIS WORLD THAN I ONCE THOUGHT, SO I TRIED TO ENGAGE WITH IT.
I TRIED TO HELP AND DOVE IN HEADFIRST.
YOU AND I BOTH DID THAT.
WE FELT THE LONELINESS OR THE PAIN OF THE DEAD AND WE TRIED TO FIX IT.
BUT WE'RE JUST KIDS, FOR HELL'S SAKE. WE DIDN'T HAVE ANY ANSWERS.
AND NOW IT COMES TO... THIS.
YEAH...

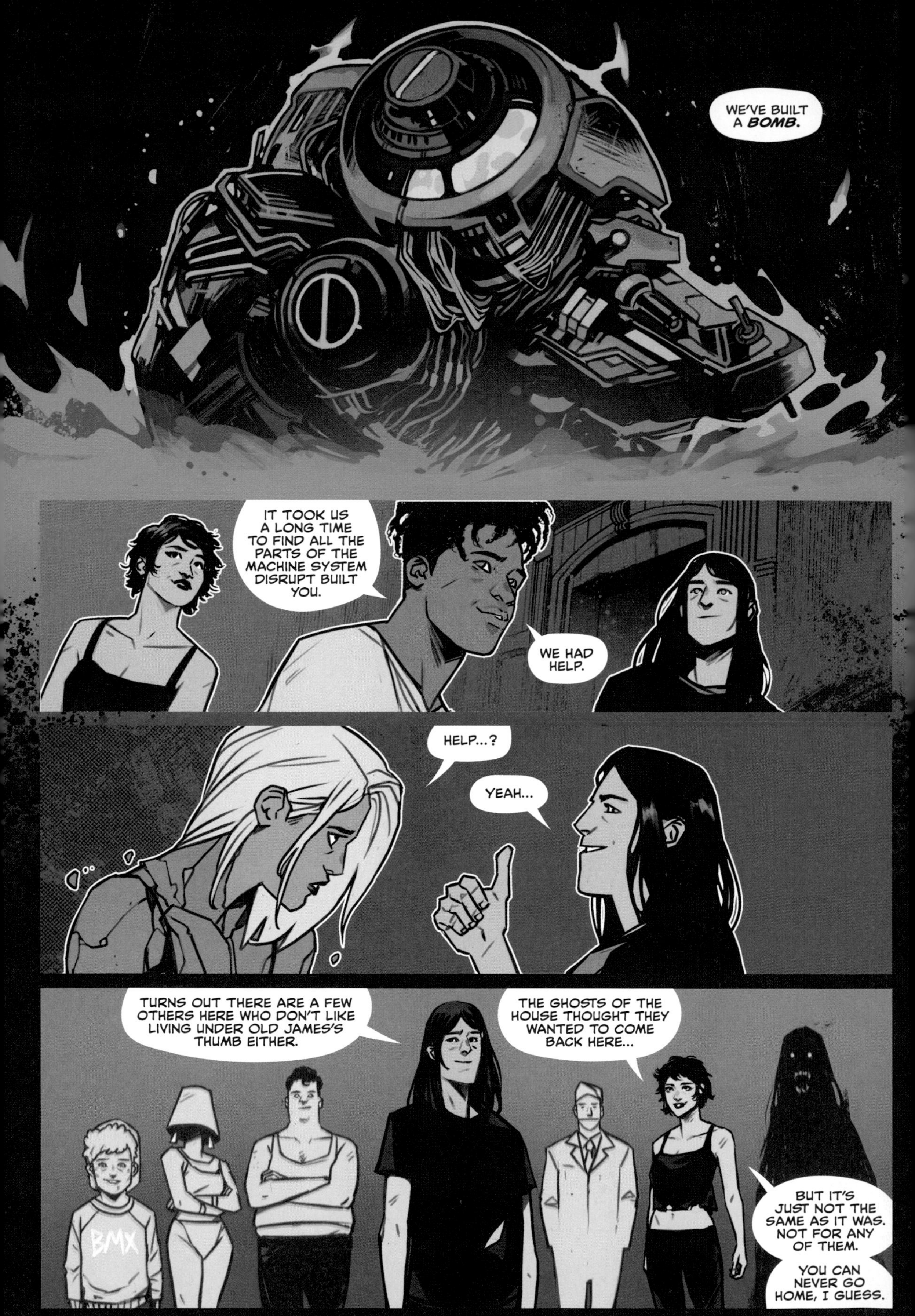
WE'VE BUILT A BOMB.
IT TOOK US A LONG TIME TO FIND ALL THE PARTS OF THE MACHINE SYSTEM DISRUPT BUILT YOU.
WE HAD HELP.
HELP...?
YEAH...
TURNS OUT THERE ARE A FEW OTHERS HERE WHO DON'T LIKE LIVING UNDER OLD JAMES'S THUMB EITHER.
THE GHOSTS OF THE HOUSE THOUGHT THEY WANTED TO COME BACK HERE...
BUT IT'S JUST NOT THE SAME AS IT WAS. NOT FOR ANY OF THEM.
YOU CAN NEVER GO HOME, I GUESS.
BMX

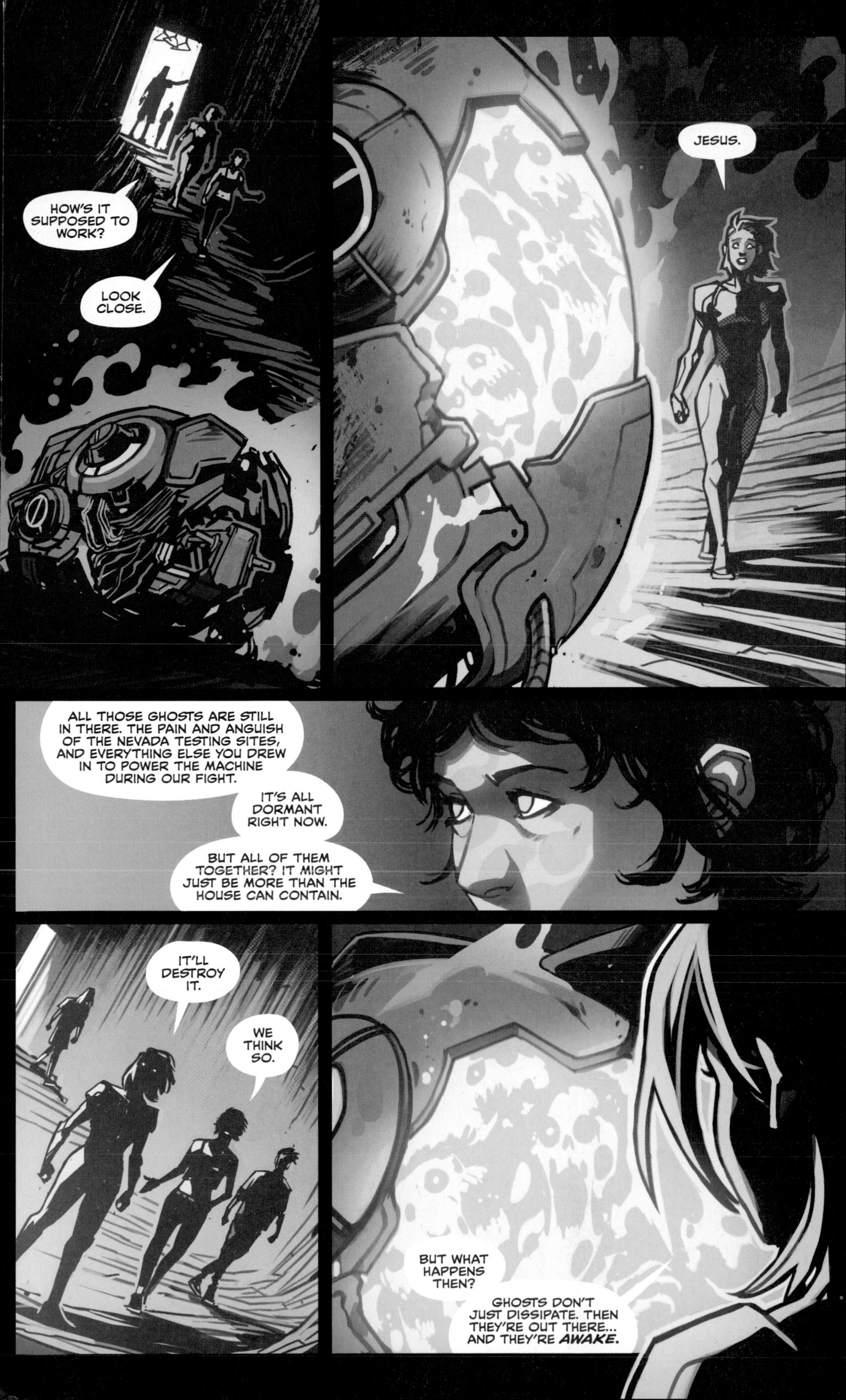
HOW'S IT SUPPOSED TO WORK?
LOOK CLOSE.
JESUS.
ALL THOSE GHOSTS ARE STILL IN THERE. THE PAIN AND ANGUISH OF THE NEVADA TESTING SITES, AND EVERYTHING ELSE YOU DREW IN TO POWER THE MACHINE DURING OUR FIGHT.
IT'S ALL DORMANT RIGHT NOW.
BUT ALL OF THEM TOGETHER? IT MIGHT JUST BE MORE THAN THE HOUSE CAN CONTAIN.
IT'LL DESTROY IT.
WE THINK SO.
BUT WHAT HAPPENS THEN?
GHOSTS DON'T JUST DISSIPATE. THEN THEY'RE OUT THERE... AND THEY'RE ***AWAKE.***

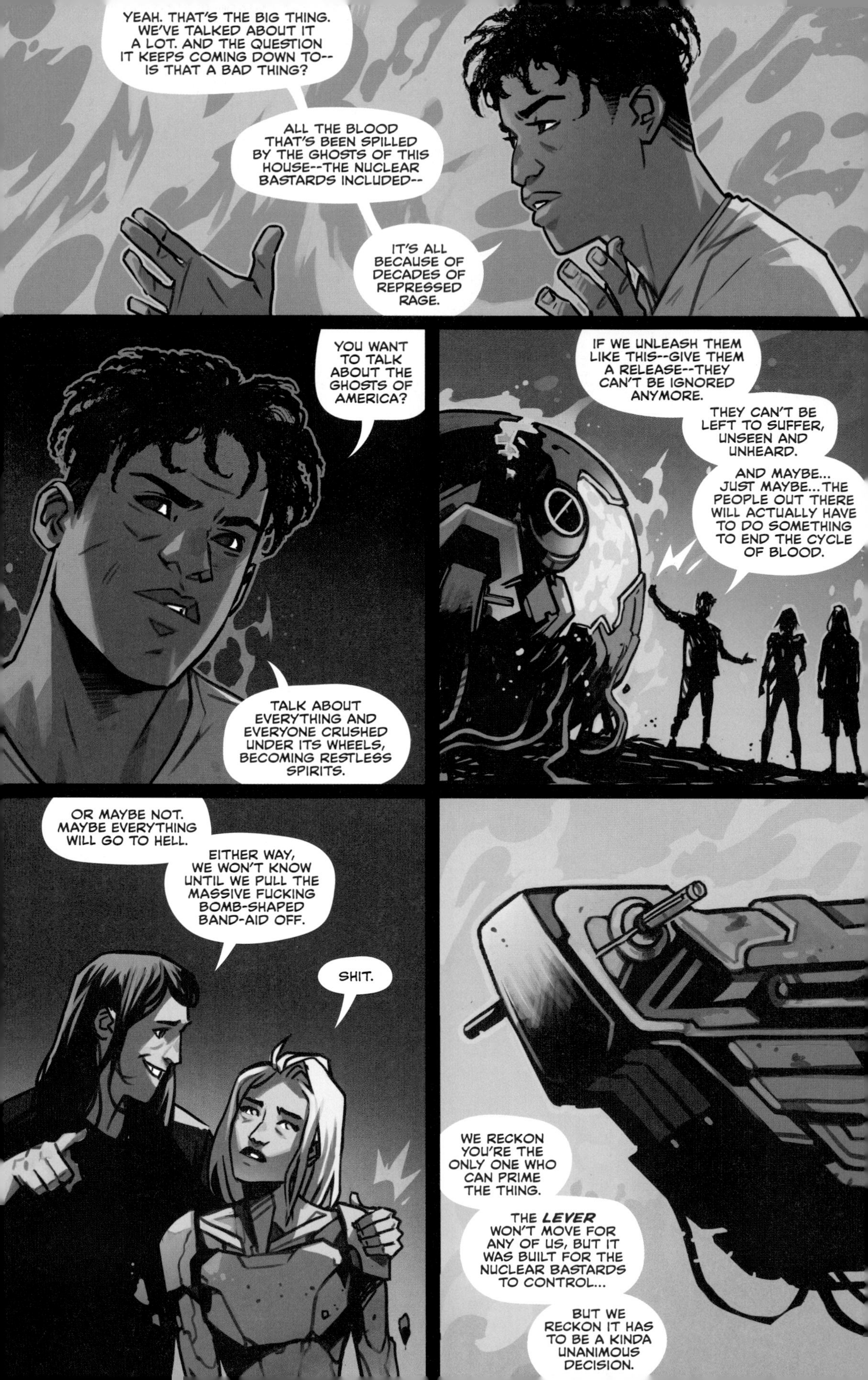
YEAH. THAT'S THE BIG THING. WE'VE TALKED ABOUT IT A LOT. AND THE QUESTION IT KEEPS COMING DOWN TO-- IS THAT A BAD THING?
ALL THE BLOOD THAT'S BEEN SPILLED BY THE GHOSTS OF THIS HOUSE--THE NUCLEAR BASTARDS INCLUDED--
IT'S ALL BECAUSE OF DECADES OF REPRESSED RAGE.
YOU WANT TO TALK ABOUT THE GHOSTS OF AMERICA?
TALK ABOUT EVERYTHING AND EVERYONE CRUSHED UNDER ITS WHEELS, BECOMING RESTLESS SPIRITS.
IF WE UNLEASH THEM LIKE THIS--GIVE THEM A RELEASE--THEY CAN'T BE IGNORED ANYMORE.
THEY CAN'T BE LEFT TO SUFFER, UNSEEN AND UNHEARD.
AND MAYBE... JUST MAYBE... THE PEOPLE OUT THERE WILL ACTUALLY HAVE TO DO SOMETHING TO END THE CYCLE OF BLOOD.
OR MAYBE NOT. MAYBE EVERYTHING WILL GO TO HELL.
EITHER WAY, WE WON'T KNOW UNTIL WE PULL THE MASSIVE FUCKING BOMB-SHAPED BAND-AID OFF.
SHIT.
WE RECKON YOU'RE THE ONLY ONE WHO CAN PRIME THE THING.
THE *LEVER* WON'T MOVE FOR ANY OF US, BUT IT WAS BUILT FOR THE NUCLEAR BASTARDS TO CONTROL...
BUT WE RECKON IT HAS TO BE A KINDA UNANIMOUS DECISION.

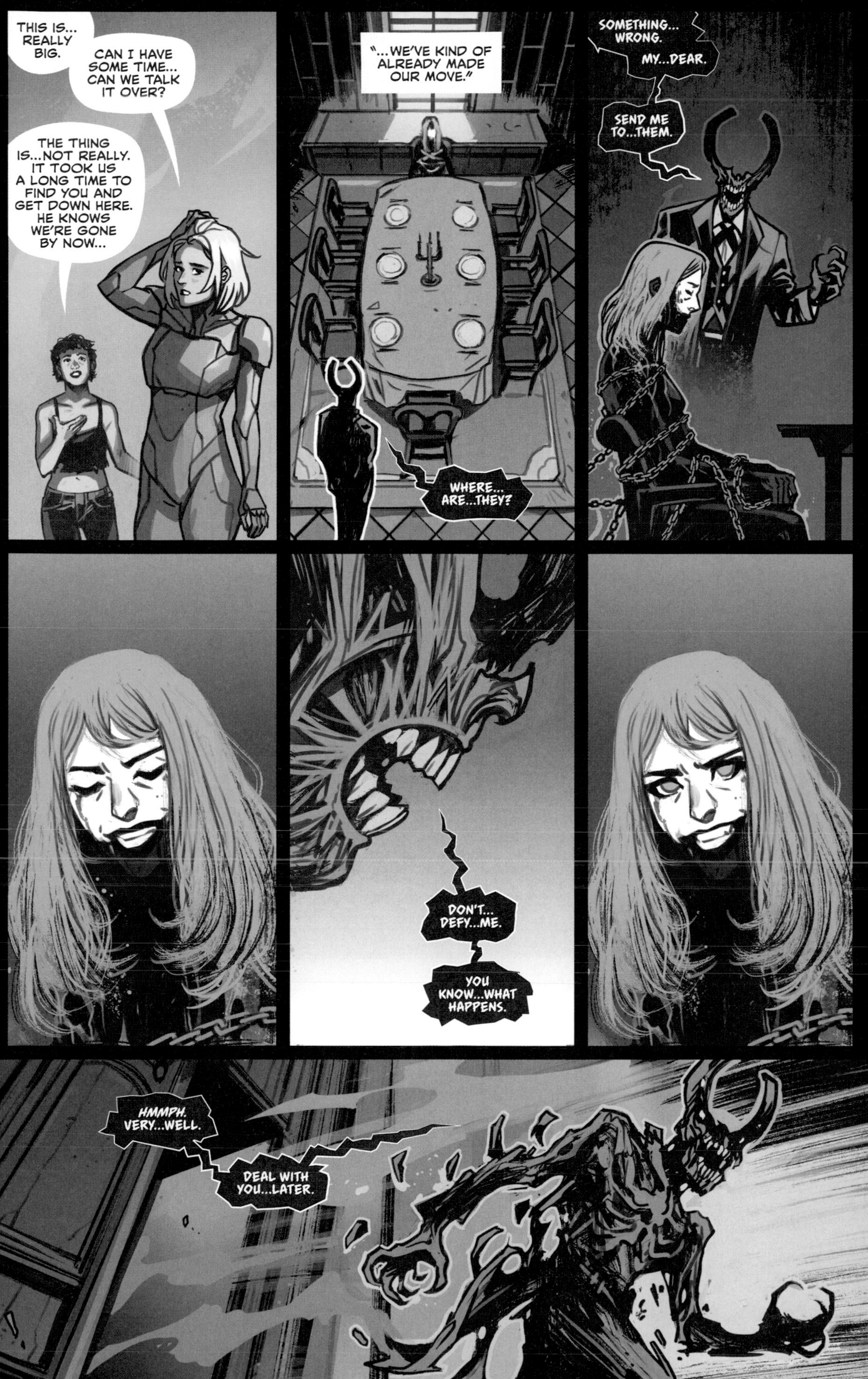
THIS IS... REALLY BIG.
CAN I HAVE SOME TIME... CAN WE TALK IT OVER?
THE THING IS...NOT REALLY. IT TOOK US A LONG TIME TO FIND YOU AND GET DOWN HERE. HE KNOWS WE'RE GONE BY NOW...
"...WE'VE KIND OF ALREADY MADE OUR MOVE."
WHERE... ARE...THEY?
SOMETHING... WRONG.
MY...DEAR.
SEND ME TO...THEM.
DON'T... DEFY...ME.
YOU KNOW...WHAT HAPPENS.
HMMPH. VERY...WELL.
DEAL WITH YOU...LATER.

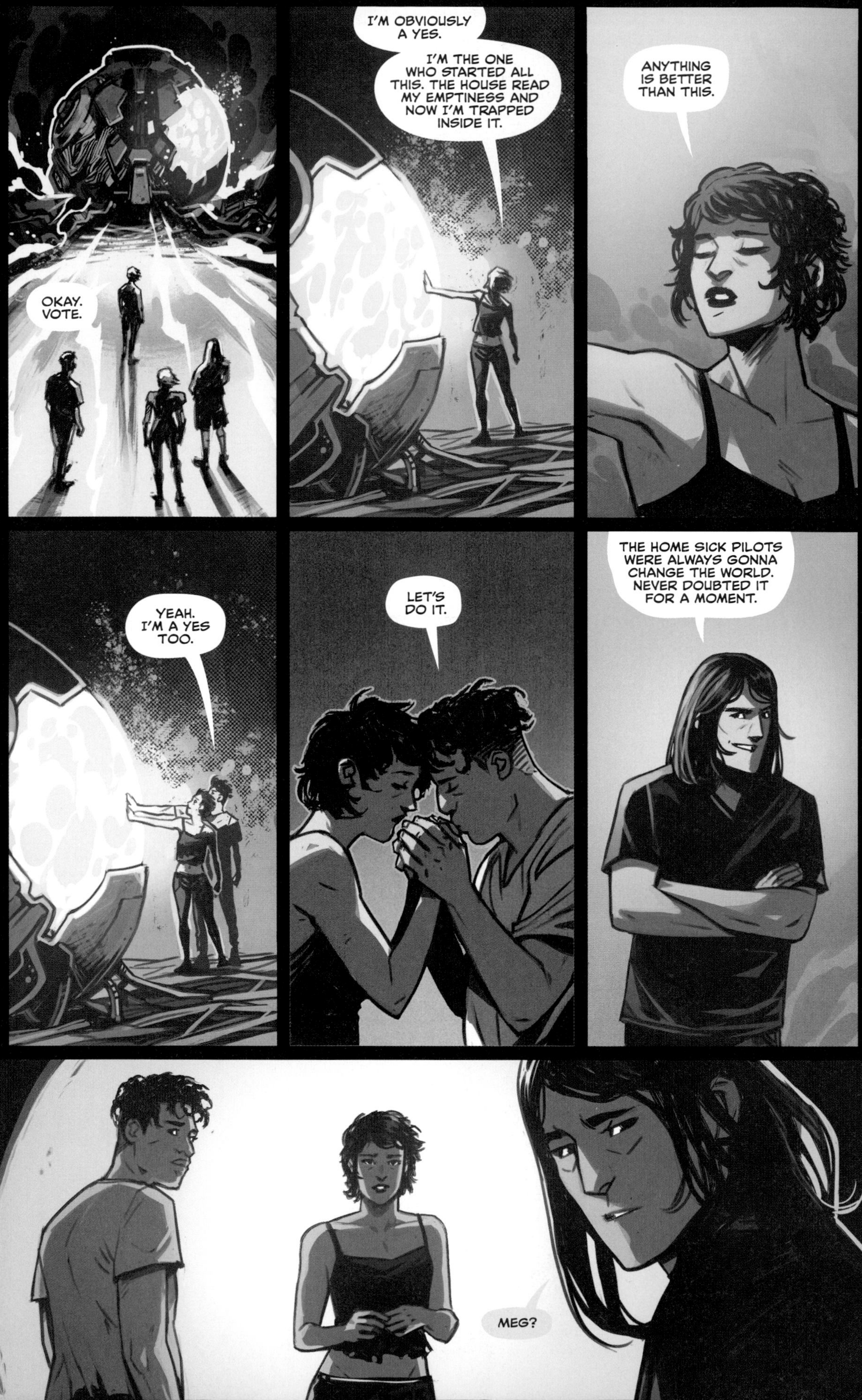
OKAY. VOTE.
I'M OBVIOUSLY A YES.
I'M THE ONE WHO STARTED ALL THIS. THE HOUSE READ MY EMPTINESS AND NOW I'M TRAPPED INSIDE IT.
ANYTHING IS BETTER THAN THIS.
YEAH. I'M A YES TOO.
LET'S DO IT.
THE HOME SICK PILOTS WERE ALWAYS GONNA CHANGE THE WORLD. NEVER DOUBTED IT FOR A MOMENT.
MEG?

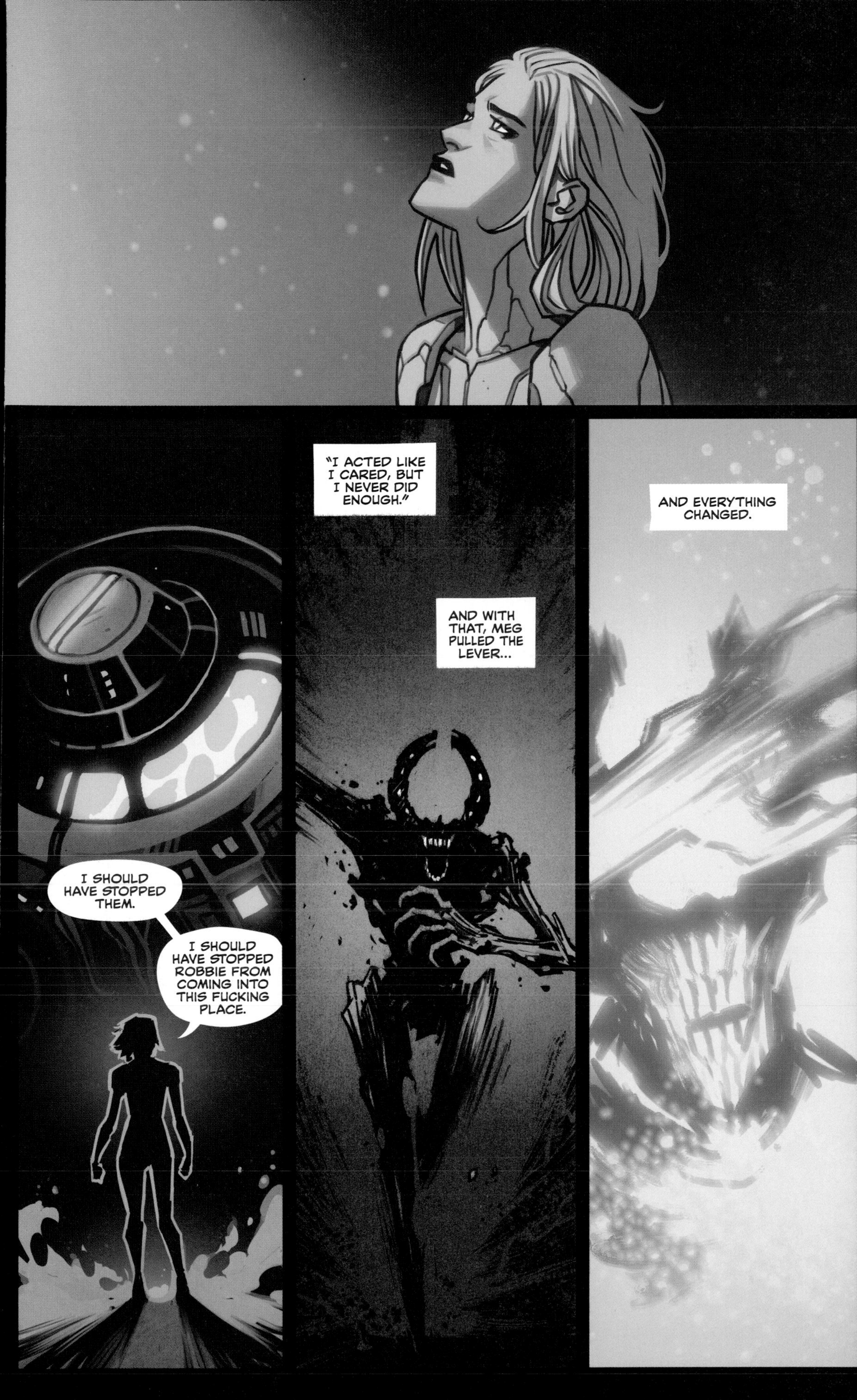
I SHOULD HAVE STOPPED THEM.
I SHOULD HAVE STOPPED ROBBIE FROM COMING INTO THIS FUCKING PLACE.
"I ACTED LIKE I CARED, BUT I NEVER DID ENOUGH."
AND WITH THAT, MEG PULLED THE LEVER...
AND EVERYTHING CHANGED.

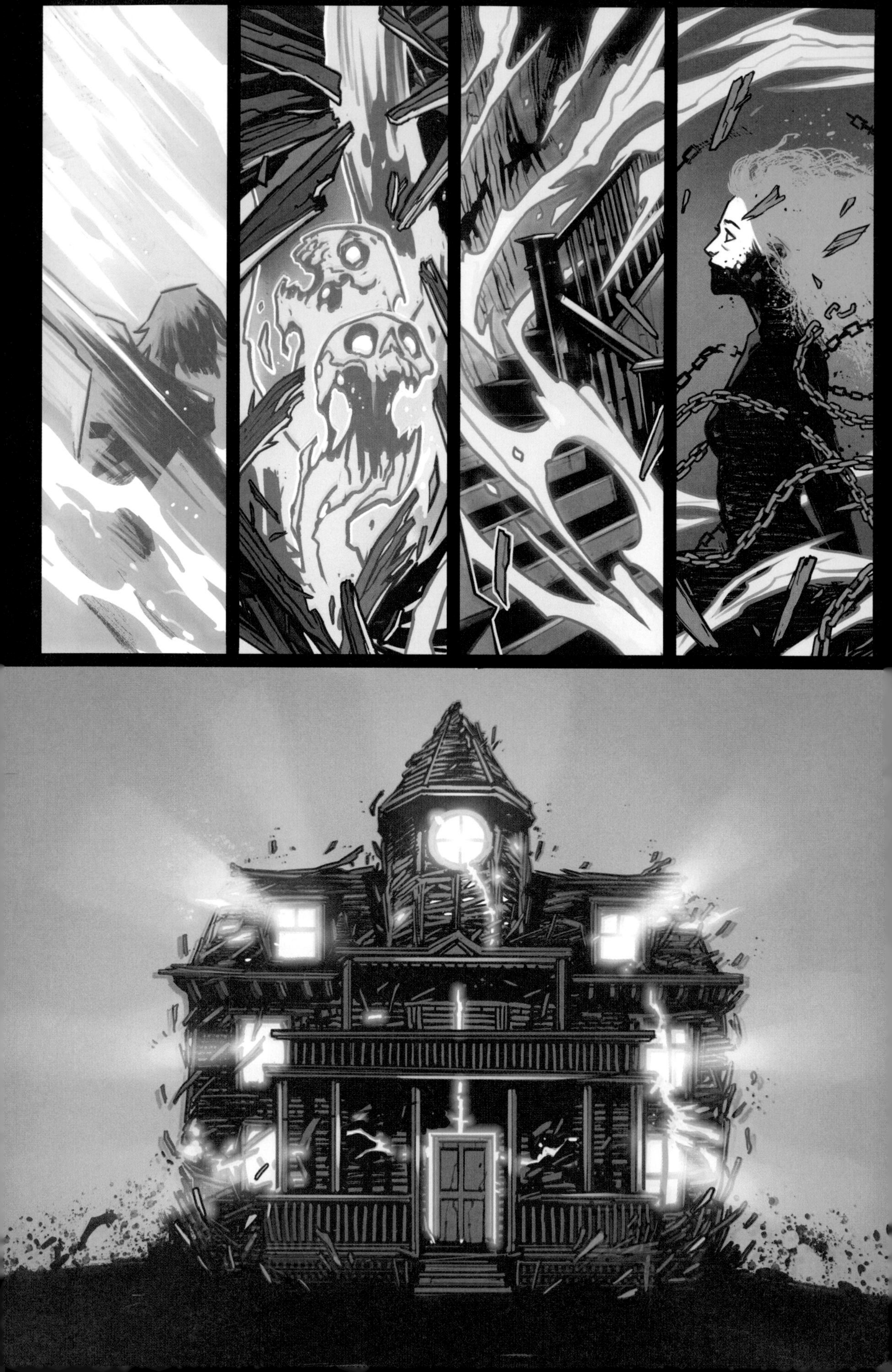

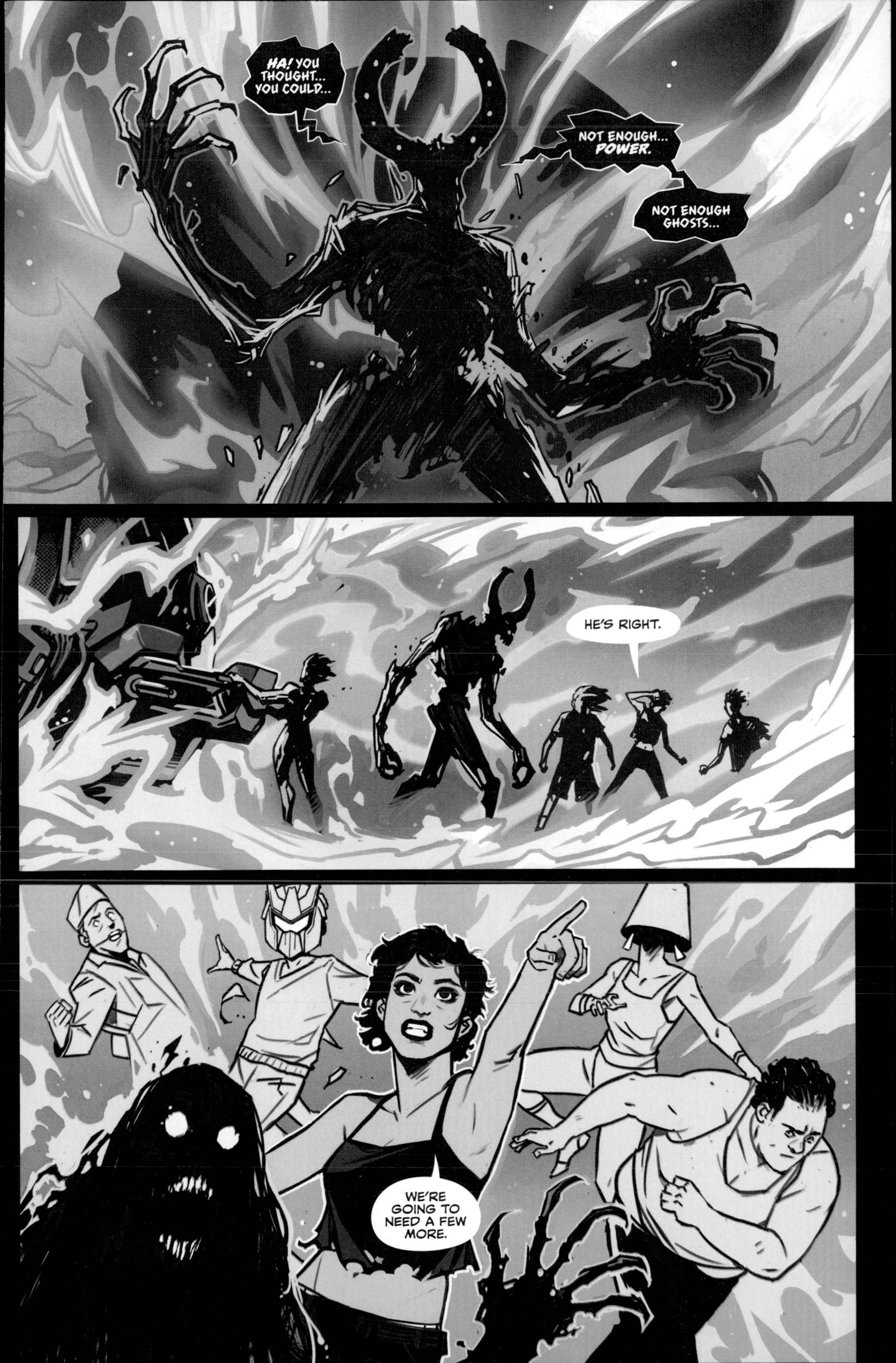
HA! YOU THOUGHT... YOU COULD...
NOT ENOUGH... POWER.
NOT ENOUGH GHOSTS...
HE'S RIGHT.
WE'RE GOING TO NEED A FEW MORE.

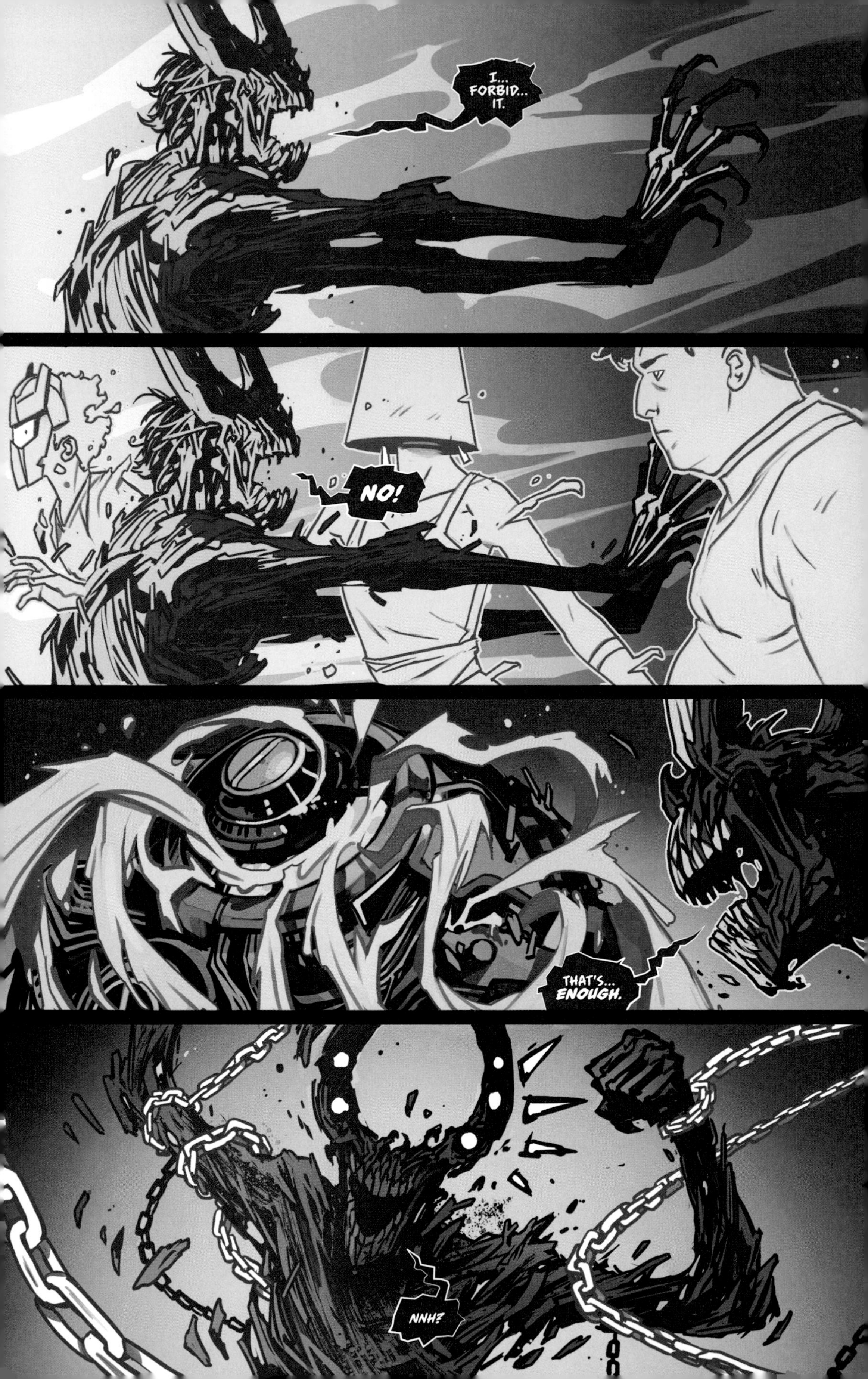
I... FORBID... IT.
NO!
THAT'S... ENOUGH.
NNH?

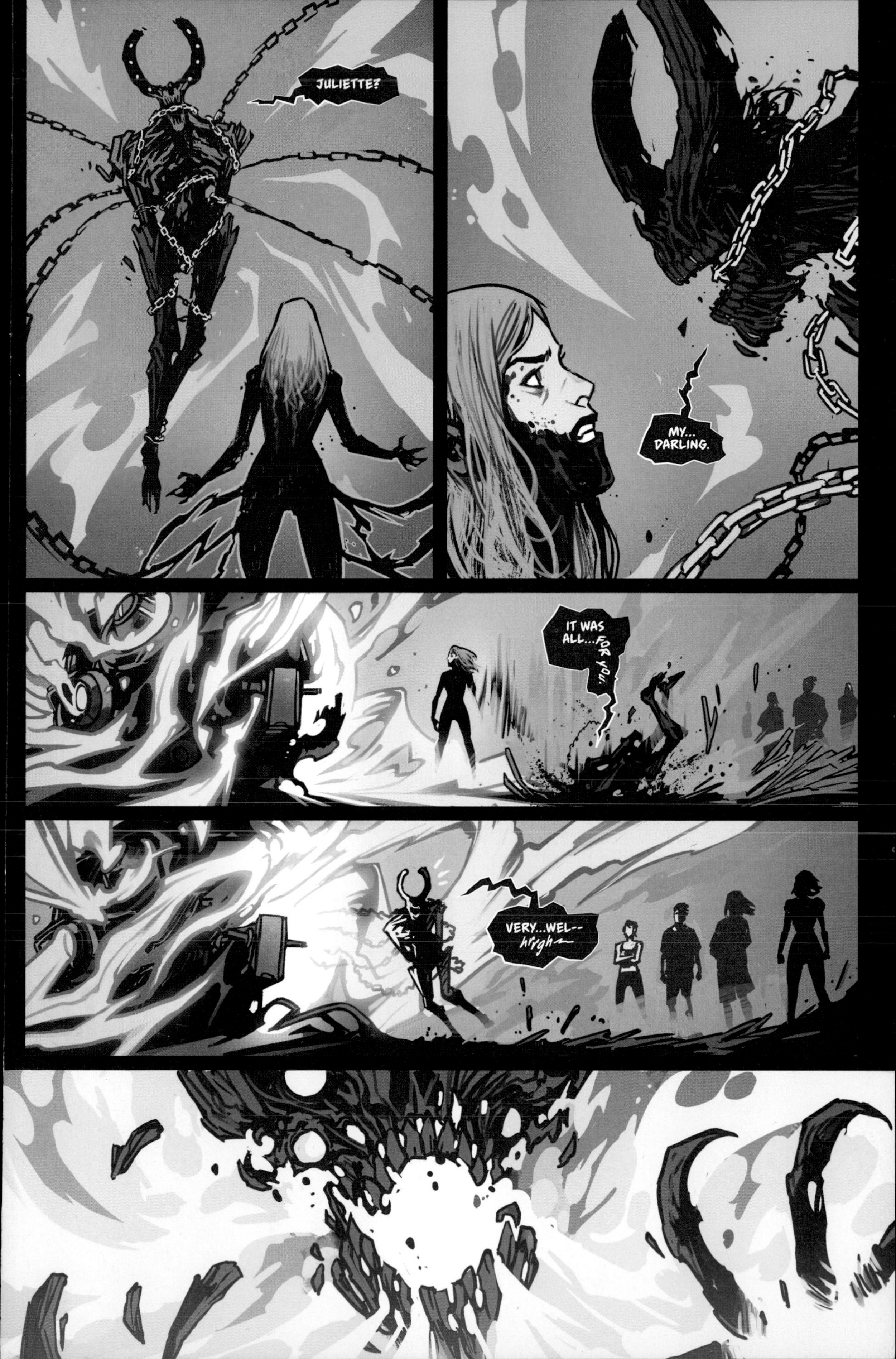
JULIETTE?
MY... DARLING.
IT WAS ALL...FOR YOU.
VERY...WEL-- hrrgh--

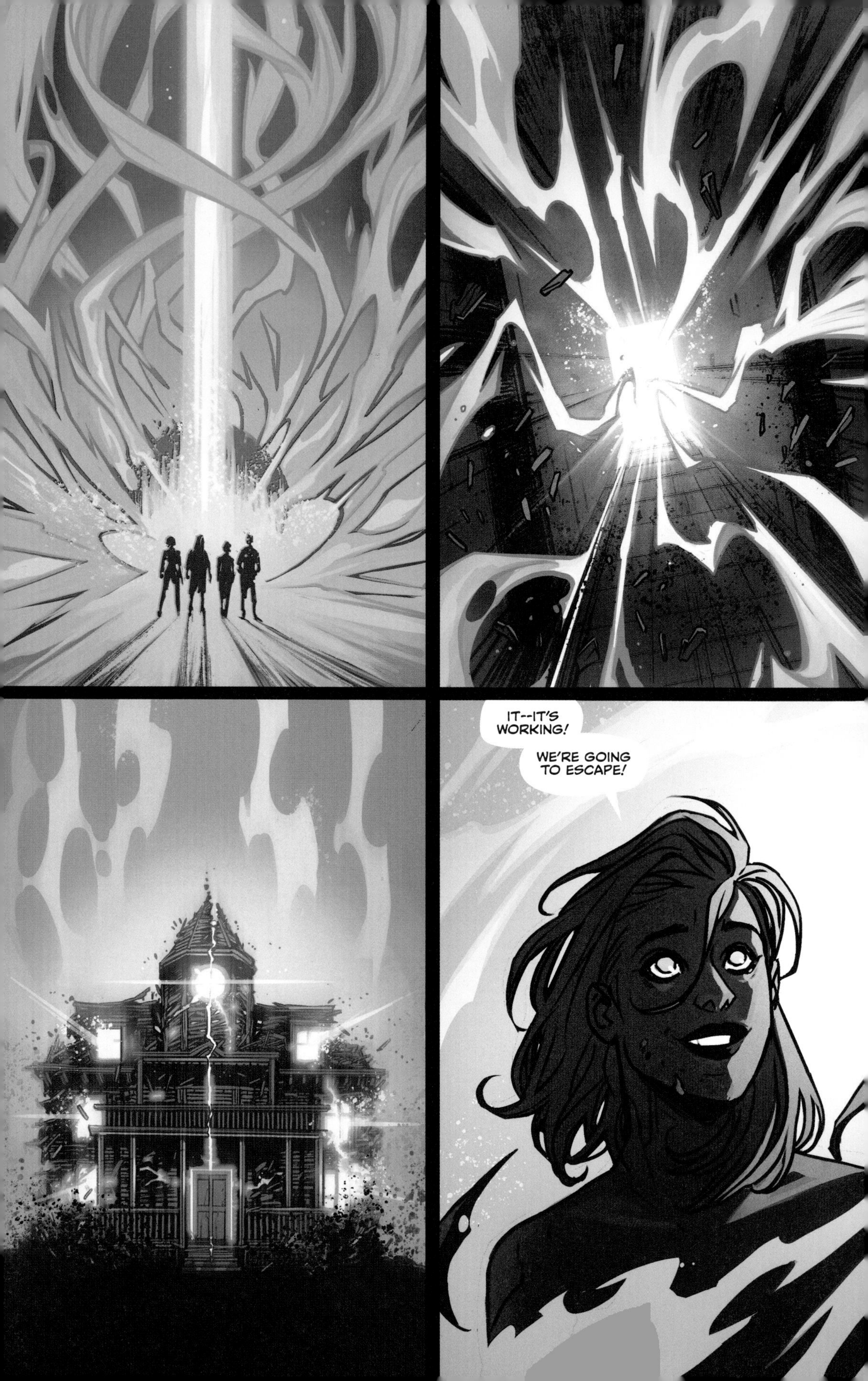
IT--IT'S WORKING!
WE'RE GOING TO ESCAPE!

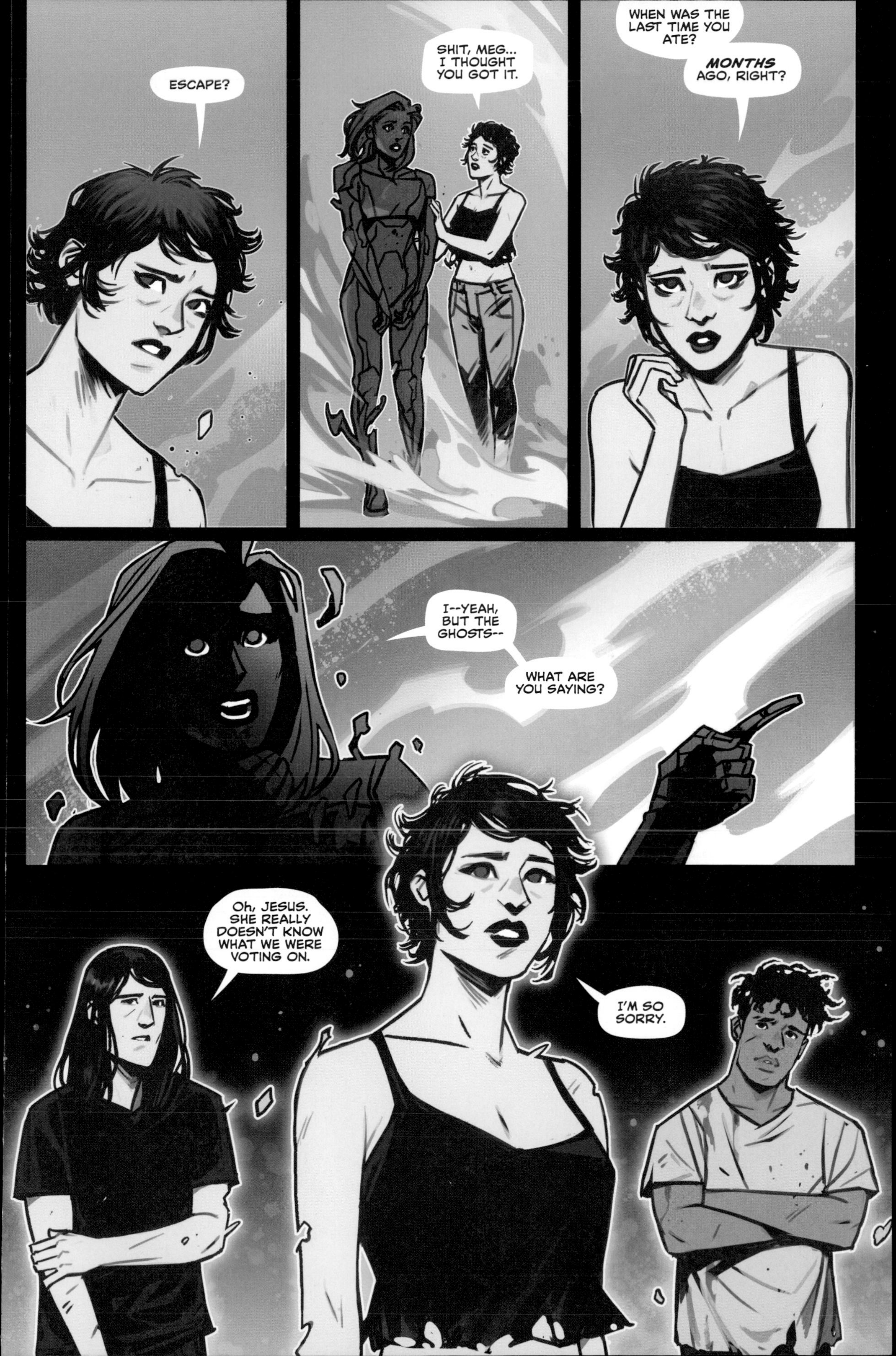
ESCAPE?
SHIT, MEG... I THOUGHT YOU GOT IT.
WHEN WAS THE LAST TIME YOU ATE?
MONTHS AGO, RIGHT?
I--YEAH, BUT THE GHOSTS--
WHAT ARE YOU SAYING?
Oh, JESUS. SHE REALLY DOESN'T KNOW WHAT WE WERE VOTING ON.
I'M SO SORRY.

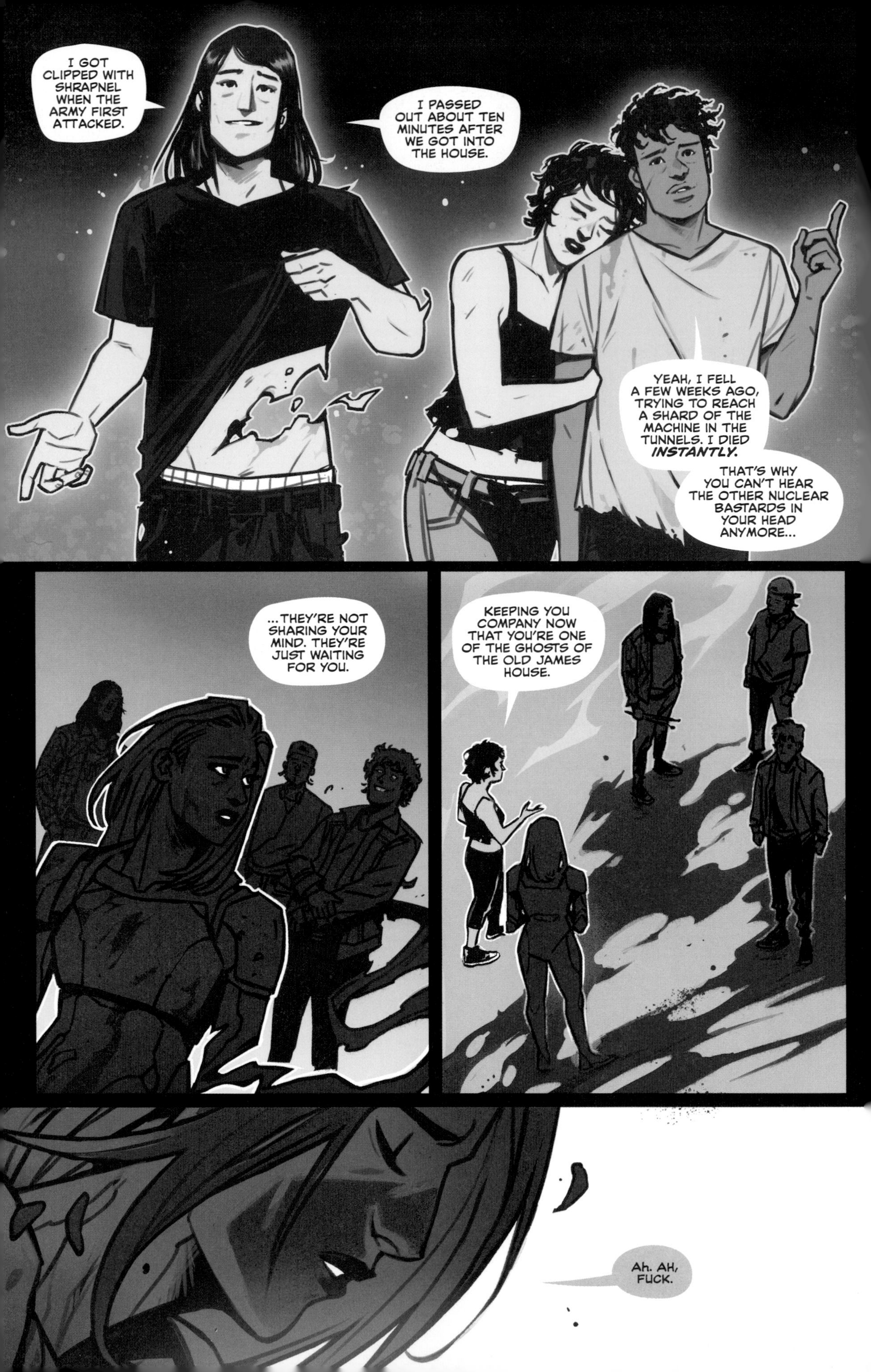
I GOT CLIPPED WITH SHRAPNEL WHEN THE ARMY FIRST ATTACKED.
I PASSED OUT ABOUT TEN MINUTES AFTER WE GOT INTO THE HOUSE.
YEAH, I FELL A FEW WEEKS AGO, TRYING TO REACH A SHARD OF THE MACHINE IN THE TUNNELS. I DIED *INSTANTLY.*
THAT'S WHY YOU CAN'T HEAR THE OTHER NUCLEAR BASTARDS IN YOUR HEAD ANYMORE...
...THEY'RE NOT SHARING YOUR MIND. THEY'RE JUST WAITING FOR YOU.
KEEPING YOU COMPANY NOW THAT YOU'RE ONE OF THE GHOSTS OF THE OLD JAMES HOUSE.
Ah. AH, FUCK.

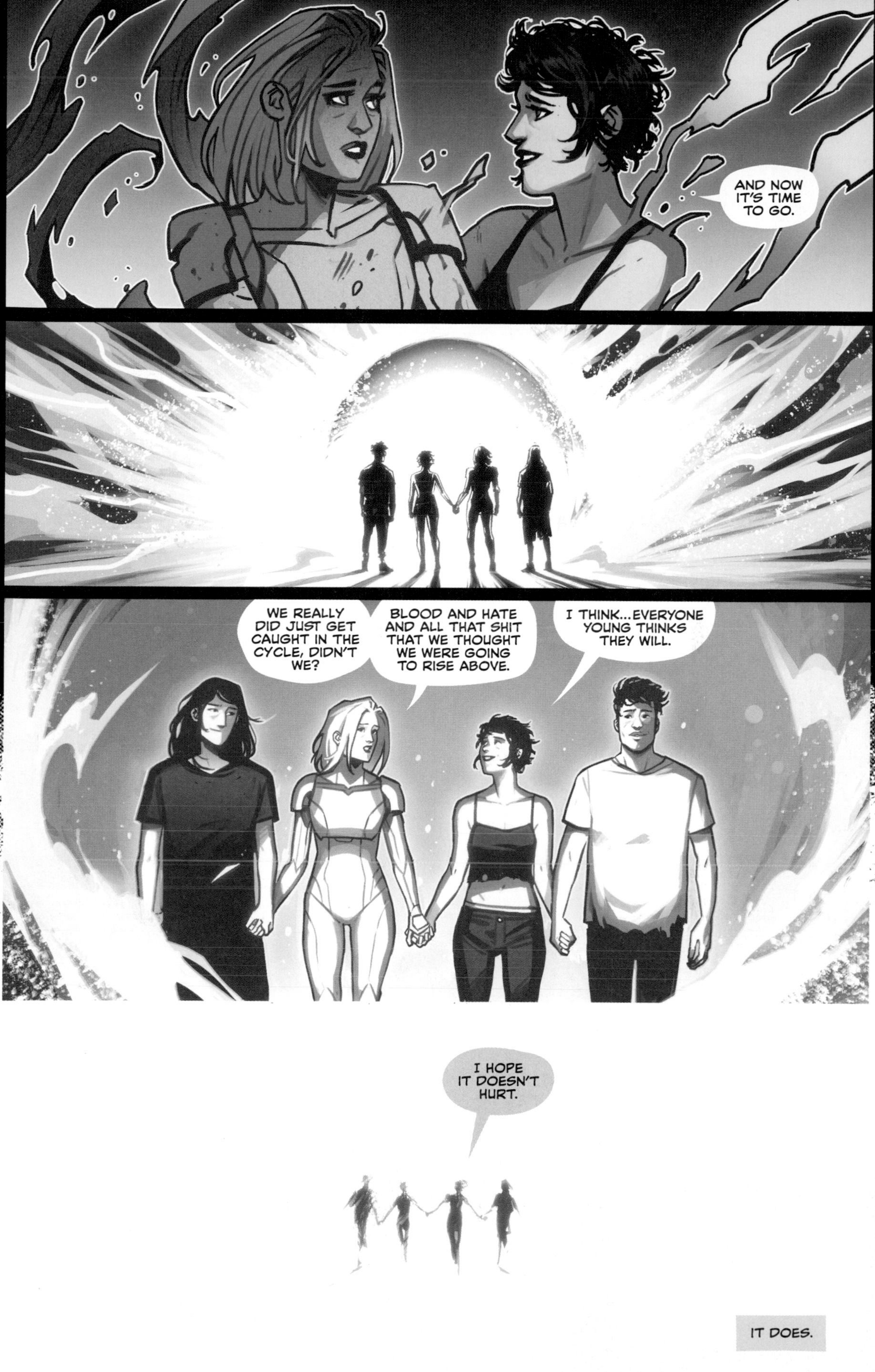
AND NOW IT'S TIME TO GO.
WE REALLY DID JUST GET CAUGHT IN THE CYCLE, DIDN'T WE?
BLOOD AND HATE AND ALL THAT SHIT THAT WE THOUGHT WE WERE GOING TO RISE ABOVE.
I THINK...EVERYONE YOUNG THINKS THEY WILL.
I HOPE IT DOESN'T HURT.
IT DOES.

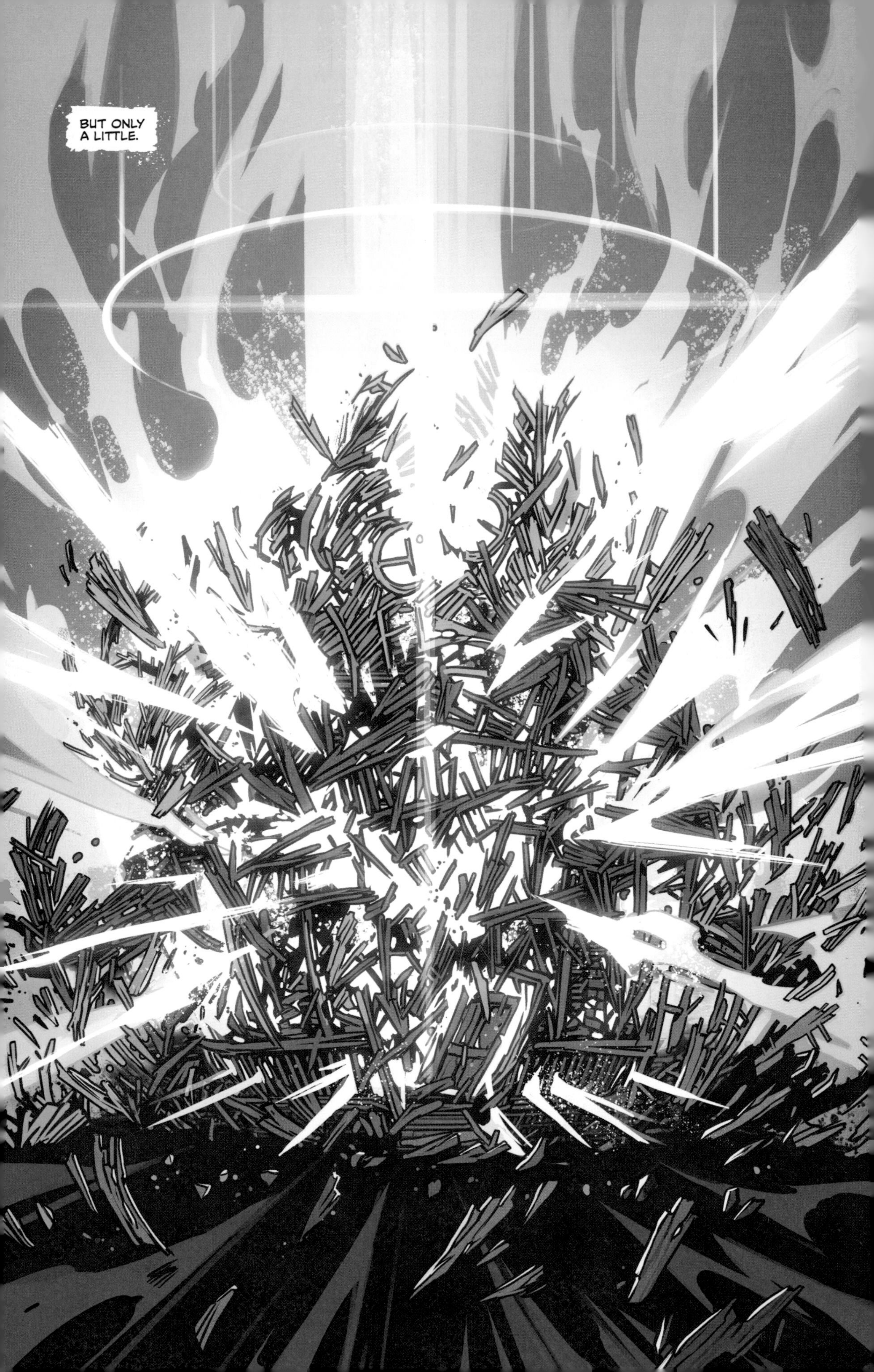
BUT ONLY A LITTLE.

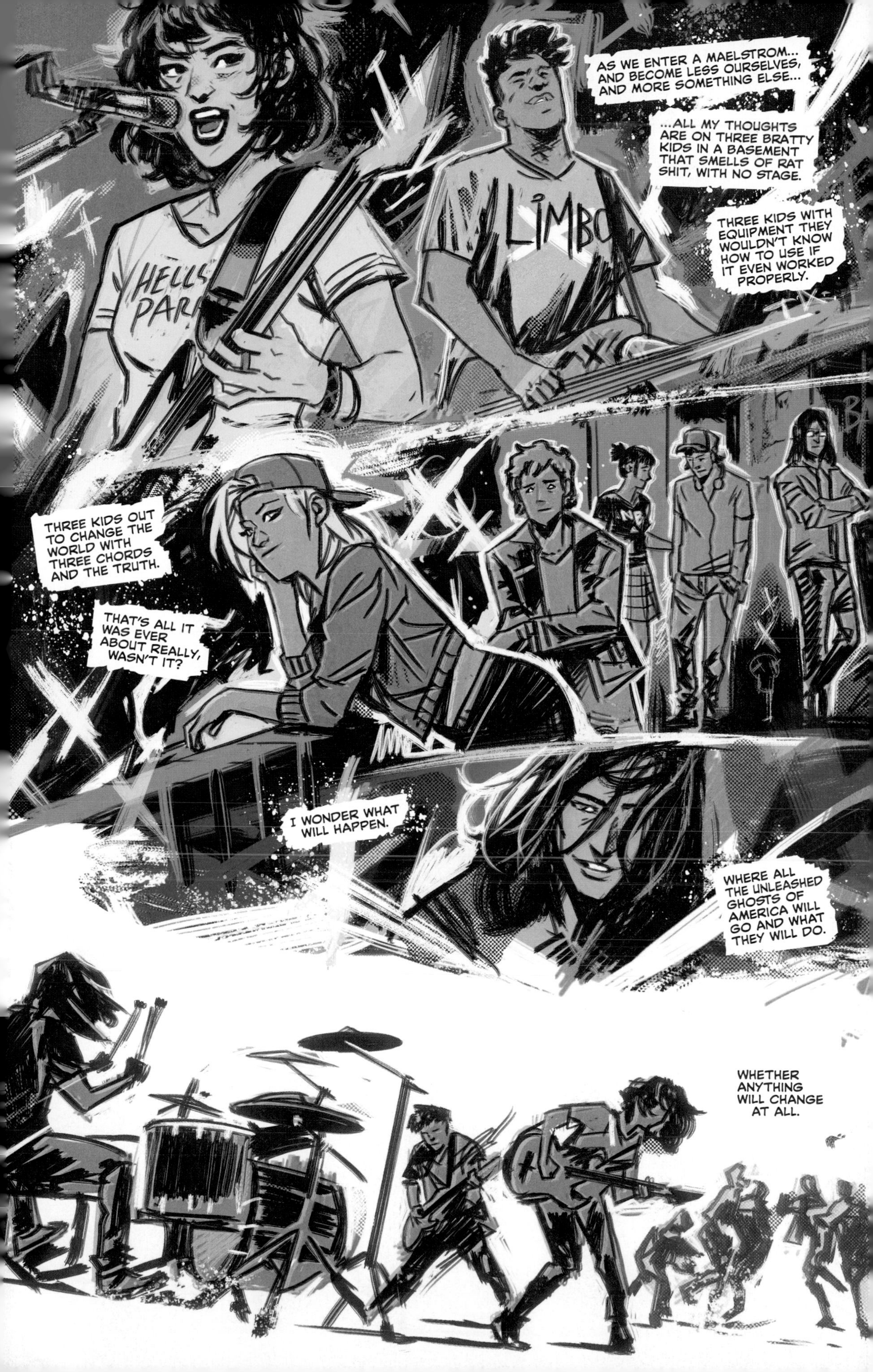
AS WE ENTER A MAELSTROM... AND BECOME LESS OURSELVES, AND MORE SOMETHING ELSE...
...ALL MY THOUGHTS ARE ON THREE BRATTY KIDS IN A BASEMENT THAT SMELLS OF RAT SHIT, WITH NO STAGE.
THREE KIDS WITH EQUIPMENT THEY WOULDN'T KNOW HOW TO USE IF IT EVEN WORKED PROPERLY.
LIMBO
THREE KIDS OUT TO CHANGE THE WORLD WITH THREE CHORDS AND THE TRUTH.
THAT'S ALL IT WAS EVER ABOUT REALLY, WASN'T IT?
I WONDER WHAT WILL HAPPEN.
WHERE ALL THE UNLEASHED GHOSTS OF AMERICA WILL GO AND WHAT THEY WILL DO.
WHETHER ANYTHING WILL CHANGE AT ALL.

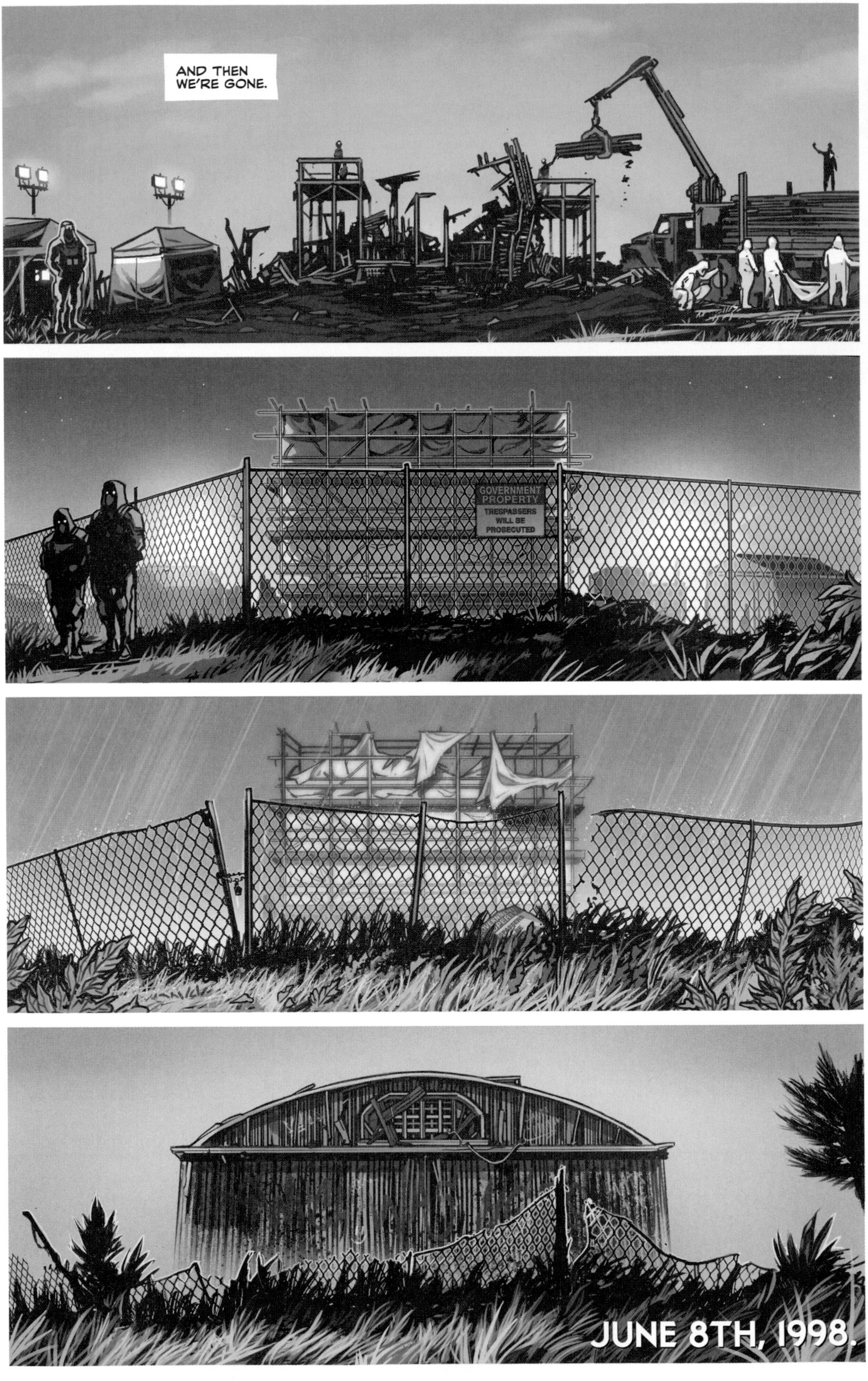
AND THEN WE'RE GONE.
GOVERNMENT PROPERTY
TRESPASSERS WILL BE PROSECUTED
JUNE 8TH, 1998.

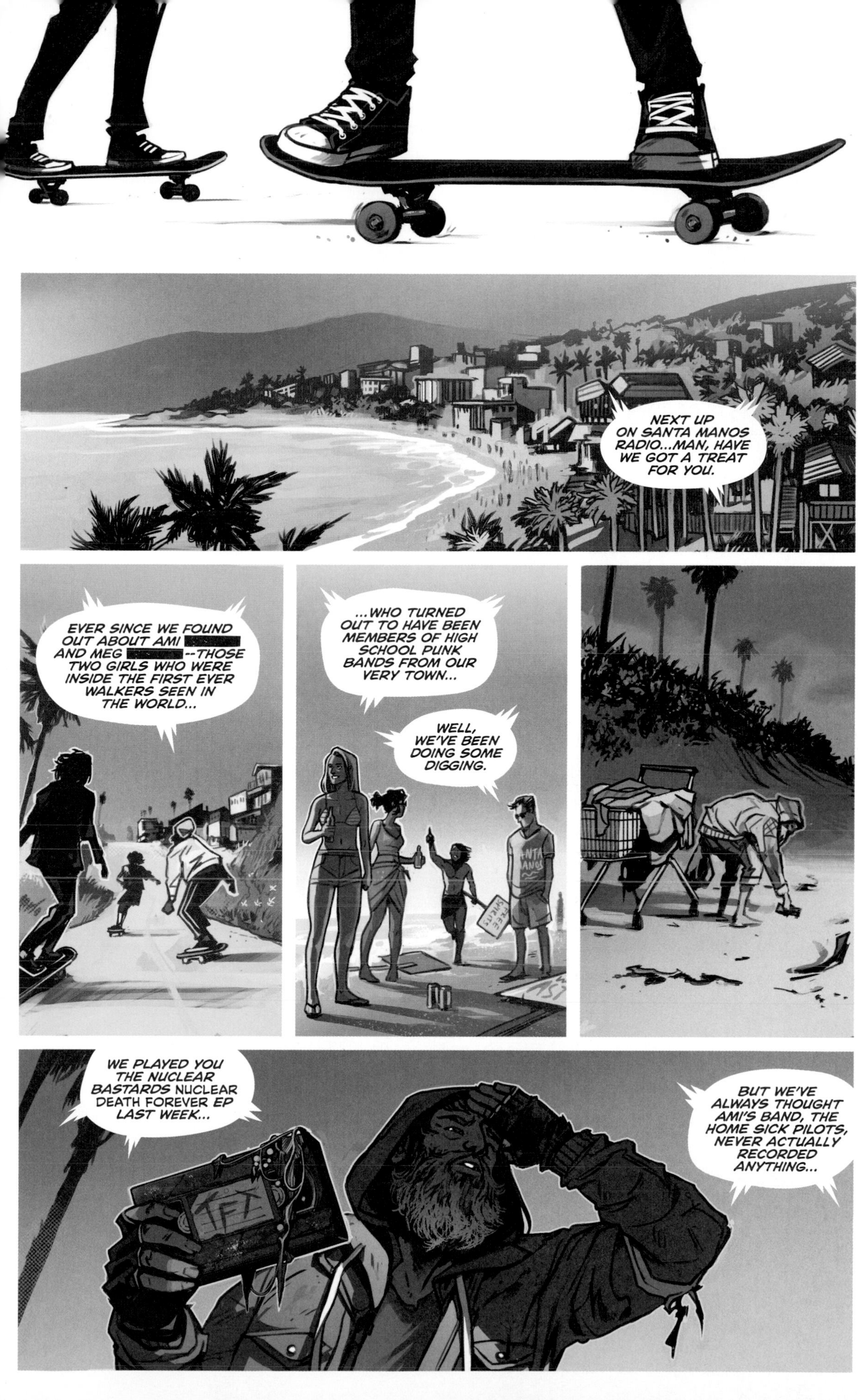
NEXT UP ON SANTA MANOS RADIO...MAN, HAVE WE GOT A TREAT FOR YOU.
EVER SINCE WE FOUND OUT ABOUT AMI [redacted] AND MEG [redacted]--THOSE TWO GIRLS WHO WERE INSIDE THE FIRST EVER WALKERS SEEN IN THE WORLD...
...WHO TURNED OUT TO HAVE BEEN MEMBERS OF HIGH SCHOOL PUNK BANDS FROM OUR VERY TOWN...
WELL, WE'VE BEEN DOING SOME DIGGING.
WE PLAYED YOU THE NUCLEAR BASTARDS NUCLEAR DEATH FOREVER EP LAST WEEK...
BUT WE'VE ALWAYS THOUGHT AMI'S BAND, THE HOME SICK PILOTS, NEVER ACTUALLY RECORDED ANYTHING...

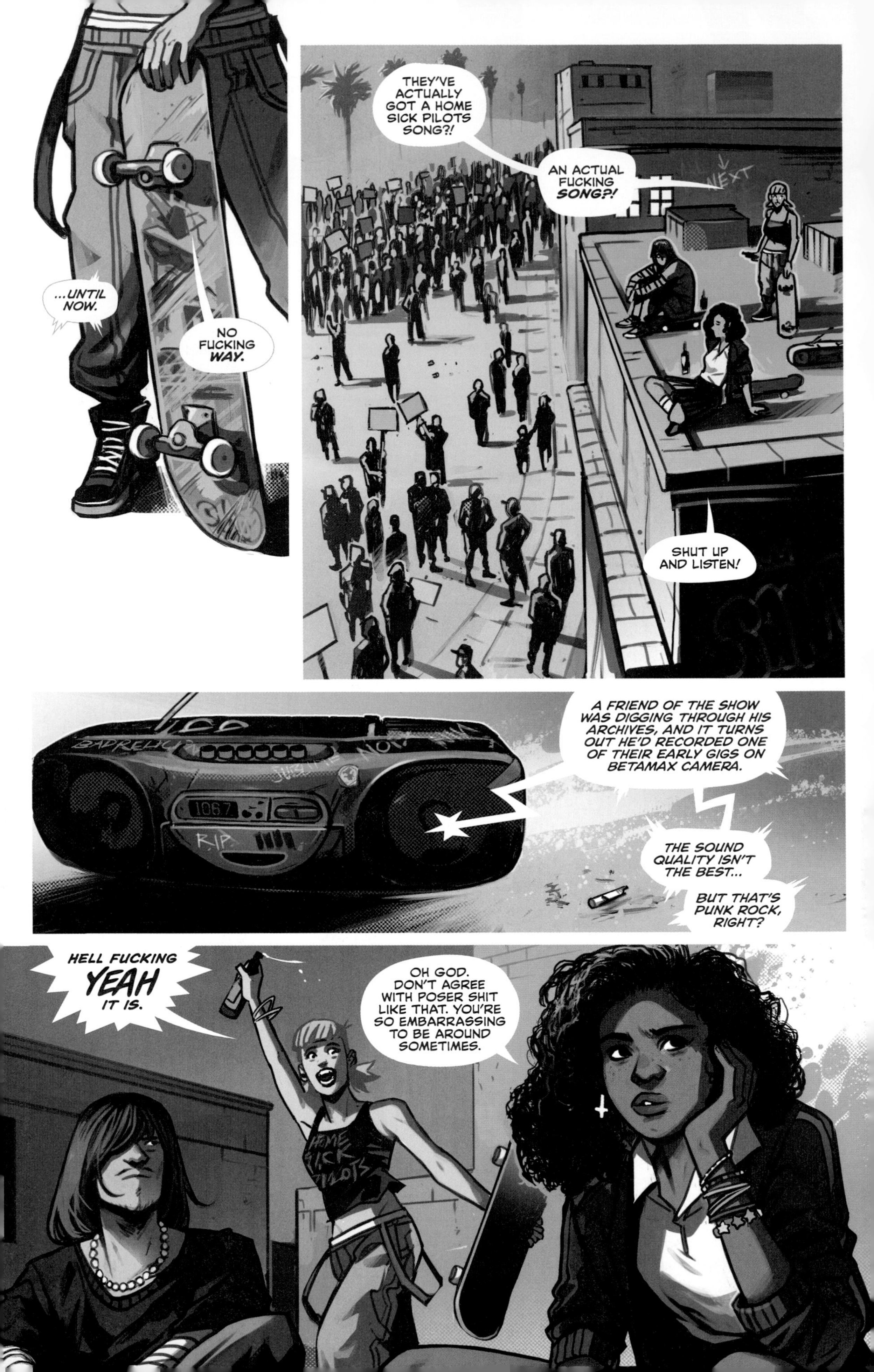
...UNTIL NOW.
NO FUCKING WAY.
THEY'VE ACTUALLY GOT A HOME SICK PILOTS SONG?!
AN ACTUAL FUCKING SONG?!
NEXT
SHUT UP AND LISTEN!
A FRIEND OF THE SHOW WAS DIGGING THROUGH HIS ARCHIVES, AND IT TURNS OUT HE'D RECORDED ONE OF THEIR EARLY GIGS ON BETAMAX CAMERA.
THE SOUND QUALITY ISN'T THE BEST...
BUT THAT'S PUNK ROCK, RIGHT?
106.7
R.I.P.
HELL FUCKING YEAH IT IS.
OH GOD. DON'T AGREE WITH POSER SHIT LIKE THAT. YOU'RE SO EMBARRASSING TO BE AROUND SOMETIMES.
HOME SICK PILOTS

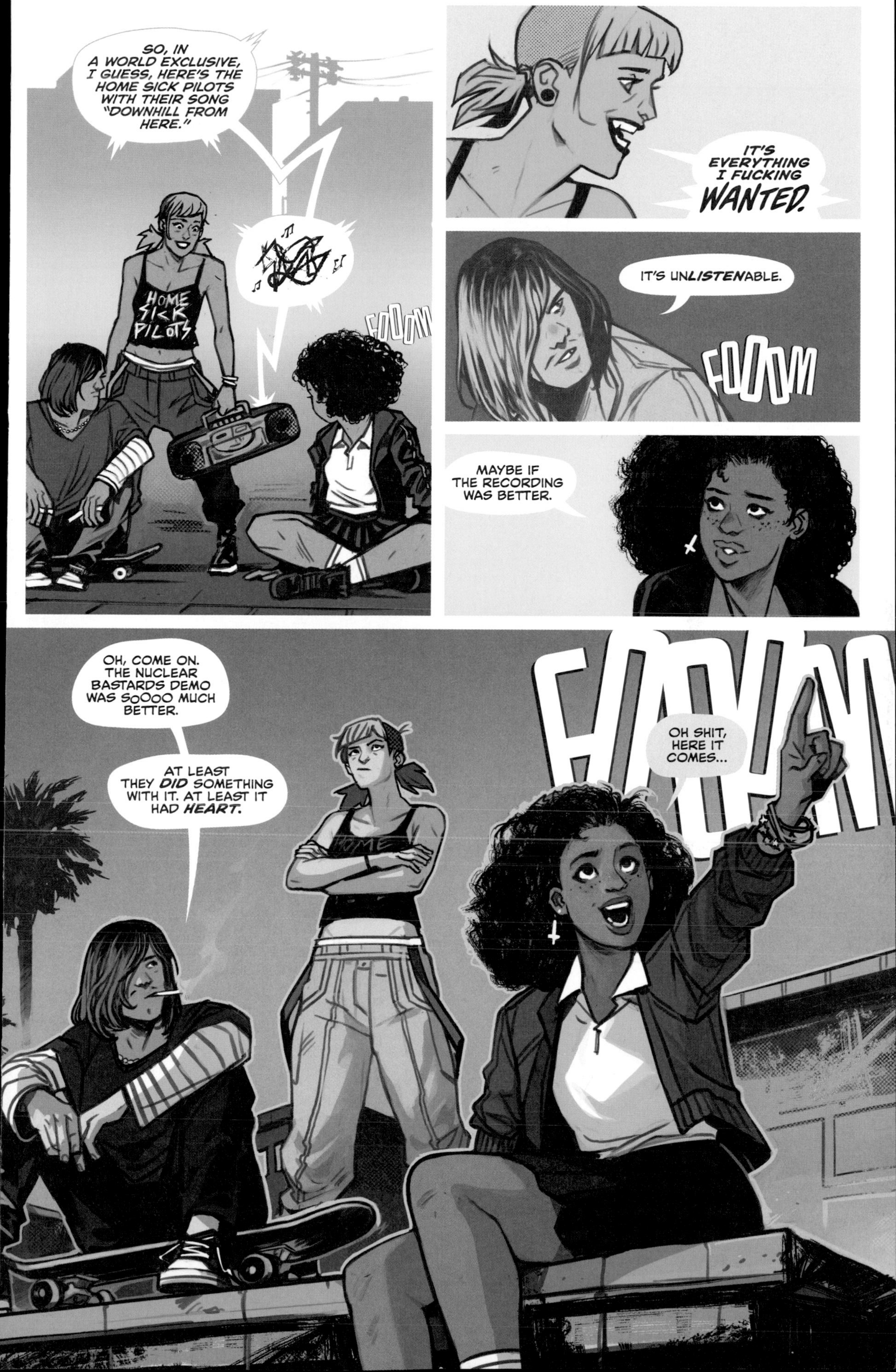
SO, IN A WORLD EXCLUSIVE, I GUESS, HERE'S THE HOME SICK PILOTS WITH THEIR SONG "DOWNHILL FROM HERE."
HOME SICK PILOTS
FOOOM
IT'S EVERYTHING I FUCKING WANTED.
IT'S UNLISTENABLE.
FOOOM
MAYBE IF THE RECORDING WAS BETTER.
OH, COME ON. THE NUCLEAR BASTARDS DEMO WAS SOOOO MUCH BETTER.
AT LEAST THEY DID SOMETHING WITH IT. AT LEAST IT HAD HEART.
OH SHIT, HERE IT COMES...
HOME

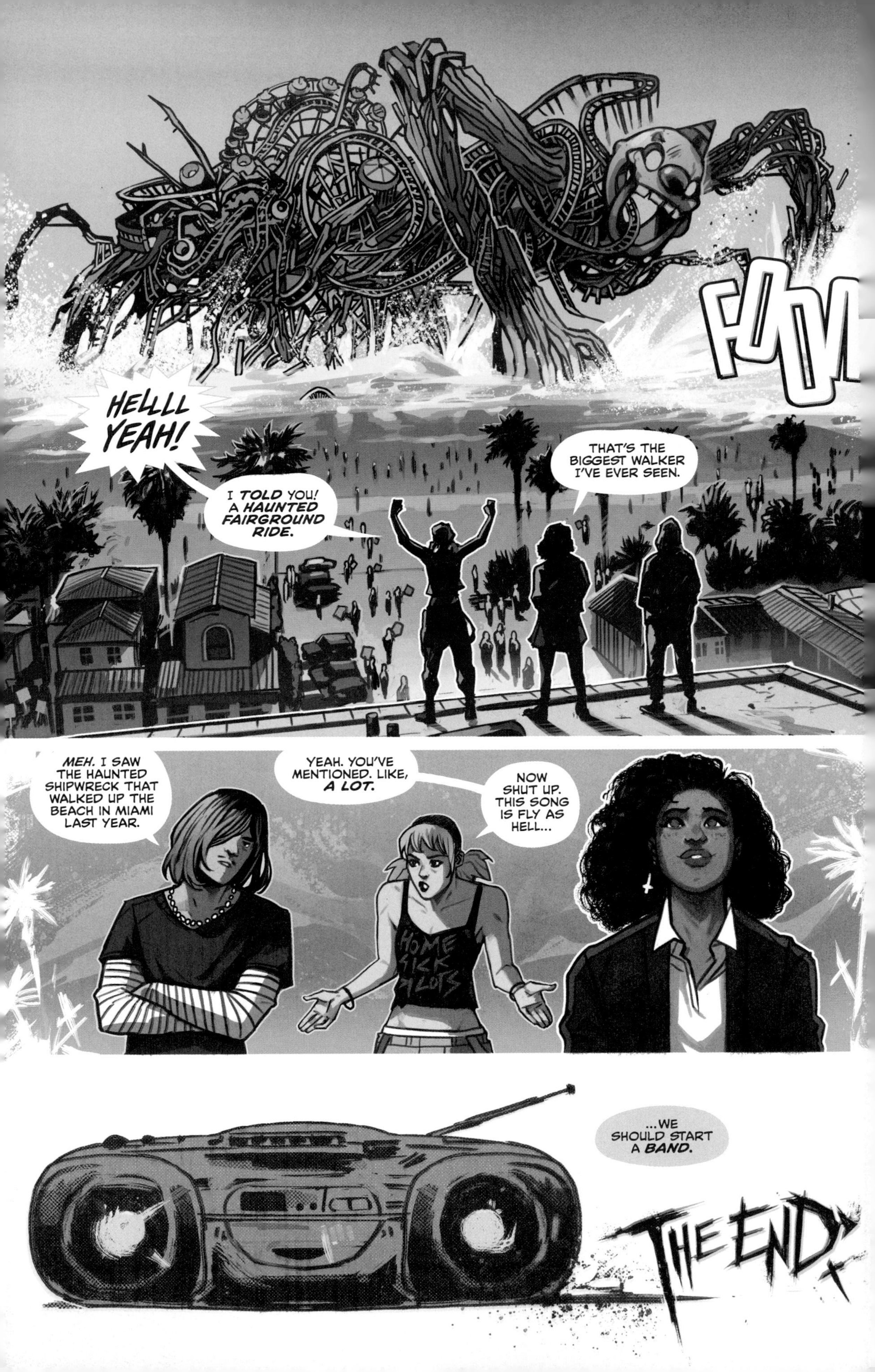
FOOM
HELLLL YEAH!
I TOLD YOU! A HAUNTED FAIRGROUND RIDE.
THAT'S THE BIGGEST WALKER I'VE EVER SEEN.
MEH. I SAW THE HAUNTED SHIPWRECK THAT WALKED UP THE BEACH IN MIAMI LAST YEAR.
YEAH. YOU'VE MENTIONED. LIKE, A LOT.
NOW SHUT UP. THIS SONG IS FLY AS HELL...
...WE SHOULD START A BAND.
HOME SICK PILOTS
THE END

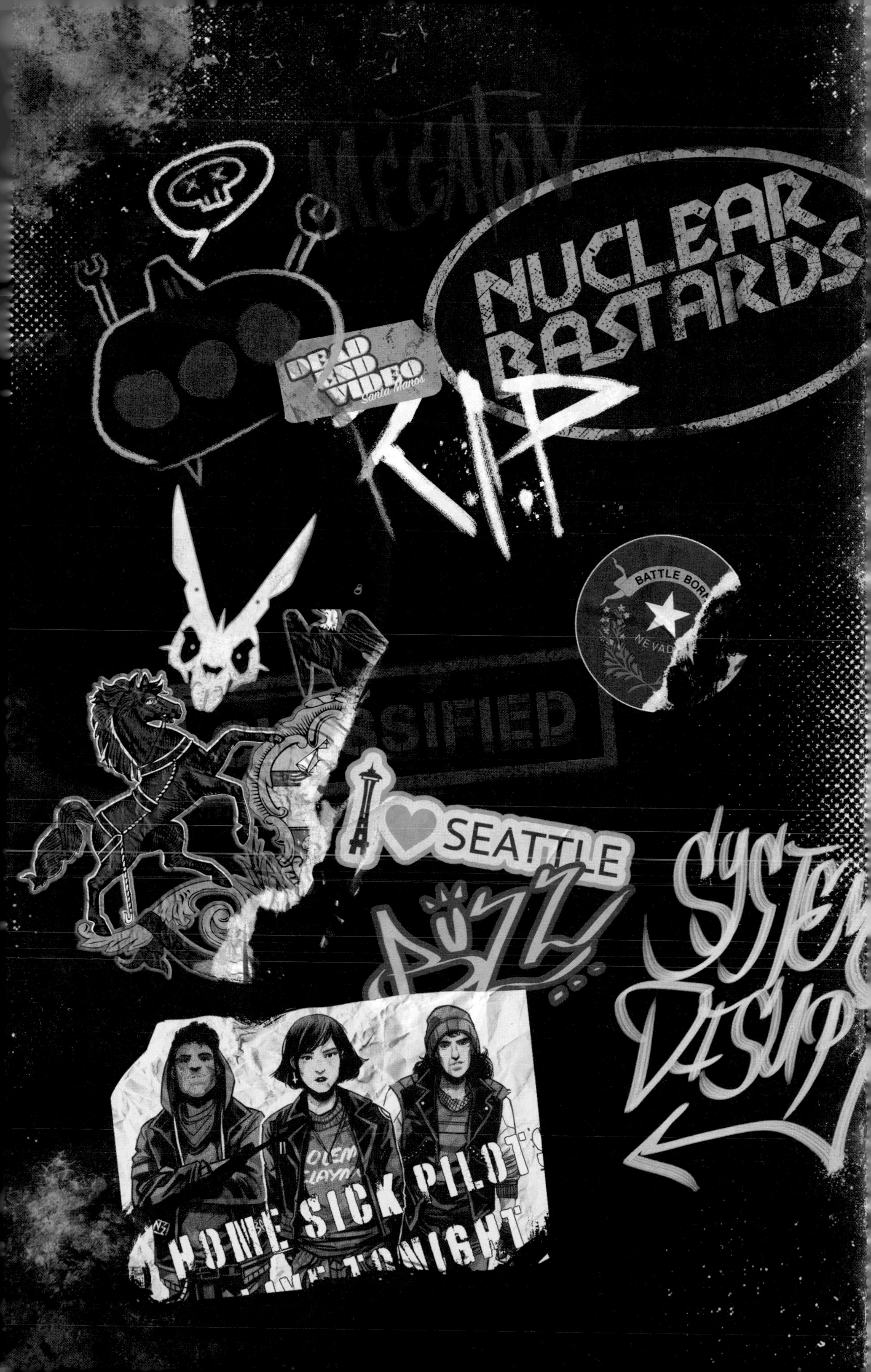
MEGATON
NUCLEAR BASTARDS
DEAD END VIDEO
Santa Manos
R.I.P.
SSIFIED
BATTLE BOR
NEVAD
I ♥ SEATTLE
HOME SICK PILOT'S
TONIGHT

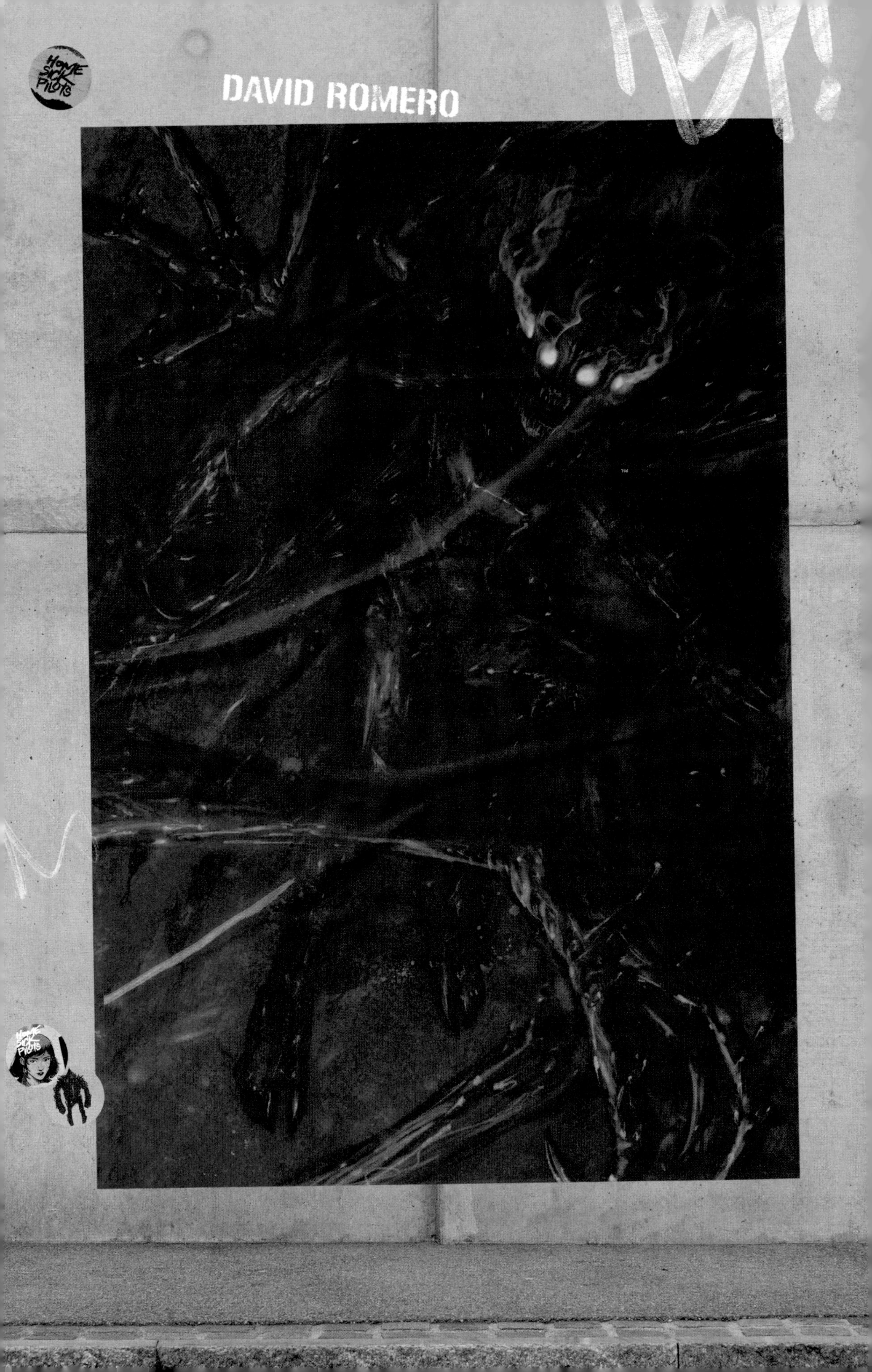
HOME SICK PILOTS
DAVID ROMERO

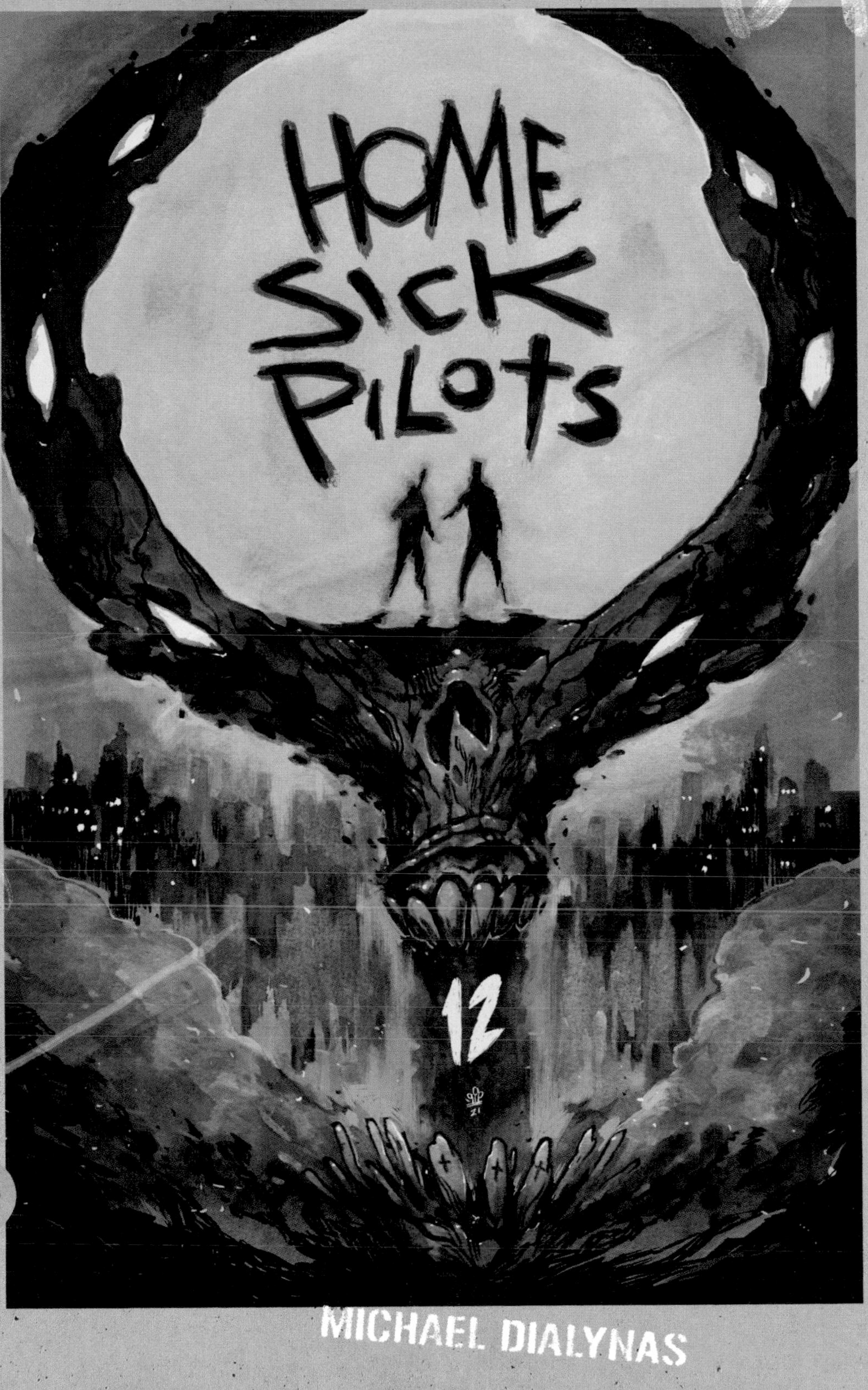
HOME
SICK
PILOTS
12

MICHAEL DIALYNAS

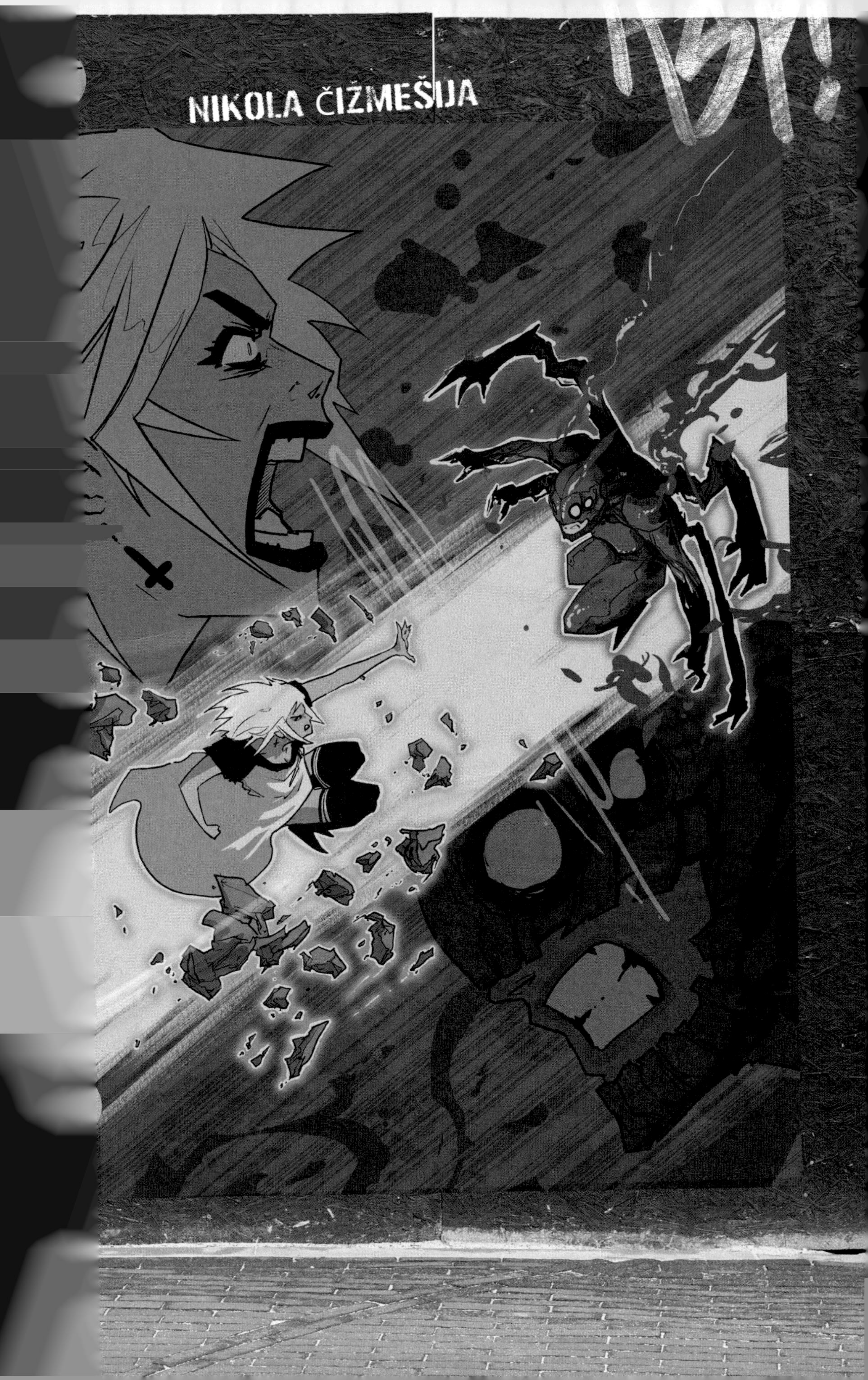
NIKOLA ČIŽMEŠIJA

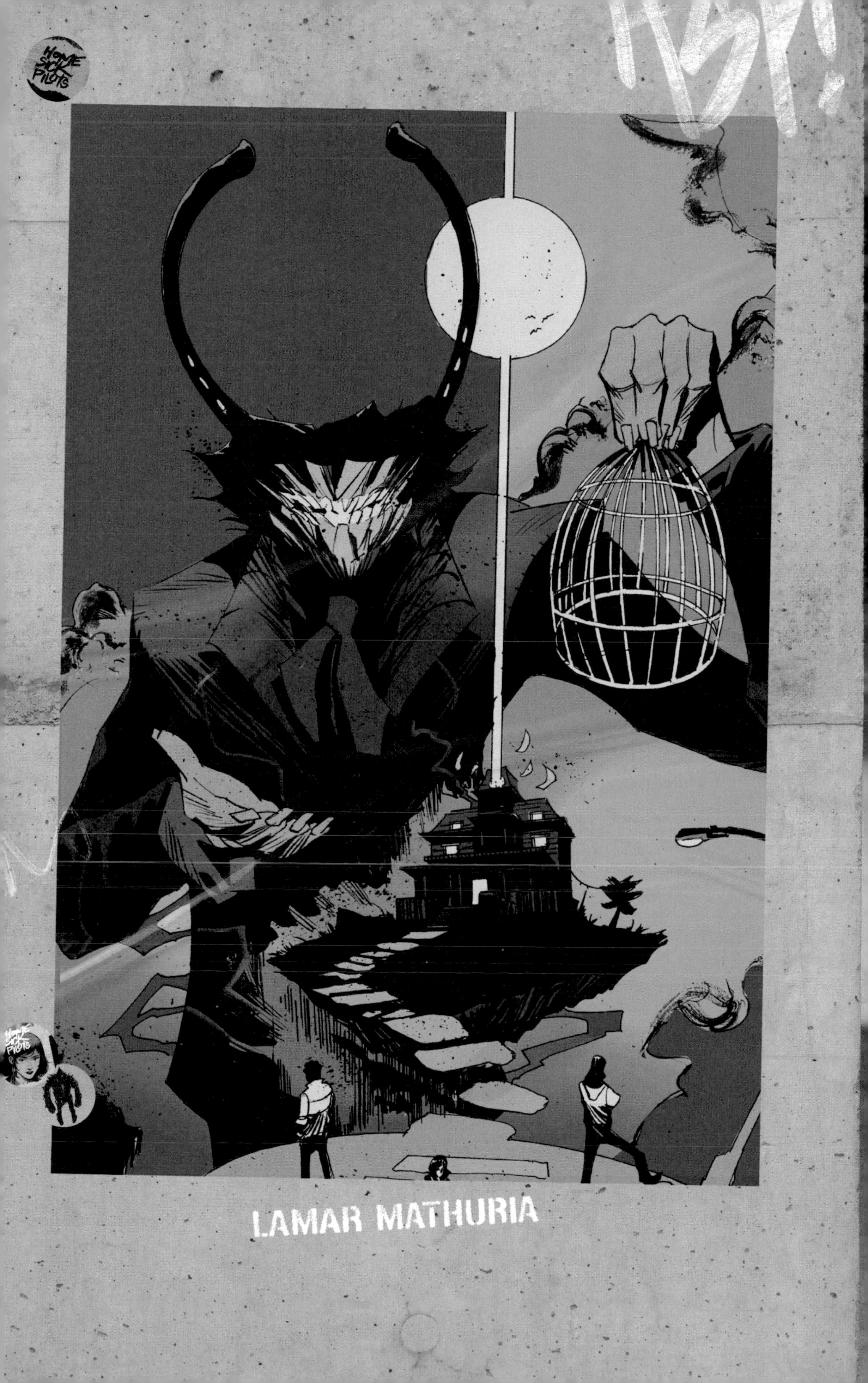
HOME SICK PILOTS
LAMAR MATHURIA

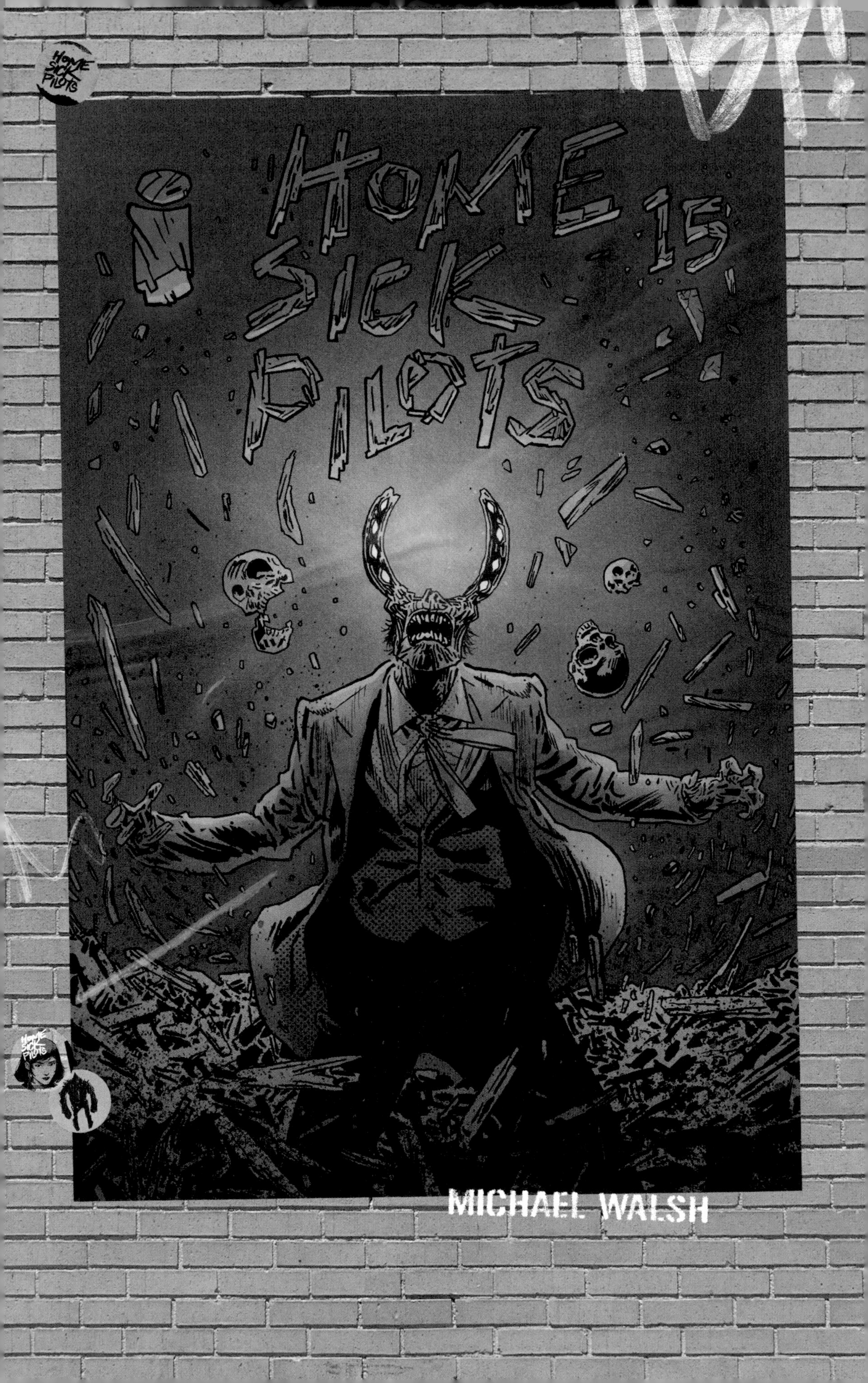
HOME SICK PILOTS
HOME SICK PILOTS 15
MICHAEL WALSH

THE HOME SICK PILOTS!

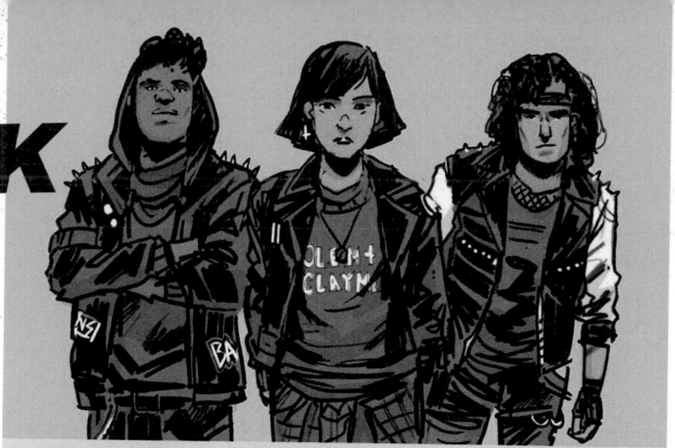

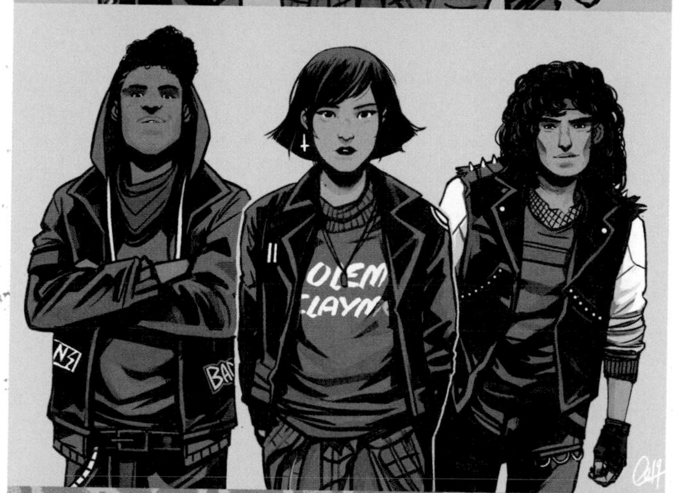

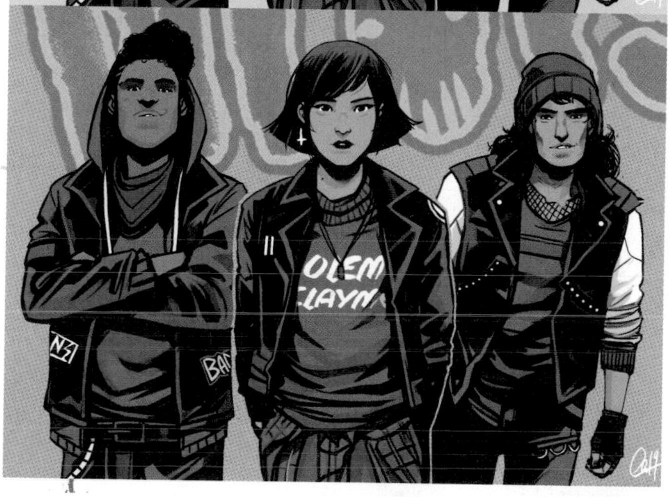

Ami, Buzz and Rip were originally intended to be characters in a follow up to our Image Comics series LIMBO (2016) before we decided to the develop the foundations of the follow up into HSP. I drew my inspiration for the trio from the German Techno Punk group Atari Teenage Riot, however I styled each to look more inline to a grungy punk group from the US.

Additionally, Ami's ghost suit was a nod to Super Sentai and Evangelion.

MEG

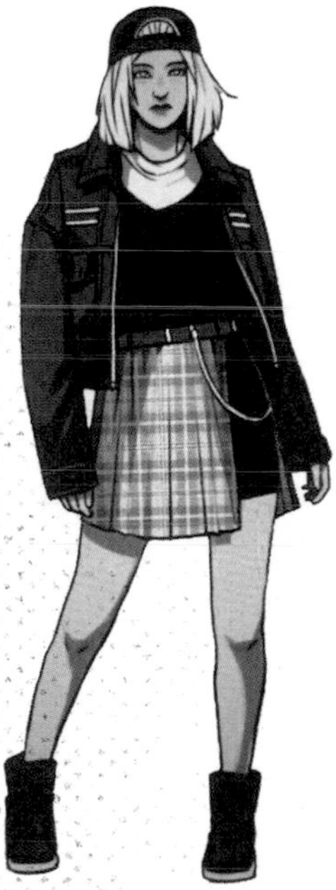

Meg was an amalgamation of 90s Drew Barrymore and Gwen Stefani. A supposed pop punk poser in a Thrash band. A kind, sweet girl from the valley that got caught up in some horrible shit.

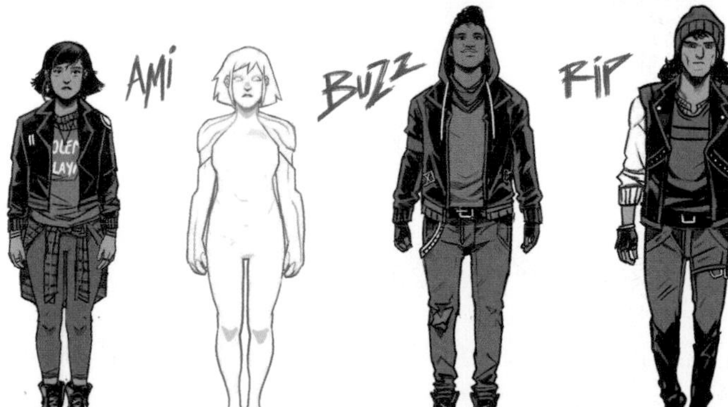
AMI
BUZZ
RIP

Liner notes by Caspar Wijngaard!

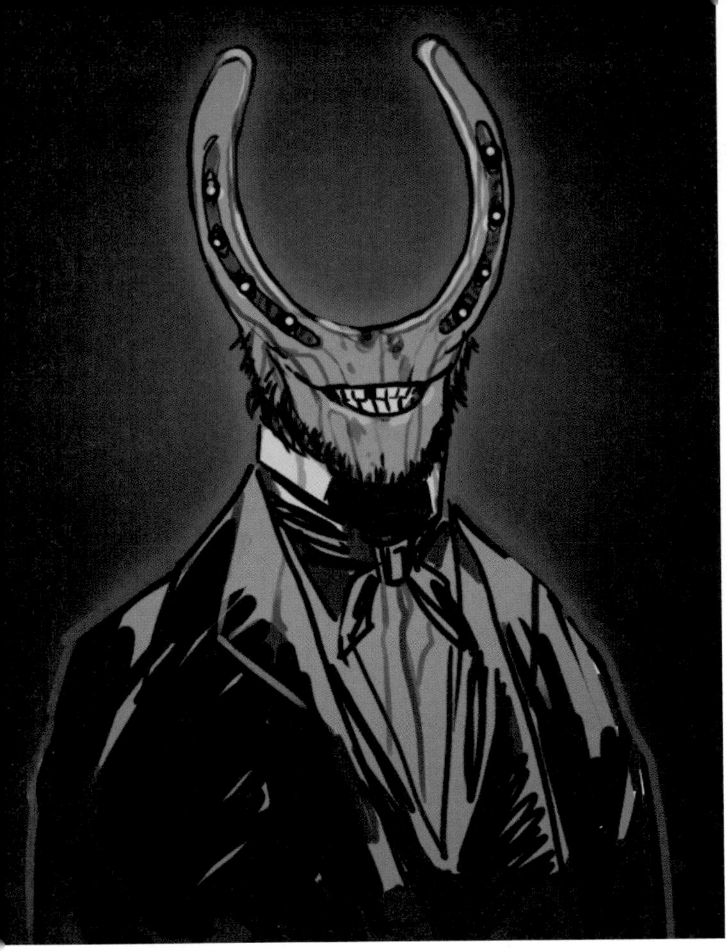

OLD JAMES

Dan suggested I incorporate a horse shoe into his body and I replied "hold my beer". He was initially more tame, however as he gains more power he is stripped back into a pure horror form. Once I drew him without the suit in issue 5 and it was hard to go back.

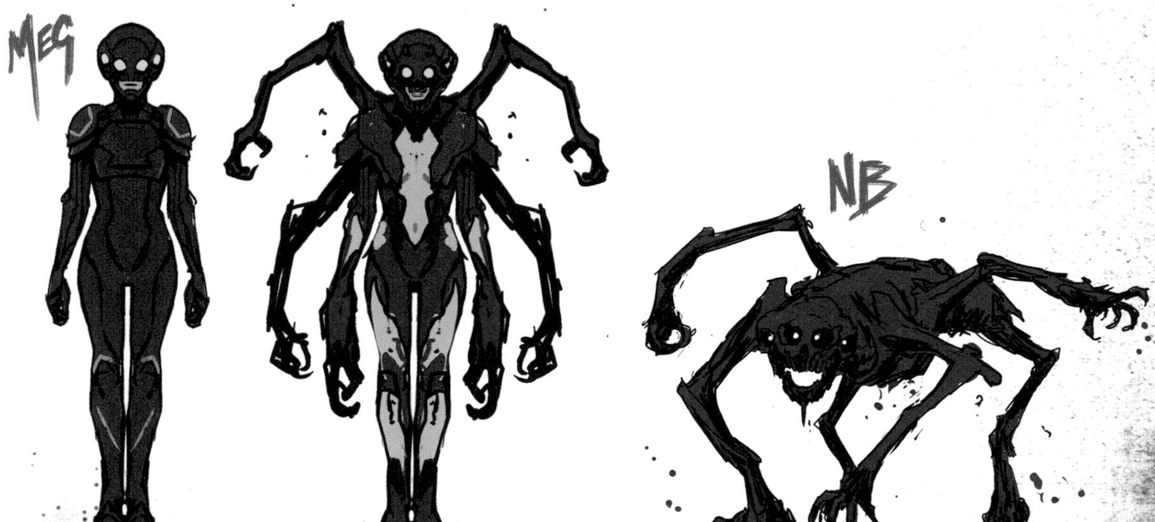
MEG
NB

BLOOD SUIT

The polar opposite to Amida's ecto ghost suit, still pulling inspiration from Super Sentai but with a more horrific twist. I suggested to Dan that the NB suit could possibly detach from Meg and become a six armed sentient horror, unfortunately it never made the cut.

THE BIG WITCH

I wanted to keep her design Simple enough that it had elements of a twisted house which still remained humanoid, I drew inspiration from the Robots from Laputa: Castle in the Sky by Hayao Miyazaki as I always adored their sympathetic design.

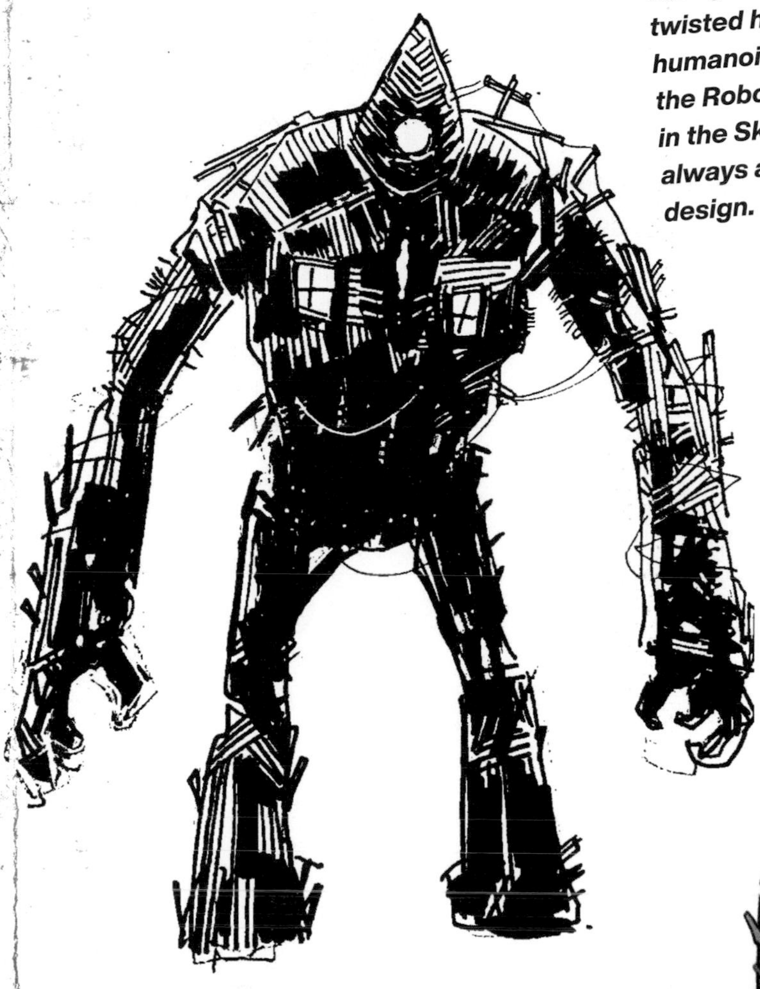

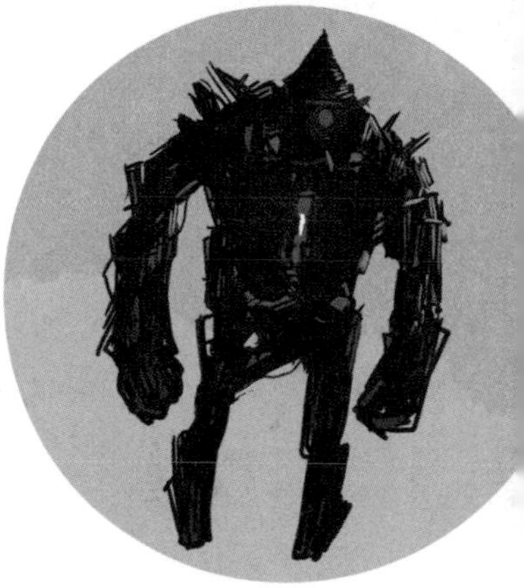

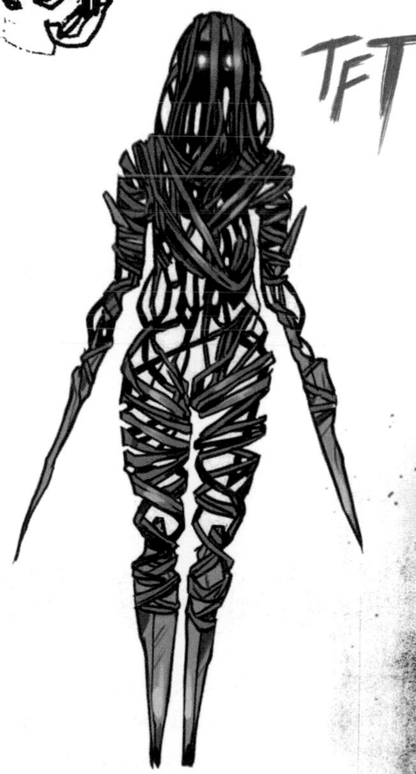
TFT

TFT

That Fucking Thing was another homage to our first book LIMBO. Celluloid tape was used in buckets in that series and before we had even started developing HSP I wanted to create a villain entirely of tape. TFT was a perfect antagonist for our misfit heroes.

THE LOGO!

Dan and Caspar had a clear vision for the look of the series, including the branding — aiming for a blend of punk metal, DIY flyers, 90s electro punk with a bit of pop — so I started to write, scratch and paint versions of the title. If I was in a punk band in the 90s I'd use markers, ink and a photocopier to assemble my band logo (important for DIY mixtapes!) so that's what I did!

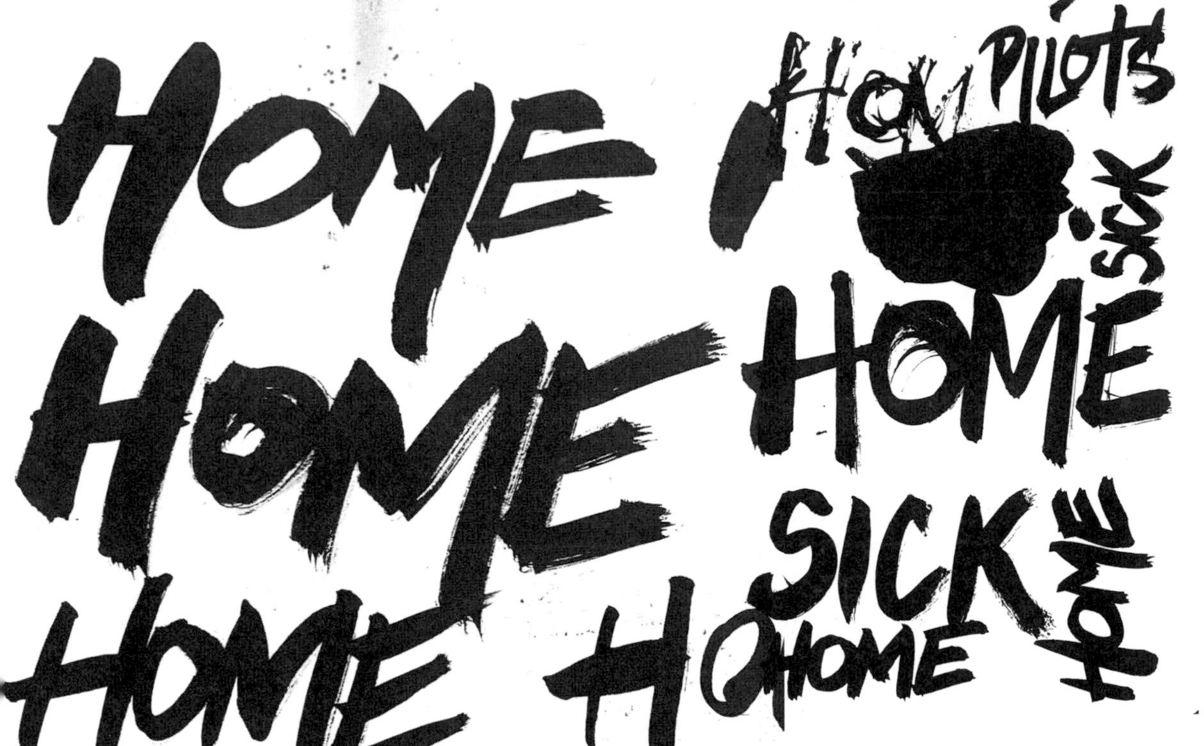
HOME
HOME
HOME
HOME PILOTS
SICK
HOME
SICK
HOME
HOME

Early version of the logo where I experimented with photocopy textures and noise to create the right look.

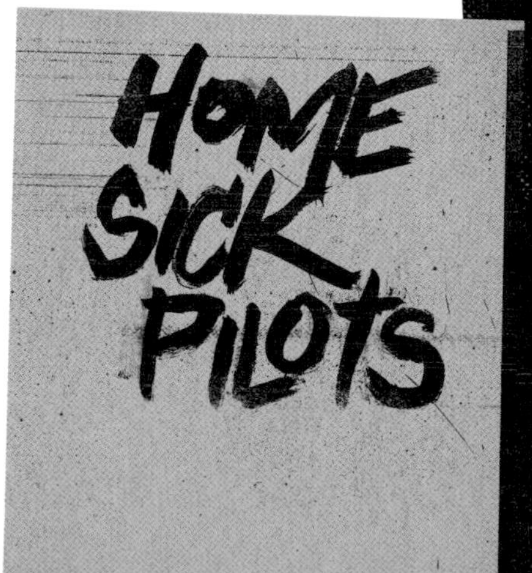
HOME
SICK
PILOTS

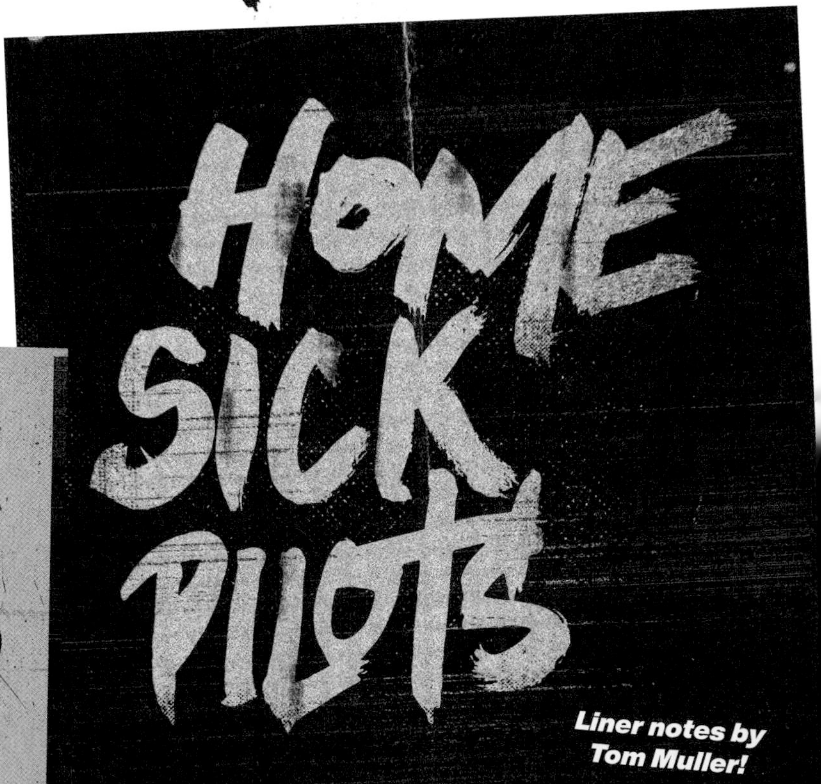
HOME
SICK
PILOTS

Liner notes by Tom Muller!

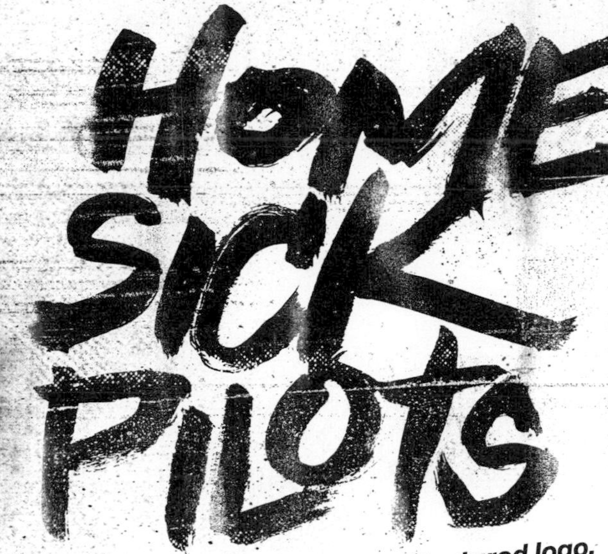
HOME
SICK
PILOTS

The final textured logo.

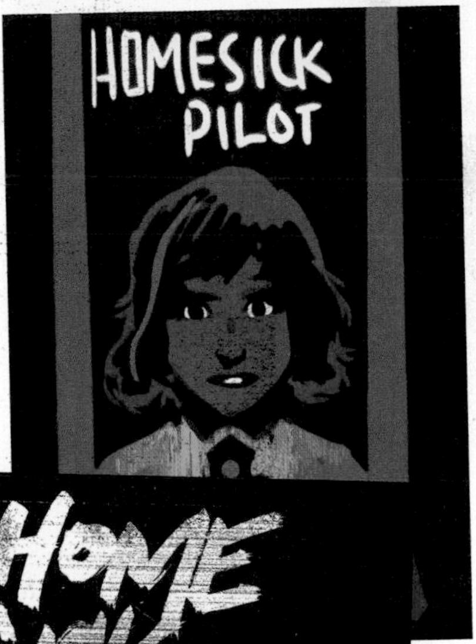
HOMESICK
PILOT

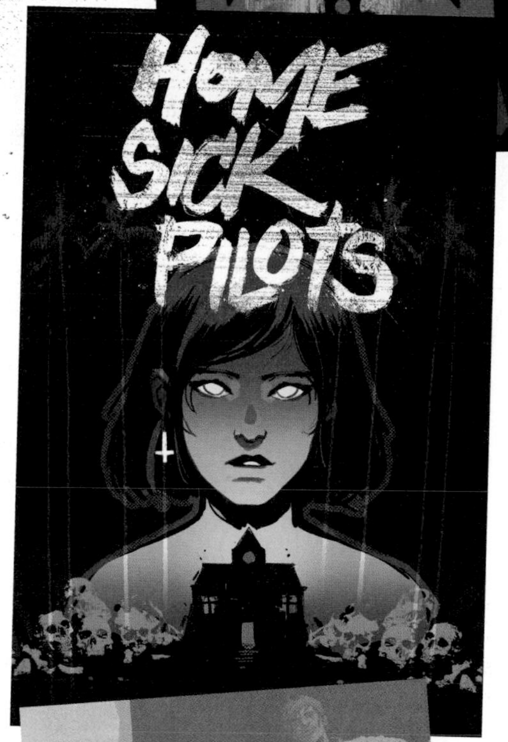
HOME
SICK
PILOTS

Early cover concepts from Caspar working out the placement of the logo. Through iterations we worked out the size, position and the textures we'd use on the trade dress. Once locked, we didn't deviate from the format — resulting in a cohesive, impactful series of covers!

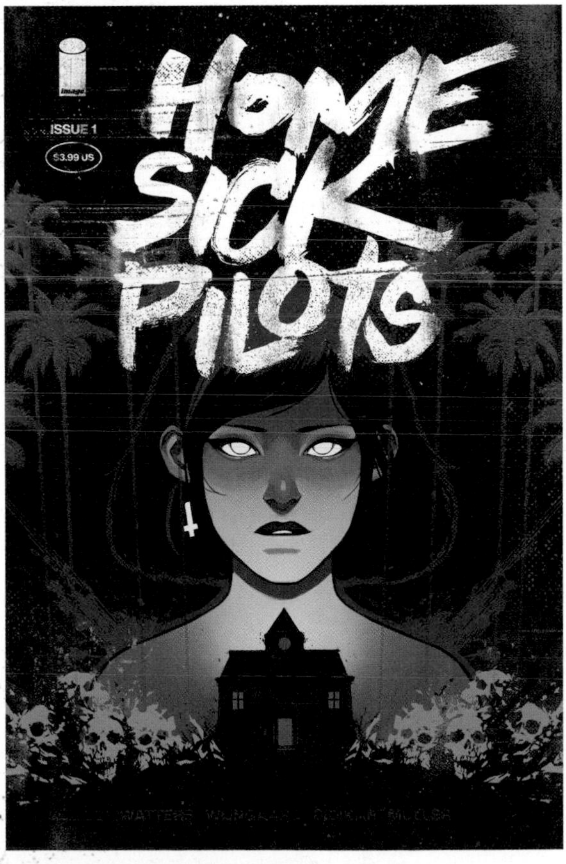
HOME
SICK
PILOTS
ISSUE 1
$3.99 US

The cover to issue 1, which set the standard for the series.

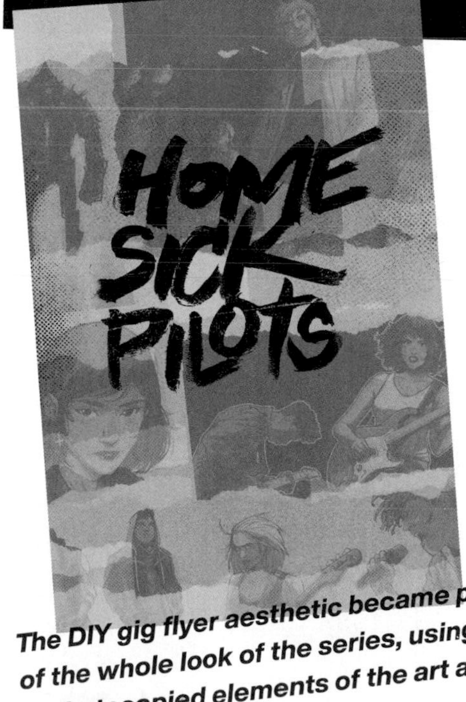
HOME
SICK
PILOTS

The DIY gig flyer aesthetic became part of the whole look of the series, using torn & photocopied elements of the art as textures for our 'liner notes'.